Dedicated to the People of Darfur

Dedicated to the People of Darfur

Writings on Fear, Risk, and Hope

EDITED BY
LUKE REYNOLDS
JENNIFER REYNOLDS

FOREWORD BY
GEORGE SAUNDERS

RUTGERS UNIVERSITY PRESS

NEW BRUNSWICK, NEW JERSEY, AND LONDON

LIBRARY OF CONGRESS CATALOGING-IN-PUBLICATION DATA

Dedicated to the people of Darfur : writings on fear, risk, and hope / edited by
Luke Reynolds and Jennifer Reynolds; foreword by George Saunders.

   p. cm.

Includes bibliographical references.

ISBN 978–0–8135–4617–9 (alk. paper)

ISBN 978–0–8135–4618–6 (pbk. : alk. paper)

1. Sudan—History—Darfur Conflict, 2003– 2. Ethnic conflict—Sudan—Darfur.

I. Reynolds, Luke, 1980– II. Reynolds, Jennifer, 1981–

DT1593.6.D27D43 2009

962.404′3—dc22

2009000769

A British Cataloging-in-Publication record for this book is available from the
British Library.

Visit our Web site: http://rutgerspress.rutgers.edu

Manufactured in the United States of America

For the people of Darfur

CONTENTS

PART THREE
Where I Come From

PART FOUR
Creating Change

PART FIVE
Leaving Safety

FOREWORD

GEORGE SAUNDERS

As a writer, I enjoy working with words. Words make meaning. Changing words changes meaning.

Which comes in handy sometimes.

Say I blurt out a problematic phrase like "genocide in Darfur." This is problematic; if there's a "genocide" in Darfur, shouldn't we be doing something to stop it? And for various reasons, we in the developed nations don't want to stop it.

Why not? Some have suggested racism. They say: Remember Rwanda? You were indifferent when one group of black people butchered another for months on end. To which I respond: Ha ha, yes, but remember Bosnia? We were indifferent there too, for years on end, when one group of white people butchered another.

Furthermore, among the many nations indifferent to this so-called "genocide" are people of every conceivable color. Black, white, brown, yellow, all have proven themselves equally indifferent to stopping the so-called "genocide" in Darfur.

Ergo, we are not indifferent to the genocide in Darfur because the victims are black.

We are indifferent because they are poor and far away.

Still, the resulting sentence doesn't sound so great: "We are ignoring the genocide in Darfur because the victims are poor and far away."

Enter the "power of revision."

Consider the opening pronoun. Are "we" ignoring the genocide? I'm not. I'm writing about it. Let's be more precise: "*They* are ignoring. . . ." And are "they" really "ignoring" it? Aren't they more accurately "deferring action with regard to" the genocide in Darfur?

Also: "genocide" is such a charged word. While, ok, yes, certain armed members of one racial group are systematically trying to eliminate all the members of another group, including the children, including the women, many of whom are being raped before their murders, let's not jump to conclusions. Let's wait until all the evidence is in—like fifty years or so. Once the killers have been given a chance to do what they are trying to do, we will be better equipped to see what it was they were attempting.

Also, let's change "genocide" to "tragic recent events shrouded in the inevitable mist of unverifiable information," which makes our sentence: "They are deferring action with regards to the tragic recent events shrouded in the mist of unverifiable information in Darfur because the victims are poor and far away."

But would we do that? Ignore someone just because they were "poor and far away?" I know I wouldn't. What I *might* do, however, is "make the strategic albeit heartrending decision to refrain from violent military intervention in the recognition that war is not to be entered into lightly."

Now we're getting somewhere. Especially if we go into passive voice, to avoid sounding accusatory: "Action with regards to the tragic recent events shrouded in the mist of unverifiable information in Darfur has been deferred, in a strategic albeit heartrending decision to refrain from violent military intervention in the recognition that war is not to be entered into lightly."

Good. Almost meaningless.

Yet sounds almost uplifting.

Kind of like: "Never again."

PREFACE

LUKE REYNOLDS AND JENNIFER REYNOLDS

The first time we read about the genocide in Darfur we were sitting in our warm apartment drinking tea. That day, the *New York Times* reported on the wide-scale injustices that were occurring in Sudan, specifically the massive numbers of soldiers who were raping women: mothers, daughters, sisters. We stopped drinking our tea.

We were two graduate students with little in our bank account, but we felt a deep desire to help change this situation. As Communication and Creative Writing students, what could we contribute to a world crisis that at first glance appeared completely removed from our everyday life? We signed petitions, made phone calls, donated what we could, and cast our vote. And yet our spirits sought more. But what? Other than the actions we had already taken, we felt powerless.

We had (and still have) no money. We had (and still have) no fame. We had (and still have) no influence in the national media. We have yet to be called to appear on *Larry King Live*, *Good Morning America*, or *Oprah*.

As we considered this dilemma, we reviewed our passions: writing, reading, volunteering, connecting with others, and bringing people together to make an impact. We asked ourselves, *What do the combination of these passions suggest we do?*

A response rose up in us. We could create an anthology that raises funds to support ending the genocide in Darfur. It would bring together some of the writers and activists whose words and work have ignited our own lives. They could sing as one chorus—though each would reveal a different avenue for creating change through risk taking.

Immediately after committing to the project, our minds were flooded with questions that had the potential to paralyze our efforts: *What if we attempt this and fail? What if no one is interested in contributing? What if everyone thinks this is an unworthy idea? What will happen if these words fall on apathetic ears?* These fears that we rehearse in the quiet places of our lives become mantras for every decision we make. We may not share them in the classrooms of the university, the corner offices of corporate enterprises, or glowing kitchens on winter evenings. Yet we allow them control over our lives.

Despite our fear, we wanted to see this anthology come to life. We wanted to live out what poet Theodore Roethke wrote: "I learn by going where I have to go." Through this risk, we discovered authentic power.

We wrote to authors, poets, professors, social activists, and others and asked them to share their insights on fear and risk. All of our contributors responded with enthusiasm. You now hold in your hands the result.

In bringing together these voices, we desired to create two layers of meaning: first, to inspire change and reignite passion within the reader and, second, to make the book itself have a tangible impact on the world. But can singing a song—however profound or moving—do this? There's no guarantee, but it's worth the risk.

Therefore, the royalties from this anthology will be given to the Save Darfur Coalition. In Darfur, Sudan, more than 600,000 people to date have been killed, mutilated, or raped (as stated in the powerful book *Not on Our Watch* by John Prendergast and Don Cheadle). According to the Save Darfur Coalition's website, "In all, about 2.3 million Darfuris have fled their homes and communities and now reside in a network of internally displaced persons (IDP) camps in Darfur, with over 200,000 more living in refugee camps in Chad." Change is vital. Now.

As George Saunders so eloquently and forcefully claims in the foreword to this volume, words have power to acknowledge or hide reality. The ways in which we choose to recognize or ignore everyday truth define who we are as people to our family, to our community, to our country, and to our world.

The essays in *Dedicated to the People of Darfur* explore how we can fight fear by taking risks through our words and actions. In its own way, each essay refuses to support a culture that welcomes apathy and ignorance.

In "One Man's Risk," Peter Turchi contemplates what might seem to be the smallest of all decisions, the tiniest challenge: he and his family are hiking, and they must cross a small river. Turchi sees himself standing on one of the rocks, and he must make a slight leap to reach the next. Instead of making the jump right away, he stops; he considers; he thinks about what might happen were he to slip and fall. Would his head pound one of the smooth, hardened entities below? Would there be blood? This pause freezes him and forces him to consider *why*. Why does danger creep into us so subtly only to command so wildly?

In "Life Drawings," Beth Alvarado explores the nature of how our writing demands that we forego the consequences of what may come from it. Alvarado is highly vulnerable as she explores her own relationships and those of other authors; how does each writer push past the censor of *shouldn't* to create the real people she wants to—needs to—create in order to bring forth the art demanded of her? Risking recognition from family or friends, the writer somehow must put pen to paper to form the souls that people her story, regardless of outward reaction.

Phillip Lopate navigates the fears we live with every day, those that join us constantly, like the old coins that fill our pockets. In "Real Risks" he explores the fear of death. Will we have accomplished what was necessary for us, what was demanded of us, before we leave this world? Will others ensure that our names live on?

Other essayists explore the ways in which our interests, cultures, and political machines facilitate danger: Sarah Stone examines politics and how we might authentically become involved; Andrew Greig describes a mountain-climbing expedition; Gail Dines pries open the corporate culture and its perpetuation of abuse against women; John Robinson grills the educational apparatus that often crushes our students in the public school system; Tom Grimes documents a writer's depression; Debra Spark explores the many faces of fear; Robert Boswell's words burn with the redemptive power of escaping from drugs.

Ultimately, this anthology shows us the fears we face and the risks we might take to push past our fears into action. Some may believe the market on risk has been cornered by daredevils; but this book offers a fresh perspective, exploring risk as a necessary component of the journey toward authentic transformation of ourselves and our culture.

In short, these essays offer a way in which to rescue the fire of risk from the rain of the status quo. In a world where passions are persistently extinguished, may these words ignite a belief in humanity, a belief in life.

ACKNOWLEDGMENTS

Our immense gratitude goes to the following people:

- Ann Cummins, whose belief trumps all and whose energy and encouragement throughout every phase of this project was remarkable. This book would not exist without her.
- Our contributors, all of whom were willing to speak their truths powerfully and passionately in these pages and whose belief in the cause behind this anthology is inspirational.
- Jenny Bent, an extraordinary agent, whose vision for this anthology gave it the substance and stamina to grow.
- Rachel Friedman, our editor, whose commitment and dedication propelled the book to its finish.
- The staff of Rutgers University Press, whose support and clarity along the journey was essential.
- Dawn Potter, for all of her time and attention to detail as our copyeditor.
- John Robinson, whose undying ability to believe in both dreams and daring sustained us.
- Our families, who love unconditionally and endlessly encourage us to reach for the stars. You are powerful examples of generosity, persistence, and faithfulness. All of your excitement and support for this project has meant so much. You are right: anything is possible.
- Tyler, you are an amazing blessing in our lives. We are so thankful for the light you bring to us each day.

PART ONE

∞

The Fears Within

Weeping Unfamiliar Tears

Long ago, when there was no day or night, when the wind was only felt and not heard, there lived a people who walked and flew. They didn't have sight and it wasn't out of blindness. They chose to tie their eyelids with soft ropes as soon as their innocence was washed away with age, which happened before a child could talk. This way no one could describe what the others had never seen. They felt that with the departure of innocence, they could no longer see the purity of the world. After their eyes were tied shut, they learned to feel, hear, and smell. They went about their daily activities, hunting and flying to the sea to fish. When they heard an unfamiliar sound, they attacked and destroyed its source, if they felt it was threatening. They lived peacefully as much as they knew without sight.

No one knew why or how it happened, but they suddenly couldn't hear, smell or feel anything. They became frightened, took up their armors and waited in hiding around the village. They waited and waited, and some of the population began to die of hunger or sometimes by walking into the spears of others. One little girl who was the youngest in the village decided to untie the ropes around her eyes. The rays from the sun rushed into her eyes and she immediately closed them, she feared the light, as she had no memory of what it was. Slowly she learned to open her eyes and saw her people dying. She cried as loudly as she could as this new sight of death caused her pain even though she didn't understand it. She could not hear herself and no one else did so she only watched helplessly as her people died. She cried for days and then started hearing herself, and slowly her people began to hear her as well. She started to sing in her lamentation, calling the names of her people and also describing what she was seeing, the sun, its rays, its setting, the night, the stars. She eventually saved her people and gave them the chance to discover that the departure of innocence didn't destroy the purity of the world, rather it deepened it; and to understand that depth came the complexities that her people had feared.

This was one of the many stories I was told as a child that illustrated risk as discovery, freedom from fear of the unknown, the possibility of living, a provision of hope in otherwise hopeless situations, and the only way life progresses in a meaningful manner. The lessons from this story have become ingrained in my veins because of the experiences that have shaped my life.

Since 1993, when the war in my country, Sierra Leone, began affecting my life to the present, the possibility and continuation of my existence has been based on risk. The chances I took to stay alive during the war, the people who opened their hearts and homes to me when my life had no direction, had a profound impact on not only my survival but also in shaping who I have become. When we take risks on others and ourselves, we open the doors to discover our humanity, and our capacity for recovery and goodness.

When I was 12 years old and saw first hand the brutality of the civil war, I didn't think I would be able to survive it. The dynamics of my culture and of everything about its functionality changed abruptly. A land where once my innocence as a child was celebrated now became a place where that innocence was deeply feared. There was no longer a sense of community and care for all, and the very sacrosanct nature of life was disregarded. It seemed hope itself had died hence living became temporary as one could be killed any minute.

My older brother, Junior, friends, and myself could have decided that it wasn't worth running to escape what seemed to be inevitable death. However, we took a chance to run and hoped that we would stay alive. The strength and determination to at least stay alive if only for a day exposed us to myriad dangers and susceptible to recruitment to fight in the war, death and all the madness that the war brought. That risk also made it possible for me to be alive today.

The chances that we took had consequences of losing family and friends, witnessing massacres and the temporary loss of our humanity, all of which happened. However, with all of those losses and exposure to the extremities of human capacity for violence also came the possibility of living and a deep appreciation of life. With that risk also came the understanding of the true nature of violence and its impact on the human spirit, and more importantly, a discovery of the resilience of that same spirit. This knowledge also became realized by the intervention of others in my life, the risks each person took to intertwine their existence with mine.

The non-governmental workers from UNICEF, the United Nations and local organizations in Sierra Leone who decided to intervene and remove someone like me from the war laid the foundation for my life now. Their decision was tremendously risky as they were engaging with commanders and warlords whom the rest of the world had condemned and labeled impossible to have any sensible discussion with. These workers, by risking their lives, faced these warlords and created a relationship that saved the lives of so many children. In addition, an understanding of how to speak and deal with commanders who recruit children was discovered. What if all such workers had simply opted out of trying anything? The fear of warlords as completely irrational people would have become an accepted norm and many children and myself would not have been rescued but left to perish.

During my rehabilitation, there was a predominant belief that children who had participated in the war would never recover. But this didn't deter some remarkable individuals, such as Esther, the nurse at the center who had a profound impact on restructuring how I understood the world and learned to live in it again, to care for us, the former child soldiers. At the rehabilitation center run by Children Associated with War (CAW), and sponsored by UNICEF, we attacked and seriously hurt a good number of the staff members. Most returned to still help us and that chance they took on us ignited our broken spirits and sparked our humanity that had seemed lost. Through their perseverance and determination to not give up on us, we began to realize the possibility of another life besides the violence that we had known for many years. Most of these workers were chastised by society for helping us; it wasn't a popular vocation to help former child soldiers at that time.

When I came to live in the United States with my mother, Laura Simms, she took a risk of providing a home for a child who was still recovering from war, a child whom she knew little about. Many people at this time feared that I could become violent and cause her serious damage. The risk she took gave rise to the other possibility that most refused to acknowledge, which was that a home and family would rescue me from the restlessness I felt. And this was exactly what happened. I learned to live again with meaning and a deep appreciation of every moment of my life.

A negative and perhaps pervasive connotation of taking risks is the exposure to danger, the welcoming of something unpleasant. Granted, this understanding is part of this endeavor but these aren't the only outcomes when we take risks. My life has and continues to be composed of a series of risks and though each comes with its consequences, each risk also comes with possibilities to learn, to desist from unwarranted fear and to discover the beauty in the complexities of our existences as human beings.

Moreover, risk shows us our capacities to impact the lives of others and to find hope in hopelessness itself. Risk can also stimulate positive thinking and outlook. When risks are taken, whether for others or personally, we create the possibility for transformation, for reassessment of older methods of doing things, and thereby the occurrence of beneficial change, one that strengthens the understanding of our common humanity. And when we have such understanding, there arises a responsibility for each other's lives.

Scared

I haven't saved the e-mail, but it must have said, "Would you be willing to contribute an essay. . . ." *But, of course*, I'm sure I thought, before I'd even finished the sentence. ". . . on the topic of risk?"

The sticking point being that I've never taken a risk in my life. But that doesn't stop me from assenting to the request. Saying "no" is its own risk: don't want to appear ungenerous and don't want to miss an opportunity. A friend once suggested that my general caution might have to do with my sister Cynthia and her death, at 26, of breast cancer. This loss might have made me inclined to think things would always turn out badly, for whenever there was a chance for something to go right with her illness and treatment, it didn't. But this is far from the case. I was nervous long before Cyndy died. Indeed, my anxiety—about the evening news, about tragedies, near and far—so irritated my sister that she chastised me, more than once, during her illness. Not about my anxiety about her, since I knew enough not to burden her with my fears. It was my family's way . . . a little whistling, everyone pretending that the cancer in the brain and the back of the mouth, not to mention her failure to eat more than half a bagel a day, didn't signify. But Cyndy chafed at my worry about other things.

Cyndy was the sort who took risks, from the minor (smoking cigarettes in high school, dressing outlandishly) to the more major (immersing herself in London's theatre world; moving alone to California for graduate school, though still in the midst of her illness). Once, my twin sister, Laura, was out to lunch with Cynthia, seated in the smoking section of a little coffee shop in our hometown. Cynthia and Laura didn't smoke, but they needed to eat and the only free seats were in the smoking section. Laura turned to a man in the booth behind her and asked if his current cigarette could be his last. "The smoke," Laura said, "is kind of bothering me."

The man refused her request. And not politely.

Of course, Laura was simply trying to protect Cynthia, whose lungs might have had cancer cells by then. Who knows? Every part of her had cancer in the end.

But Cyndy needed no protection. She heard the man telling Laura off, and now *she* was the avenging sister. She walked over to him, pulled her wig off her head, and started yelling, assuming he'd be affected by a suddenly bald, 25-year-old cancer patient, a young woman who could take a lot—her body bloated by steroids, her mouth full of sores, her lungs exhausted—but couldn't take him being mean to Laura.

The man kept on smoking. He was in the smoking section, after all. He had his rights.

As for me, as for risk: I've never done anything. Drugs? I don't think so; my mind is a scary enough place without assistance. Extreme sports? Let's consider the unextreme that I can't handle: ice skating, skiing, or even driving in winter, which I consider a dangerous sport, given the latitude in which I live. Travel? I do it now, without much problem, but can remember my trembling college-self confronted with the labyrinthine underworld of New York subways or eschewing an early trip abroad out of sheer nervousness about the unknown. I suppose I once expressed romantic interest in someone without them handing me a signed affidavit that they were interested in me first. That qualifies as a risk, doesn't it?

So I'm not a daredevil. What of it? I may have missed a chance to experience something by being cautious, but I don't feel truly ashamed of my failure to take *stupid* risks. I'm glad I never was involved in drugs, less pleased by my middle-aged fondness for white wine, and I don't feel my life has been hampered by the hours I haven't spent whizzing down ski slopes. Sure, I feel embarrassed about the way I tremble at the edge of rooftops or falter when life places me on the end of a diving board (which it doesn't, thank the Lord, anymore), but that's all.

Still, there's a fair amount of shame attached to my risk-adverse personality. And that shame has to do with history. When I read, I identify with the hero of what I read. I assume everyone does this. No matter what you see in the mirror or discover in gym class, you are the beautiful girl of the fairy tale and the gallant knight who performs feats of strength to win back the castle. And as it is with fiction, so it is with history—from the founding fathers on. I'd like to think I'm the kind of person who would take the sort of risks that really matter: the scientist or artist who risks disapprobation in order to pursue an untested idea, the nun who hides Jews in her convent during the Third Reich, or the black woman who moves to the front of the bus and sits down. But really by choosing the life I've chosen—as a writer and teacher—I've opted out of a life of serious risk.

If I take risks, it is the risks that are too risky not to take. I couldn't live with myself if I didn't speak up when I saw a parent hitting her child or if I didn't react when I heard someone say something that struck me as offensive. This could be a risk, I suppose. People don't exactly *like it* when you suggest they are being a racist or a bad parent or a bully. But there's no real fear to overcome here, even though I can produce anecdotes of myself upbraiding this one or another. It would be too terrifying *not* to say something. What kind of ugly person would I be then?

This is what I am, instead: a decent and cautious person, committedly left-wing, who opposes war in Iraq, wants a two-state solution for Israel and Palestine, buys organic produce, uses eco-friendly light bulbs and washes her hands then washes her hands. Yes, that's me—secreting my follies (risks taken, but not to be divulged) and appreciating (this is the most I can claim for myself) the people, their legions numerous, who have made the world (well, my sliver of it anyway) a relatively (nominally?) safe place in which to be scared.

LYNNE KELLY

The Risk of (Not) Communicating

We all know some of them. The in-your-face risk takers who climb mountains, jump out of airplanes (Who came up with that idea, anyway?!), travel to remote and little known destinations, always seeking the next thrill. Ooh-ing and ah-ing at the stories of novelty and danger recounted by our fear-nothing friends, those of us who psychologist Marvin Zuckerman calls "low sensation seekers" feel envious of their adventures and shame that we have no such stories to tell. Announcing "I rode my bike on a rails-to-trails path" is a sure-fire loser in the game of adventure one-upmanship.

Yet there is a different kind of risk that we all take, with varying degrees of awareness of the dangers that lie ahead. Rarely does this risk involve any threat of physical harm, but it can skyrocket our heart rate and instill enormous fear in all of us on occasion and, in some, on a daily basis. It is the risk inherent in the small and often mundane act of reaching out to another human being by communicating. Who has not felt a twinge of nervousness in anticipation of speaking to a stranger or using words to become emotionally closer to someone or asserting our disagreement with a person of authority? Who has not felt shaky or even panicked at the prospect of standing before an audience to speak?

How much awareness we have of the risk of communicating and, thus, how much anxiety it provokes varies, of course, from person to person. I consider myself to be a formerly shy person. As a child and until I emerged from graduate school diploma in hand, I felt afraid of and restrained from communicating. (For those of you wondering how I "got over it," I'm guessing my gradual increase in confidence can be attributed to my experience as a teacher of undergraduate college students and, if I may humbly add, their frequent laughter at my attempts to be humorous.) I think that those who are shy are most aware of the risk of communicating. A pioneer in the scholarly study of shyness (which he called "reticence"), Gerald M. Phillips claimed that reticent people avoid communication because they believe they have more to lose by talking than by remaining silent. Clearly, Phillips was talking about a kind of risk assessment that leads the shy to often choose silence.

But it is not just the shy person for whom communicating is risky business. Each time we open our mouths to speak we risk rejection, disagreement, or reproach. More subtly and perhaps more importantly, when we communicate we offer a self-definition, what Goffman called "face," an assertion of how we see ourselves as people. When I make a witty remark I am saying, "I am a clever person with a sharp wit." If no one laughs or, worse, everyone ignores my comment, my sense of self is disconfirmed in that moment. These tiny onslaughts against the self can be mildly embarrassing to devastating. In a paradoxical way, another risk of communicating is acceptance and intimacy, which can bring about incredible joy and self-fulfillment. However, this may be referred to as, like my grandmother used to say, the be-careful-what-you-wish-for risk. The acceptance, emotional closeness, and mutual dependency produced by communicating and developing relationships with others can give way to feelings of privacy invasion and lessened freedom as well as heartache, disappointment, and loneliness. Enough said.

There is danger too in hurting, rejecting, disappointing, angering, and disconfirming others—even those we love—with our words. I can't erase the image of the shadow of sadness that crossed my daughter's face when I scolded her, nor will I forget my mother's stunned look the first time I actually vocalized my rebellious teenage response. For years, by the way, that interchange was recounted as a family story of how Lynne, the goody-two-shoes daughter, shocked her mother.

Before you think that the lesson here is to not communicate so as to avoid the risk, I need to point out that, not only is that probably impossible, but it carries other risks. Although, as Phillips pointed out, shy people feel they have more to lose by talking than by remaining silent, shy people are well aware of the risks of not communicating. Their self-definition as shy is too often disconfirmed by others who label them "stuck up" or unfriendly. Then there is the pain of feeling on the fringe of a group or the isolation and loneliness of having few, if any, truly close relationships. Even those who do not experience shyness have suffered the loss of potential intimacy by not making a move, or not voicing the feeling, or not expressing the honest opinion.

If I had to take a stand, I'd argue that the risk of not communicating outweighs the risk of communicating. I risk being trite here but there is no greater joy than the emotional bond created with other human beings through communication. Sitting around with family and extended family trading stories of family members' antics, spinning silly fantasies with friends over lunch, sharing painful parts of my past with my spouse, and the many poignant and playful interactions with my daughter are the life events that have delivered the most happiness and the greatest meaning to my life. You, of course, have your own memories of the joys of communicating.

So perhaps you, like me, are not an adventure-and-thrill-seeking kind of risk taker. Like me you have a hard time even watching other people do bungee jumping and you'd rather have your foot run over by a car than jump out of a plane wearing a parachute. Yet the danger we face is no less real, although it rarely results in any broken bones. Each day we face and accept the risks to self and others of communicating and not communicating. The next time, then, that you find yourself in a game of adventure one-upmanship, go ahead and announce, "You think rafting down the Amazon is scary—I told my friend a secret that I had never shared with anyone before."

Real Risks

Every time I momentarily lose a sense of orientation, like asking myself in the midst of some domestic family squabble what am I doing here or who am I (such moments of vagueness do not decrease with aging), I think back to the last piece I wrote and tell myself, "Aha, I am the author of—" it could be a lengthy tome, or a book review or semi-hack article I wrote last week, doesn't matter, the point is that I experience an instantaneous congealing of self-confidence. Sometimes I walk about the streets of Brooklyn and tell myself, like a parent reassuring a child, that I am the author of a whole shelf of books, it was always my dream to take up a shelf in the library, and I'm almost at that point, having written maybe a dozen titles, edited a half-dozen more, and contributed ten more introductions to picture books or other authors' reissued texts that get my name put on the cover and/or spine of the volume. You would think that anyone who had already generated so prolific a corpus (we will defer the question of quality for the moment, or indefinitely) would be mature enough not to need to have to resort to such petty incantations, but such is not the case. I need to pat myself on the back constantly because without this reminder of my literary output I fear I would vaporize.

The negative corollary of this phenomenon is that every time I finish a book, I become very morbid and think I am going to die soon. It is as though, having cleared the decks, or the desk, I no longer have an excuse to live. Actually, even before finishing a book, when I am still in the final stages, I begin to have the hit-by-a-truck fantasy: walking through the streets of Brooklyn, I ask myself if my manuscript has reached a point sufficiently far along that, were I hit by a truck and killed instantly, it could still be published, with a short note, of course, by my widow or agent or editor explaining the circumstances. I brood about where I left my manuscript, and if it is in an overt enough place on my desk or the piles of papers beside the desk so that my wife could find it, after she has gone through the necessary grief-and-burial period, or so that she could locate it on my computer, and initiate the search for a publisher, assuming she liked it enough not to suppress it (one can never be sure about such things). Then the day comes when I have definitely finished the manuscript, for better or worse, and it is a book, or potential book. I take it to the photocopy shop and have three copies made. I give one to a friend and another to my agent. The third I leave with my wife. And I begin to think of death.

Sometimes these thoughts take the form of fantasizing approaching some friend, and asking him to become my literary executor. This fantasy of the chosen friend is shot though with Hawthorne-Melville unconsummated homoeroticism, except the brunt of this romanticized turn in the relationship will start from the moment I die, necrophiliacally, so to speak: Who will love me enough, once I become a ghost, to put up with the bother of being my executor? First I have to go through a rigorous analysis of all my friendships and ask which one of them I trust the most. Many have let me down in the past; these are easily eliminated; but I must also cross off the list those dependable friends who are older than myself and who might not be around long enough to agitate to keep my books in print, or, even more improbably, get the out-of-print ones re-issued. There is also a large stack of my uncollected work (journalistic articles, film and book reviews, ephemeral essays, poems, juvenilia) which a really alert, industrious literary trustee might find a way to see into print. How to locate all that material? I have made the problem easier by tossing new pieces as I write them into a folder which I keep on the ledge of my bookcase, but the process is very unsystematic, and to compile a full dossier of my unpublished work, the chosen literary executor would have to burrow into my files, a process that could easily take half a year. In any case, if the friend is successful, he will have added to my library shelf, which is all I care about.

The irony is that I have still not gotten around to making a will, though my wife and my mother-in-law regularly tell me it is my responsibility to do so. They are quite reasonable in nagging me to make out a will, but this step would entail envisioning my extinction, and while I am happy to do so in terms of settling my literary remains, or as an act of gothic imagination, I am less drawn to the idea of making life easier for those who will survive me. Let them suffer. Oh, I am sure in due course I will make out a will, but the prime motivation for it will be to settle this question of my literary executor.

When I finish a book I am dead, empty. It is at such junctures that I wish I had a knack for living. E. M. Cioran once wrote a book with the beautiful title *The Temptation to Exist*. I, too, have frequently been tempted to exist, but I am no good at it, and so I plod through the hours of ordinary life with a pretense of graceful acceptance and participation which does not fool for a second those closest to me (my wife and daughter), and I wait impatiently for the next opportunity to sit at my desk and write. Anything. For it is only when writing that

I begin to exist. In that sense I take no risks by writing: intensely honest self-exposures come easily to me, the most provocative positions that go against the grain of conventional morality are a breeze, complex researches and ambitious structural challenges are, finally, child's play next to the difficulty of getting through daily life, trying to love one's family members on a consistent basis (despite the lack of respect they show me compared to the literary community at large), listening to the neighbors' small talk, and deciding which telephone company provides the best service package.

ANN HOOD

Holding a Little Girl's Hand

Our lives had fallen into a new but now familiar routine. Once again morning meant the bustle of getting kids to school, packing lunches, finding hairbrushes and matching socks. I was still fragile enough to find these ordinary things extraordinary. Sometimes I stood in the basement, my hands pulling warm clothes from the dryer, and paused to marvel at how simple and satisfying this task was: the soft pink shirt, the twisted fairy underwear, my son's size large T-shirt wrapped around his little sister's Hanna Andersen striped pajamas.

On this morning, the Monday after Thanksgiving, we were running late, as if our overload of turkey and pie still slowed us down. The house was littered with the damp towels and extra linens of too many houseguests. Homework had to be found, backpacks retrieved from under pillows. Exasperated by my slowness, Sam convinced his father to take him to school. "I can't be late for Algebra," he grumbled. That left just me and Annabelle, our two-year-old daughter.

A year earlier, Sam and Lorne and I had traveled to China to bring her home from an orphanage in Hunan, a squat, bland concrete building overflowing with children. Our house, by comparison, had gone mournfully silent in April of 2002, when our five-year-old daughter Grace died suddenly from a virulent form of strep. Since that warm spring day, our lives had been marked more by what used to be than what could be. Where there used to be four brightly colored Fiestaware plates on the dinner table, sat an awkward three. The backseat of my Passat used to be crowded with kids and dog, crayons and books; after Grace died, Sam sat alone back there, the black seat seemingly endless and empty as he hummed the songs from *Oliver!*. I used to run, from ballet to swimming, from art class to play rehearsals. Then I was suddenly still, my hands finding comfort in yarn and needles, my foot tapping restlessly while I waited for the clock to finally dip its hands toward the time I could pick up Sam and hear a joke or song, get a sticky hug.

Until Annabelle.

"Our family is revived," Sam pronounced in our stuffy hotel room in Changsha as we watched our eleven-month-old daughter—daughter! Did I dare to even use that word again?—grin at us from the bed. Since she was unable to sit up yet, we placed pillows all around her like a princess on a puffy throne. We scattered books and toys, a cornucopia of baby things. What would catch her eye? She had already, immediately, caught our hearts.

Back at home, strangers stopped me in the supermarket and on the street. "Your daughter is beautiful," they said. She was, with her mop of black hair, her Cupid mouth, and dollish face. "Thank you," I managed.

Daughter. I was too afraid to believe that I was indeed the mother of this baby girl. For me, the word daughter was fraught with anxiety, even terror. How easily I had tossed it around with Grace. "My son is eight and my daughter is five," I would say. "I can't talk. I need to pick up my daughter at school." "My daughter," I would say proudly, and hold out a picture of Grace, a miniature of me with her blond hair and glasses.

Then, on that night in April, a doctor looked at me hard and said: "Your daughter is not going to make it." Within thirty-six hours, my daughter was dead. The word became sharp and painful. Friends uttered it with pride and exasperation about their own daughters as the months passed. And I, daughter-less, smiled at the sports trophies and test scores, tried to sympathize with the hurt feelings and temper tantrums of all the daughters out there. Without Grace, hearing little girl stories or watching the proud or even exasperated expressions of mothers made my hollow heart seem even more so. Sometimes as I lay awake at night, I silently practiced the words that I couldn't bear to say out loud: My daughter is dead.

On that Monday after Thanksgiving, after Sam and Lorne left, I urged Annabelle onto the potty and left the bathroom. Her new favorite saying was, "I need privacy," and that few minutes gave me time to dress quickly and drag a comb through my hair. When I went back to get her, I found Annabelle lying in a crumpled heap on the floor. Despite the panic rising in my gut, I tried to avoid catastrophizing, something I had found came easily after Grace died. "Stop kidding around," I said, forcing my voice to be light.

When Annabelle didn't move, I dropped my calm façade and began to call her name, over and over. How could I not remember that night three years earlier when I screamed Grace's name until my voice grew hoarse and my fists bruised from pounding the plexiglass that kept me away from my dying daughter? With those images racing across my mind, I scooped Annabelle into my arms. She flopped like cooked spaghetti. Somehow I dialed Lorne's cell phone, yelling for him to come quick. "Something is very wrong with Annabelle," I said, and the sound of my own words caused a fierce trembling to course through me.

A friend of mine whose father was murdered when she was just a teenager, told me that when her infant son was diagnosed with a terminal illness, she told the doctor, "You must be mistaken. I've already had mine." Hadn't I already had mine? Could it be possible that this daughter who changed my sorrow to hope could suffer some unspeakable tragedy too? Of course it was possible, I knew. Since Grace had died I had met enough families with losses heaped upon them with Jobian frequency and intensity to understand that no one was safe.

It was that understanding that almost kept me from having another child. The risk, it seemed, was too great. Before I was a mother, I leaped into love with my arms and heart wide open. When a romance failed, I mourned loudly and deeply. But I never hesitated to leap again. Love—romantic love—meant soaring highs and seemingly depthless lows. But I embraced the emotional twists and turns of love, knowing its risks, bearing a heart that had been disappointed, even broken. When a new man caught my attention, I did not think; I jumped.

Losing Grace did the opposite. Always social, I retreated. Happy to walk around my house with a phone pressed to my ear, I stopped answering calls. Any exchange held the risk of loss of some kind. As a teenager, I went on a date with a green-eyed boy. He sailed us across Narragansett Bay, then stopped under the Newport Bridge and dared me to jump overboard. Without hesitating, I stood on the stern and leaped. The current beneath the bridge was so strong that within seconds it had sent me far from the boy and the boat. I saw his stunned face, his tanned shirtless body quickly working the lines to come rescue me. When he finally reached me, I laughed in his strong arms as he pulled me aboard. I would do it again, I remember thinking. For years afterwards, when I sailed those waters, I always thought of my sixteen-year-old self, how willing I had been to jump off that boat into the unknown. The memory pleased me. But after Grace died, that girl seemed like a stranger. I was no longer trusting, hopeful, brave.

When we decided to adopt a baby from China, that girl I once was flickered in me. To love a child again was surely riskier than jumping off that sailboat thirty years earlier. I knew that no matter how tightly I held her, no matter how wide my heart opened to bring her near, no matter what I had already lost, there was nothing certain in this act of mothering again. With each paper I filled out and each form I filed, that braver self emerged more. On the flight to Beijing, I wondered when the terror would come. I wondered when I would think about retreat. But that never happened. On a cloudy March day in 2005, a Chinese official called my name, and I stepped forward with as much bravery as I had when I stood on that stern in Narragansett Bay. I held out my arms for my daughter. And happily, eagerly, I jumped.

But racing to the Emergency Room where our ordeal with Grace began, cradling Annabelle in my arms, that terror I had waited for took hold. How could

I have dared to attempt to raise a daughter again? To love a little girl? To think I had it in me to do this simple thing? As we moved through the familiar routine of telling the morning's story to each new puzzled doctor and nurse we saw; as we held Annabelle's limp hand through X rays and blood tests; as we struggled to hold ourselves together, give the right answers, be helpful and strong, I remembered navigating these same corridors, my other daughter's hand in mine. I remember how hard I tried to find hope in each terrible illness they ruled out. Just as this time we are told a list of nots: It is not pneumonia, meningitis, appendicitis, a brain tumor.

Annabelle lay semi conscious on a gurney, an IV in one arm, an oxygen reader on her finger, a hospital Johnny ridiculously big around her. A gaggle of serious-faced doctors arrived. I recognized one of them. He was the same doctor who had declared Grace fine just moments before the other doctor told me my daughter wasn't going to make it. He had the same red-rimmed eyes and untrimmed beard, the same weary expression. When our eyes met, he gave me no flicker of recognition.

A doctor cleared his throat.

I could hear my heart beating in my ears.

And then I heard Annabelle's voice, clear and strong: "Is that Tigger up there?" she said.

My eyes followed hers to a bouncing Tigger chasing Pooh on a poster above her.

That night here with Grace, I had bargained with God. "Just let her say Mama. Just let her say Mama." She did. Her final words.

But here was Annabelle, grinning at Tigger and at me and at all of these doctors. Like Snow White getting the kiss from the Prince that woke her, Annabelle seemed to grab on to all the hope and fear I had and come back to me. A foolish thing to think, perhaps, because surely that much and more had gone out to Grace those long hours in the hospital and she did not come back. But that rainy November day, in that same Emergency Room, surrounded by those same doctors, my life took a different turn. Even now no one knows what happened to Annabelle that day or why she recovered so fast and thoroughly.

What I do know is this: there is no safe route through parenthood, or even through life. When we offer our heart to others, we do not know what will happen to it. It might break. It might grow. It might take us places we never imagined. But isn't that the risk of love? To be willing to stand on the stern on a beautiful summer day and, not knowing the outcome, leap.

UZODINMA IWEALA

Safe Passage

I am not afraid. And then suddenly I am afraid. The sky is cloudy with white that wants to be grey, clouds that at present innocent, want to be more powerful than they are. Innocent becomes sinister in an instant. Transformation, transition—whatever you wish to call it. That is the risk you take in living. You are who you are and then suddenly you are not.

The airplane has stopped and I stand on the tarmac beside it. It is white with a silver underbelly and has wings but no engines beneath them. The engines are in the back, suspended there beside the tail. The tail is also white, but it is dirty where the plane once flew through the clouds and the clouds were not white but grey and sinister and full of water and dust. The paint on the tail is peeling. The words Sosoliso spread across it in red and blue, fading. I am so small beside the airplane. In this sun I am so black but I am not sinister. I am afraid.

My cousin's cousin's brother is dead. How am I supposed to feel? It is too close to Christmas for death. Christ, the bringer of light and life was born on Christmas therefore, in these periods, there should be no death. I have always believed this as a child and I still want to believe it despite a Tsunami that told me otherwise. That happened the day after Christmas, the day after the light came into this world but I didn't believe it because I was in university and therefore I was still young. Now my cousin's cousin's brother is dead and though we have never met I have been told to go and comfort him. I stand next to my father's car shivering because it is December and it is cold. I look up at my cousin's apartment where they stand on the balcony looking down at me. I have to comfort a man I have never met because he is family and in this world that is all that is certain. I check the date and time on my phone and yes it is still almost Christmas.

My mother's body guards laugh at me because I am so afraid to fly. They are also afraid to fly but because they wear black suits and carry guns, they pretend not to be. When I am with them I also pretend even if my face cannot turn to stone like their faces, even if my hands still shake. My hands shake now—my whole body shakes now, my linen shirt, my jeans—because my mother's security is not with me and I have no reason to pretend. Now I can afford to show fear because I am standing beside life or death and it looks like an airplane. Who would not be even a little afraid when he sits in the center of steel and aluminum on seats that are imprinted with the behinds of too many passengers even if it's painted white on the outside to make it look nice and has a sweet name like Sosoliso on its tail? This plane is so large and I am so small but it can fly and I cannot. I take a chance on something I do not fully understand so I am afraid. I am told that I will not be afraid if I place my trust in Christ. With Christ all things are possible. But I do not fully understand Christ. Who can understand how Christ died near Easter even if he rose again? It is near Easter and the sun is hot even if the sky is cloudy.

My cousin's cousin is family and that is the only thing that is certain. But what do you say to a man who is family that you have never met? Whose brother has died? I am so sorry for your loss? My condolences? He is wretched looking—my cousin's cousin. He is black but he has been crying so much that around his eyes and nose is red. My girlfriend's face grows red when we fight and she cries, but she is white. My cousin was black but now he is red because his brother has passed and he cannot stop crying. He is a big man with broad shoulders, thick arms and a heavy belly. He is too big to be crying like this so automatically I am moved. I also cry but silently. And because the dead brother is not someone I know, I am not red—even if it is certain that he was family. We sit in my cousin's apartment—powerless. My cousin's face is rock but his eyes dart about and he holds himself ready like prey being hunted. Anything can happen at any moment that is the risk you take in living. Innocent becomes sinister in an instant. You are who you are and then you are not. They say that through Christ all of this uncertainty vanishes because he is the light and life of this world. But it is near Christmas and my cousin's cousin's brother is dead, like all of those people washed away in one large wave. We do not understand this so we sit on the brown leather couch—the three of us staring out a window to the highway and its cars full of people and the shopping bag of gifts bought because it is almost Christmas and time to share happy memories. We stare at a television that shouts commercials at walls that were once white in the sunlight and are now dark with the night. Everything can change in an instant.

But for my mother I would not face this choice. She is a good woman but pushy and I am her son so I obey her. I was asleep and she woke me. She wore blue the color of the sky with gold embroidery streaked like sunlight across the front. Your grandparents miss you and your uncle is a big man in the town with the airport. You should go and visit them there. I want our driver to drive me because it is only six hours from my bed to a bed in my grandparents' house. I will not be in control, but I will not be powerless because our driver gets paid by my mother therefore he has to listen to me if I tell him to slow down, speed up, or stop so I can take a picture of my country near Easter when the sun is hot but not vicious. My mother is a powerful woman that is why she has security who follow her wherever she goes. That is why she needs the driver to drive a car full of her security. I am powerless that is why I do what my mother tells me to do. But my mother is a good woman even if she is pushy and she gave me enough money to fly this plane to visit my grandparents and enough money to fly this plane back. But now we are not yet flying back even if the lane was full and the pilot was ready to go. The pilot is white and his shirt was also white. Now it is grey. It is grey because he sweats. His face is red even if it is like rock because something is wrong and he is afraid.

That the walls of my cousin's apartment are not white bothers me and I want to leave. That my cousin's cousin's face is red bothers me and I want to hug him close and whisper that we are family and that will always be certain—even if one of us is dead. But a man cannot hug a man he does not know even if they are family. And he can only hug a man he does know if there is a handshake between. I cannot shake my cousin's cousin's hand because his hands are limp and lifeless beside his torso. And I cannot hug him because his torso rests lifeless against the brown leather couch. Instead I sit, my cousin sits, and my cousin's cousin slouches between us and we stare out the windows at the darkness that was once light and the many red tail lights that blink through it carrying people home with gifts to celebrate the coming of Christ the light and the life. Last Christmas there was the light and then there was a Tsunami. This Christmas my cousin's cousin's brother is dead. Innocent becomes sinister in an instant but it is certain that we are family so we sit next to each other on this couch with the blue light of the television flickering on the grey walls in place of happy memories.

He was not always afraid, this pilot. We who stand before him, next to his plane, growing restless in the hot sun, we were also not always afraid. Or maybe we were but we had Jesus Christ to hold our collective fear and because of him we could pretend that in this life everything is certain. It is almost Easter and Christ is dead so he cannot collect our fear. That is why the pilot's face is red as he rushes from the nose of the plane to its engines beneath its once white tail. Is there a problem? Is there a problem? There is a problem but the pilot does not speak English so he cannot make us less afraid. And he is also himself afraid therefore he cannot make us less afraid. There is commotion. These people, my people, are all in black and they are becoming sinister. They are shouting and their clothes flap in the wind. Their clothes are of many colors so they look like wild flowers and I am amused. I am black but I am not yet sinister though I wish I could be because it would make me less afraid. This pilot does not know what to do because there should be no problems and he and his passengers should be on his plane halfway to our families and happy memories. But nothing except family is certain and what was once powerful can in an instant become powerless. That is why I am standing outside the plane with engines by its tail that were once powerful and now are powerless. That is the problem.

My cousin's cousin's brother was not always dead. I know this because I have seen pictures of him alive with a smile or teenager's half smile across his face. My memories of him are uncertain because I did not know him well even if he was family and that is certain. He wore hip clothes to complement his smile or teenage half smile—black or red football jerseys, shorts or trousers made of denim. And he had a laugh that sounded like fresh water rushing over stones though he didn't laugh much. He only laughed at the things he considered funny like how my cousin's cousin would slurp his Indomie noodles and flinch at the hot water that sprung up to his face. Otherwise he smiled or half smiled because he was a teenager and much of that life is filled with awkwardness and silence. He was a clever boy, but he liked football. He was top of his class and he sat in the middle of the room with his hands on the desk and his fingers cradling his chin while he thought about football and girls—but mostly football. That is why he wore football jerseys. Or maybe he was none of these things. How can I know if we have never met? Perhaps he was some of these things before he died. I will never know because now he is dead and he is not who he was.

I am who I am but not who my father wants me to be. I am too reckless. That is why I speak more freely with my mother. My mother is not too reckless, but she is pushy and you cannot be pushy without being a little reckless. My mother pushed me to fly this plane. My father would have said drive. But I speak more freely with my mother therefore I am standing here looking at the men in green who have come to fix the problem. They spoke to the pilot and he spoke back even if they could not understand each other. The men in green spoke to us and told the commotion that the problem was gone. The commotion became calm and I no longer thought of wildflowers in the wind. The plane was now powerful again and I was confused because it was near Easter and who can understand how Christ died even if he rose again. I am afraid but they tell me I will be less afraid if I believe in him because he takes all the risk away from life. My fear is heavy and my body strains against its weight as I step into the plane. My father would not get on this plane because he does not risk his life unnecessarily. But I am not who my father wants me to be therefore I get onto this plane. A police man in a black suit but with no gun pushes me into the plane. If God wants us to live in this plane we will live. If God wants us to die in this plane we will die, he says. Trust in God it will make you less afraid.

My cousin's cousin's brother died on that same plane but not with me. I flew near Easter. He flew near Christmas. We flew to family because that is the only thing that is certain. We flew with gifts and happy memories even if we were afraid. And like me he stood before the plane with its white and its silver and its red and blue Sosoliso—fading—and prayed to God for safe passage. The passage was safe until it was not. Innocent becomes sinister in an instant. The clouds were white and then they were grey and full of rain and dust. The plane was powerful and then it was not. My cousin's cousin's brother was and then he was not. The only thing that is certain is we are still family. The rest we leave to God.

Rescuing Fire from the Flood

I blanket the poems with reservation mud and call it saad.

I listen for the crackling of dried earth under foot—it is the story's
     memory of the first four worlds. Beyond this are just strip malls
     and casinos acting like suns around which we moth.

The silence above "here" is an escape hole that I use to keep myself free
     from this text. (As to not be bound.) (As to be risking my life so the
     page may not return with me and shake me loose from sleep again.)
(otherwiseIwouldspeaklikethiswithoutmuchbreathuntilI _____.)

I imagine x's drawn over my eyes, and say no, do not look at the poem
     again. The poem looks for air inside a paper bag, finds a worm,
     clenches its rubbery lips around it, feels for a hook, and is shocked
     that the worm is only a worm, that its meal—the hook—was just
     an image the poet imagined.

Saad naashch'2 = words I draw with.

When I entered this world, all the words I heard stood up straight:
     nihízaad bee hozhon7.
tıd7d77n bee 'at77n, etc. But recently they've begun to climb away from
     the page, as if they too, are afraid to be burned by the flowering of
     this new world.

There are ceremonies for this.

There are stars reflecting in pools of water where the poem slept last
night.

I've rescued nothing for myself. The poem flickered in my left hand,
then dimmed when I breathed in city air.

I've just returned from writing. The doves outside are sleeping on the
grass like anchors for clouds. The cars river up and down the
interstate near hear, and I am awakened by a poem's dreaming.
It sings: cars rivering. It speaks: splintering from a polished clay
bowl. It taught me something that I'm not entirely sure of yet.

Forgetting began my recent poetry manuscript and I've placed my hand
in fire again, waiting for its wings to carry me back to the waiting
room of hozh=.

There are songs for this.

There is a poem of fire flickering in the flood's teeth.

PART TWO

Writing Risk

BETH ALVARADO

Life Drawings

I read in an article, long ago, that Bernard Malamud's daughter was upset because she saw her toes in one of his short stories. Her *toes?* Okay, that one we can dismiss. She must have been way too sensitive, a prima donna—unless her toes were deformed, unless he put them on the feet of a whore—so I'll be charitable. Maybe there's a story behind her objection, some reason she couldn't separate her feelings about her father from his description of her toes. Maybe she thought, my *toes?* That's the only memorable thing about me? The only detail significant enough to borrow?

The materials of life, we all draw on them in different degrees, not only to describe the surface, paint a picture, get the particulars "right" but to create an emotional grounding, to make the characters and their voices ring true. But the anxiety of alienating others, this is sure to cause writer's block, at least for me. If I'm drawing from life, how do I deal with the risk of committing the unforgivable, of revealing someone else's flaws or secrets?

My friend, for instance, saying to her daughter when she complained about her stepfather, "Do you *like* living in this house? Do you *want* to move to an apartment?" And, by extension—I know her daughter heard the unspoken as well as the spoken—to a poorer neighborhood, a rougher school, one where you will have no friends? Implied in those two lines of dialogue is a story about my friend's strained relationship with her husband, her willingness to emotionally blackmail her daughter, and the subliminal lesson about what a woman might give up for financial security.

Or my mother, who was afraid my daughter would date a black basketball player: "Don't go any darker than your father!" (Who is Mexican-American.) I can imagine a Grace Paley story starting with lines like those. "Don't go any darker than your father. He's a *nice* shade of brown." Paley said that's how a story began for her, with a voice. Risk following it and a character, a life, emerges.

My ex-son-in-law, a personable guy. Funny. Athletic. Down to earth. Tinkers around the house. I like him very much, as a matter of fact. After an argument with my daughter, he tore up the photographs she had put on the refrigerator. They were, of course, snapshots of people she loved, friends and family standing with their arms around one another in front of some waterfall or marble monument. The act of tearing the photographs—one by one, in front of her? or later when she was asleep?—seems to me a defining moment. It paints a portrait of a man who would, in anger, destroy her memories and, by extension, be willing to enact violence upon her or those she loved? Was he destroying, metaphorically, her connections to other people? It's such an ominous, eerie moment, some inner rage revealed, future violence portended.

Perfect for fiction. So perfect, I might say to a good friend, wistfully, "You use it. I can't. No one will ever forgive me."

But maybe there's a moratorium. Maybe after my daughter's been divorced for seven years, I can use this gesture in a story without causing her pain. Maybe memory will then have transformed it into something less recognizable. Or maybe I should go ahead and use it now, trusting that the process of creating the fictional world will transform it into art.

(Or, maybe—and this seems the obvious solution—I should just *ask* her. But what if she says: "*No*. Mother. How could you?" Where would I ever find a gesture as perfect as that? Besides, isn't the tension between "life" and "art" something that gives creation its energy, its momentum? The risk, a kind of adrenaline, as addictive as driving a car too fast or drinking too much wine on a summer afternoon. Oh, the risk is heady. Better just to pretend no one will ever read this.)

And anyway, as you can see from the story itself, my imagination is already filling in where memory fails me. I don't know when he tore the photographs up. During the argument? Afterwards? While she was asleep seems to me most chilling. There she is, vulnerable, lying in their marriage bed, her hair fanned out across the pillow. Her fingers are curled into her palm just as when she was a child. Perhaps she has already forgotten the argument and yet he is awake, tearing up the pictures. I can hear the cold, crisp sound of paper being torn. And what does he do with the pieces? Does he leave them lying where they fall on the floor or scattered across the counter? Is he careless, blatant in his disregard for her feelings? Or, in shame, does he hide them in the trash, beneath the coffee grounds and empty cans?

Maybe it's the perfect moment because it reveals something true about all of us, not just my ex-son-in-law. When we're hurt, we want to be childish. We want to lash out, to hurt the other, to scratch, bite, hit, pull hair. We want to do damage because we somehow, mistakenly, feel it will ease the pain of the damage done to us.

Or maybe it's the perfect occasion for writing fiction because I *don't* understand it. Only if I could hear the argument between them, only if I could hear my
son-in-law's voice, might I understand his conflict. It's the not-knowing, the
mystery of the gesture that sparks my imagination and gives rise to several possible narratives—none of which may have anything to do with my son-in-law
in "real life." In fact, the gesture itself might eventually disappear from any story
it inspires.

If voice and gesture can give rise to characters, maybe an exploration of
context can bring us closer to understanding the world through others' eyes.
And here, again, I have to enter the realm of fiction through the door of nonfiction. For instance, if we see my mother's prejudice—her fear that my daughter
would marry someone with dark skin—as typical of an Anglo woman of the
WWII generation, is that enough to understand her worldview? Maybe it would
make a difference to know that, the youngest of nine children, she grew up near
a large Portuguese community during the Depression; her father, a stockbroker,
had lost everything except the house, an old Victorian, in a rural area. Had they
not owned enough land to farm, they would have gone hungry. There was a lot
of prejudice against the Portuguese then—her father, a man she adored, was
unapologetically prejudiced—and yet because of my mother's dark hair and
eyes, perhaps because of her obvious poverty, she was often mistaken for
Portuguese. People discriminated against her. At the heart of her own prejudice,
maybe, there was shame, an identification with those she had been taught were
less than she. Even as an adult, she prickled at the slightest of social slights, feeling they rendered her invisible, beneath notice. And so, to rise above her circumstances, a phrase she loved, she often asserted her superiority in terms of
class as well as ethnicity. I arrived, finally, at a place of empathy for my mother
and, by extension, an understanding of people or "characters" like her, only by
listening for what was unsaid as well as to what was said.

Sometimes there is a gesture or an utterance like "rise above" that goes
right to the heart of a person's conflict. You witness it. You remember. It's so
revealing you don't ever have to write it down. And if you follow it, you find it
has roots in the family, the culture, society, politics, and economics. All of the
"characters" I've described feel the expectations of their families and religions,
the impress of their times. Can we imagine a story by Grace Paley where being
Jewish has no weight? Or the risks James Baldwin took as he wrote openly about
race and homosexuality in the 1950's?

I recently read *Saturday* by Ian McEwan, a story set in London within the
larger context of the aftermath of 9/11 and during the buildup of going to war
with Iraq. The father, who is a neurosurgeon, says he is undecided about
whether or not to support the invasion of Iraq. In his arguments with his daughter, however, who is decidedly against the war, he finds himself articulating the
pro-war position. When I read the conversations, I found myself cringing at the

daughter's arguments. Her concerns so resembled mine and yet McEwan had reduced them to youthful idealism whereas he presented the father's points as measured and well thought out. Of course, these are characters and their arguments are meant to develop their relationship, to reveal who they are and do not, necessarily, represent what McEwan believes. Still, I kept wondering if the father was a "mouthpiece" for the author. McEwan takes the risk of being confused with his character. As all of us do. We are in tricky territory once we start writing about politics or religion or race. We run the risk not only of being misunderstood but also of misunderstanding, of appropriating or misrepresenting people in a hurtful or dishonest way. This ethical dilemma may be more pronounced in nonfiction than fiction, but I believe that if we are writing honestly about conflicts that matter, we almost always run the risk of offending—and not only those we love, who might see their toes in our story, but also our readers, editors, people who might decide to publish our work, or not.

Yet if living in a pluralistic, democratic society means we must be willing to be offended, it also means that as writers, we must run the risk of offending others. What would our culture be like if writers like Walt Whitman, James Baldwin, Allen Ginsberg, Adrienne Rich, Leslie Marmon Silko, Tim O'Brien, and Salman Rushdie hadn't been willing to offend—or provoke—others? What would I have understood about the Holocaust had I not read Anne Frank's diary? What would I have understood about Civil Rights had I not read?

I was a child when I watched Watts burn on television. My family lived in a small town in Colorado. I'd never even seen a black person. I had no way of understanding why Martin Luther King and others were marching, why Watts was burning, until I read a poem by another child. I still have the book. The poem begins "I Carolyn Jackson am a pure-blooded Negro in soul and mind." It's a very simple, narrative poem, and she tells us about living on the poor side of town, about her aunt who was arrested down south for drinking out of a whites-only drinking fountain. I distinctly remember lying in bed one night, thinking about her poem, wondering how it felt to *be* her—"to feel like a crow in a robin's nest"—and thinking about the images on television and knowing there was somehow a connection, a connection on the level of pain. Maybe that's all I understood at the time: the images and words were connected by a deep, visceral pain and, somehow, her voice created an echo of that pain inside me.

An echo, not a deep understanding, and this is an important distinction. As a white woman—you will have to forgive these lists of labels which, after all, tell you both everything and nothing—who grew up in an upper-middle-class, politically conservative, agnostic family, in a sheltered white community, I have no basis in lived experience to understand how it feels to grow up as a Mexican-American, Catholic, working-class male, and yet I've been married since I was nineteen to a man who is all of those things. By watching him, listening to his stories, being a part of his family, by making some kind of imaginative leap, I've been able to write from the points of view of Mexican-American characters. Have I got it "right"? Probably not all of the time. After all, there are as many Mexican-American points of view as there are Mexican-Americans. As Jonathan Lethem said recently, about writing from an adolescent girl's point of view: "She wasn't some representative thirteen-year-old. She was Pella. I met her. I found her. I made her my own."[1]

I find Lethem's sentiment liberating—art cannot police itself, the imagination is transcendent, there are universals about human nature—but also anxiety-producing. Doesn't the artist have a responsibility? But to what—if all truth is subjective? To, in the very least, not willfully misrepresent others? So is it a matter of intention? And what if, above all, I desire to "fasten in the memory of the reader, like a living presence, some bright human image?"[2] Isn't my first allegiance to art? In fiction, I would say yes. Creating a character is a mystical undertaking and, ultimately, out of my control, yet there is also a way in which I believe I can begin only by "reading" people in the world. And I believe I have to try to read them as accurately as I can, to make empathic leaps, to understand them as deeply as I can.

When an actor prepares for a part, she imagines her own similarities to the character as a starting point. There's a constant tension between self and other: how are we alike? How different? Writers do that, too, of course, as they create characters. But Anna Deavere Smith, a playwright and actor, wrote that the self-based technique of understanding a character is too limiting because it means the self is the only frame of reference. She wondered if there might be a way "to find a character's psychological reality by 'inhabiting' that character's words." She began to test her theory by collecting oral histories with her drama students and found that "If we were to inhabit the speech patterns of another, and walk in the speech of another, we could find the individuality of the other and experience that individuality viscerally." She believes that this is the only way actors can transcend their own limited experiences, a crucial technique if theatre is going to be able to bridge difference, especially cultural or racial difference. She writes, "[B]y using another person's language, it was possible to portray what was invisible about that person."[3] It makes sense, then, when William Gass writes that a character is, "first of all, the noise of his name, and all the sounds and rhythms that proceed from him."[4] *Hearing* that voice is a way of going outside the self, of inhabiting another, or of allowing another to inhabit us.

But what if the other is someone we *don't* want to listen to? I recently found myself facing my older brother in a hospital waiting room. Our mother was very ill. During surgery, they'd had to put her on a breathing machine and now, because she had lung disease, she could no longer breathe on her own. The question was whether or not to remove the tube; if we did, she would probably die within hours. Because my mother had a long-standing Do Not Resuscitate order, my sisters and I believed she wanted the tube removed. When I asked her if she wanted it removed, she nodded her head. *Yes.* Even though we may have to let you go? *Yes.*

Listen to my brother's voice: "The DNR was suspended once she entered the operating room." "I've talked to lawyers. We're in a gray area legally." "Mom is on morphine. She isn't thinking clearly." "The *premise* of the order is flawed."

Sitting next to him in the waiting room, I realized my brother was a stranger, as foreign as someone from another time and place. I didn't want to know him. I wanted to close myself off, to stop even the sound of his voice. I found myself asking—what does he *want?* For her to live forever? If he's a Christian, as he professes, what is he afraid of? Doesn't he believe she'll go to heaven? What *are* his conflicts? His values? And then I realized these were the same questions I would ask myself of a character. I needed to get past my brother's legal posturing, his surface characteristics. Ironically, I needed to create a character of him so I could listen with compassion, so I could understand how it felt to *be* him, so I could convince him to allow our mother to die.

It was a surreal moment, as such moments always are, where we are at once inside ourselves, limited in understanding, bound by our own emotional needs and yet, at the same time, hyper-conscious, as if floating, watching from the outside, cataloging details, analyzing gestures, even our own. Is now the right time to put my hand on his arm? To lean forward, to get him to focus on my eyes so that he can see I am fully present, ready to listen?

Finally, he blurted out, "I have to decide whether or not my mother will live or die. And I can't do it." There it was, revealed in his own language, what was invisible about him, his central conflict: the burden of the only son. *Inhabit* his words, say them aloud over and over, and you'll feel it, too. "*I* have to decide whether or not *my* mother will live or die. And I can't *do* it."

He felt he carried that burden alone and the weight, the sheer emotional weight, had blurred his vision. He could not see my sisters and me, standing by, sharing the burden. He could not, I believe, see my mother as separate from himself, as a person who deserved her autonomy even on her deathbed. He could not, I believe, separate the decision from the inevitable sorrow that would follow. In other words, there were two sources of anguish and we all shared them, but he was so locked inside his own pain and feelings of helplessness, he could not feel the pain of others, not even our mother's.

The rest of the conversation and how my brother came to respect my mother's wishes are not so important for this essay. In fact, I wonder why I further blur the line between life and writing, between nonfiction and fiction. What I'm interested in, more than that, I think, is not only the mysterious process of going out of ourselves, of how we learn to detach, to observe and listen carefully in order to create characters, but that doing this in our writing can help us cultivate empathy and build bridges in our lives.

Yet, even as I say this, I know I am betraying something intimate. Risking being hurtful. *Using* my mother's death. Did I realize I would end up here when I started the essay? No. Yet as voyeuristic or parasitic as it may feel, I can't write about my own life without writing about the lives of those close to me. And, even if everything begins in the real, writing is not transcription; instead it transforms, distills, reveals, hides, questions, crystallizes, transcends. For me, once I find the right voice for the piece, language takes over. I can only follow it. It is, perhaps, like a painter who follows a line of color or a sculptor who follows the contours in the marble. I could never say, for instance, as Lethem did of his character, Pella, "I made her my own." I would be more likely to say, "I tapped into her voice," or "He kept coming back to me." For me, then, writing, like having relationships with other people, begins with allowing myself to be receptive and vulnerable. No wonder it causes me anxiety.

NOTES

1. Sarah Anne Johnson, "An Interview with Jonathan Lethem," *Writer's Chronicle* (October/ November 2006), *http://www.awpwriter/org/login/m/awpChron/articles/sjohnson17.lasso.*
2. William Gass, "The Concept of Character in Fiction," in *Fiction and the Figures of Life* (New York: Knopf, 1970), 34.
3. Anna Deavere Smith, *Fires in the Mirror* (New York: Anchor, 1993), xxxii.
4. Gass, "The Concept of Character in Fiction," 49.

NANCY JOHNSON

Writing Toward the Center

The day is spectacular in that Oregon way—August sky an almost painful, clear blue as if made up of tiny crystals. Sun-shatters light the Douglass fir and ponderosa pine. We are slow gathering the last items for the car, wanting to luxuriate in our vacation space a little longer before heading into the rhythm of the nine-hour car ride home. My husband Arthur drives because he can't read in a moving car. I settle in with *The Amazing Adventures of Kavalier and Clay*, and my seven-year-old son Wally sits behind me with his headphones on, listening to the latest singer popular with the elementary school crowd. *Clapton Unplugged* plays on the car stereo.

By ten o'clock we are heading south on highway 97, a two-lane string of road that stretches north-south through western Oregon. We're going the 55-mile speed limit since there isn't much traffic and the road is clear. It feels like a day made for travel and soaking up the season's last bits of leisure. Just as we're passing through the village of LaPine, 34-year-old Christopher Adney, traveling north, realizes he missed the entrance to his drive and whips his wheel left to make a fast turn across the highway. This split-second movement slams his Chevy Silverado 4×4 pickup truck into our 10-year-old station wagon. He blows us apart.

Time slows as our car catapults into the air, spinning around and over, filling with dust the impact has pulled up from the road and its shoulder. The sound of the crash reverberates as the car lands first on its roof and then rights itself. The air is brown with swirling dirt that fills all the open spaces. As the car bounces back to earth, flames erupt from its engine.

The first person to the scene runs over to the wreck to see if he can pull anyone out before our car explodes. He sees my son alert in the back seat and yells at him to unlock the door. Wally's leg is broken, so this man, whom we will never know except that he saved our son, carries Wally to the side of the road and lays him down on the shoulder. When the firefighters and EMTs arrive, moments later, they put out the fire and get me out of the car. They work for more than two hours to extricate Arthur, who is trapped inside the folded-over car frame. We are all flown to St. Charles Medical Center in Bend, the nearest trauma hospital.

Time within trauma becomes liquid as the trauma itself disrupts the life of each person it touches. It swoops down and cuts a deep swath into the present. Every visit back takes place in the moment no matter when the traumatic event occurred; details are always in the present tense. As a result, most of us who have experienced a trauma will try anything, consciously or unconsciously, not to replay the impact.

Neither my husband Arthur nor I have any memory of our car crash or events immediately following. I lost two days, my husband six weeks. He says he is grateful not to have that memory. Of course, he does have it; he just can't access it. Arthur's physical recovery has taken nearly five years. He had multiple breaks in all his limbs, so he will never recover his former gait, his ability to move in the world. He cannot move his left eye, cannot track with it, so what and how he sees will ever be different. Even his signature has changed, the result of his right hand having been rebuilt.

I have been writing about this car accident and its effect on our lives in a memoir titled *The Accident Is My Mother*. Although the title echoes in different ways throughout the book, in one sense, the accident gave birth to trauma consciousness, not only for me and my family, but for those close to us as well. Such consciousness incorporates the falling away of some social graces, and in ways, changes how we think by eliminating the need for smooth connections: Thoughts are attracted to each other like magnets, pulling together quickly without regard for transition.

While working on this book, I have spent weeks in depression trying to reconstruct the time I was in the hospital after the accident, confronting feelings I suppressed at the time. When I was hospitalized, I wanted the person closest to me, my husband, to help take care of me; I wanted his presence. During that same time, he was fighting to stay alive—for a week it was not clear he would survive. Even knowing this, I am still angry that he did not help me. I feel that he deserted me. Writing brings to the center those issues between us.

My son, who is now twelve, has cystic fibrosis. There is no way to tell the story of the crash and its aftermath without explaining this. But that part of the story is his, not mine to tell. I have explained to him that I am writing about him and have to mention the CF, and even though I ask him if he is okay with it and he says yes, I don't know, nor does he, how he will feel about this when the book comes out.

A psychologist told my husband that in marriages in which both partners suffer head injuries, the divorce rate is over 95%. If I write the emotional truth,

I can't pretend there haven't been times since the accident when my husband and I couldn't stand to be in the same room, when we each thought the other had changed beyond recognition. Writing a memoir takes personal matters out into the world; the private becomes public.

In his 1995 Nobel Lecture, Seamus Heaney credits poetry "for making possible a fluid and restorative relationship between the mind's centre and its circumference. . . ." This kind of movement is created when writing about trauma as well; the writer encourages the traumatic event to move fluidly between the circumference and the center, continuing its life in the present. And while we hope for restoration, even write toward it, the possibility exists that the writing is not restorative; instead, what flows from the circumference to the center disrupts the life of the writer and becomes actual not for one time and place but over and over without end.

Like a Syrupy Sweet

The opposite of risk is security. Peace of mind and comfort. Safety and stability, shelter and snug harbor. Risk is sailing into the storm, all flags flying. It's allowing for the possibility, even the likelihood, of suffering and harm. So why would I do something so foolish? Risk is an invitation to failure, isn't it? What sense would it make to imperil and humiliate myself, possibly upset my loved ones, jeopardize my serene little world?

And yet I do take risks although I'm not the sort of risk-taker they write about in best sellers or celebrate in *Jackass* movies. I don't leap from airplanes, climb mountains, plummet over waterfalls, or drive too fast. Last night, in fact, I got into an accident while driving quite sensibly, hit from behind by Elaine F., who told me she knew a Dufresne (or Duhfrez, as she pronounced it) in Baldwin, Long Island, but apparently not very well. I did not call the cops (always a risk), and Elaine did not get a ticket. Elaine called at 6:30 this morning and left a message on my answering machine asking me not to file an insurance claim. We'll handle it between ourselves, she said. (Should I risk it?) I don't even ride those terrifying roller coasters that seem so appealing to Americans. My son, however, once rode the exposed Big Shot thrill ride at the top of the 1,149 foot Stratosphere in Las Vegas when he was twelve. I waited in the lobby. I don't put my body at risk except with fats and carbohydrates, which, it turns out, may not be as risky as spinach and lettuce.

When I was a young man I left a marriage, a family, a home, a job, and friends because I wanted to write stories, and I didn't even know if I could. You can be anything, perhaps, but you can't be everything. You have to choose. Habit makes it easy to choose the devil you know, to stay the same. I could have said to my wife, You're right, dear, it's a pipe dream, and it'll disrupt our pleasant home. But fear gave me the courage, if that's the right word, to leave. And this is why.

My father came home from the Second World War after four years in the South Pacific. He was twenty-one and miraculously alive. The world threw itself at his feet. His life was suddenly one of unlimited possibility. He and his pal Billy Hillestrom made plans to homestead in Alaska. But before they could leave, my father married his pregnant sweetheart and went to work for Worcester County Electric, stoking a coal furnace for $4500 a year. In summers he played semi-pro baseball in the Blackstone Valley League and in the Industrial League. He was a strong and gifted left-handed pitcher, and soon his talents, his several no-hitters, caught the attention of Hall of Fame outfielder and Boston Braves scout Jesse Burkett. The Braves offered my father a $5000 contract with their Evansville, Indiana, farm team in the Class B Three-I League. If he had been single, he said, he would have jumped at the chance. But he had a wife and a child and a secure job with the company, so he listened to the wife, and to his common sense, and made the wise and prudent decision. And he kept pitching for Bill Hoyle's Texaco and for Laipson's Milk. And me, I wonder what might have been.

All writing is autobiographical. Everything I write is in some way about my father and the surrender of his dream, and about my own sadness (not his, mind you) at his unlived life. He might have failed in Evansville, of course. And if he had, he'd still be an eighty-two-year-old guy with Parkinson's and diabetes and macular degeneration and high blood pressure and a gift for telling stories and a contagious sense of humor and an adoring family, but he would also have the memories of a season in the bush leagues doing what he loved to do and what he was so good at. And, who knows, he might have had that cup of coffee in the Bigs.

So my own haunting fear is that I will condemn myself to live with regret because I did not try to follow my heart, that I let the dream crust and sugar over. And this fear has turned security from refuge to prison. And I intend to stay out of prison. So maybe I shouldn't congratulate myself for my courage, if that's the right word, and just admit to being blessed with an undeniable compulsion to try the new, to welcome failure. Failure, it turns out, doesn't hurt as much as inertia. In fact, it doesn't hurt at all. It invigorates. T. S. Eliot, perhaps after reading Blake, said that only those who risk going too far really know how far you can go.

Maybe if you never risk anything, you risk everything—you risk not knowing who you are and who you might have been. And besides, when you take a risk you get to go where you have not gone, where you could not have imagined going, thinking new thoughts, meeting new people (real and made up), coming to some understanding about what you didn't even know you didn't understand. Like how your dad's story of his own flirtation with pro ball, the story he told you over pizza at the Wonder Bar when you were fourteen, how that story changed your life in ways that neither you nor he could have suspected, propelled your life off into a whole new trajectory.

EJ LEVY

An Apostate in Academe

I'm an apostate in academe, a professor of creative writing who comes to the profession equipped only with faith that in the early twenty-first century universities are America's latter day Medicis, our patrons of the arts, making it viable to make a life in words.

But I'm not a believer. I remain a skeptic among the academic faithful.

I wonder sometimes what good is done by carefully crafting stories and discussing them at seminar tables while the world goes to hell; the great performance artist Spalding Gray once quoted an ancient Roman as saying, "And everyone's writing a book"; we are the Romans, it seems, and we are all writing our books; and I wonder what we have to say that can possibly matter as much as a polar bear in peril because of global warming, a child in the *favelas* of Rio; I wonder, why write?

W. H. Auden famously said in his poem "In Memory of WB Yeats" that "poetry makes nothing happen." So, why write? In 2004 the National Endowment for the Arts released the findings of a multi-year survey (*Reading at Risk: A Survey of Literary Reading in America*) which found that literary reading in America is in dramatic decline, with fewer than half of American adults now reading literature. So again, why write?

One answer to this question is offered by the Russian poet Joseph Brodsky in his 1987 Nobel lecture: he said that art is the best bulwark we have against totalitarianism, because it strengthens the individual's private sense of the world. (Though being Brodsky he put it better than this; he said: "Every new aesthetic reality makes man's ethical reality more precise. For aesthetics is the mother of ethics . . . aesthetic experience is always a private one . . . and this kind of privacy . . . can in itself turn out to be, if not as guarantee, then a form of defense against enslavement.")

For Brodsky writing itself is an ethical exercise, strengthening the soul: "The one who writes a poem writes it above all because verse writing is an extraordinary accelerator of conscience, of thinking, of comprehending the universe."

Then again, maybe we write because there's no pleasure like it (poet Elizabeth Bishop famously described that joy as "a self-forgetful, perfectly useless concentration."). Writing, we are lost in thought—or, more accurately, we are found.

Or perhaps we write because making art is arguably what makes us human—as anthropologist Ellen Dissanayake argues in her 1992 book *Homo Aestheticus,* making art is perhaps the principal thing that distinguishes homo sapiens from all other creatures, perhaps the *only* thing. Other species, after all, communicate, ratiocinate, remember, and regret, but only humans feel the need evidently to draw on cave walls, write poems, and their memoirs.

Answers to such a question—Why write?—are obviously as various as writers are, as diverse as their work. The best answer undoubtedly lies in the work itself.

But the answer also lies in the working. In the patient practice of noticing and noting down the details of one's life and those of others, we gently stitch ourselves more tightly to the world. The act of writing restores a conversation with oneself that we are sorely in need of having in our increasingly distracted culture. It's a kind of communion with the self, which is the foundation for a communion with others and the world. A conversation we're sorely in need of having.

I often tell my students that fiction writing is a sympathetic practice—by imagining our way into others' lives, we exercise and strengthen our ability to care for and about others, transcending briefly our egoism; writing, we exercise that most important muscle, the heart.

ooo

Risks in Writing the Novel, *The Rape of Sita*

Over the three years or so that I was writing *The Rape of Sita* its title was always already there in my head. I was held in awe of the double meaning of the word "rape," as both "abduction" of the Goddess, Sita, and as "physical violation" of my modern-day fictional character, Sita, who unlike long-ago goddesses was not protected by any manner of divine prophecy. But I was never blind or insensitive to the danger of the title. I was conscious, too, that Sita is an insecure deity, thus all the more dangerous for me, the writer.

I knew all along that the words of the title were strong, very strong. I needed strong words right then. I was writing not only about all the rape victims I knew in person from my being active in the women's movement for years. All *that* anger. But I was also healing my own psyche. Dealing with my own anger. And that was something I needed to confess to the reader. From the outset. On a personal level, as concerns names, I am, you see, in a love relationship of long standing with someone with the first name Ram, the same name as the abducted Goddess's husband. So, I took the risk of strong words because I needed them. Because being Ram's wife, I am Sita, in a childish name-code. This exposure of myself made the risk of the title all the more terrifying.

But, I had to do it.

I wanted in so doing to write a story to give my friends and to anyone else who might care to pick up a copy one day, the most beautiful story in the whole world as a present. And it was to me an important present to give because it would be made up out of the most hostile central raw material imaginable: rape, anger, burial, and obsessive memory. I wanted in so doing to get as near to the epicentre as I possibly could of the most irreducible conflict of the sex war: rape. I wanted to illuminate it enough to see the light in the middle of the wheel. So that whatever awful things may have happened to you in your life, or might in the future happen to you or to me, one day something beautiful can be made out of it. With words. Between and amongst human beings. With stories, and with stories within stories.

So, that's how I did it.

I, of course, chose the least violent kind of rape for the central story. No wanton violence. Not a gang rape. No blood. No incest. No pregnancy. No vast difference in class. No special impunity for the rapist. The least violent of rapes left me free to expose all the more strongly the hideousness of rape.

But the highest emotional risk I take in an on-going way in my life, and it is the risk that offers the highest prizes of all, is, of course, political commitment. And since I am engaged in political struggles and have been since I was a child, physical rape has the resonance for me of colonization, enslavement, pillage, land occupation, slave labour, modern wage labour. I didn't have to impose rape as a symbol of collective subjugation onto the novel, as if it were a stamp from the outside of events. It came from my life experience of political struggles in South Africa against the Apartheid State and in Mauritius against the sugar oligarchy and State. And from the stories I have heard from before I could understand whole sentences. The reality was already all around me then. And until today, I see them.

Anyway.

As the time for the publication of the novel neared, the taboo subject of rape was suddenly in the news in strange and unusual ways that linked rape with politics and religion. A military attaché from India was accused of raping a very young girl in Mauritius. The Mauritian Ambassador to Australia accused of violating another very young girl. A Hindu priest accused of rape. All three events had punctual political fall-out. As the date of the launch approached, the title now seemed, by these chance events, to have become more dangerous than ever.

I have to explain that *The Rape of Sita*, like my first novel, *There is a Tide*, was published in a curious way. My friends and I sold about a hundred vouchers for 100 rupees each, representing a pre-payment for a copy, so as to raise money for the Workers' Education (LPT Books) to cover its initial printing and publishing costs. Then on the day of the launch party, everyone gathered to get their copies while celebrating the birth of a novel. The two artists who spoke at the launch of *The Rape of Sita*, Jeanne Gerval-Arouff and Vidya Golam, would forever stand by me when I came under attack for the title. They took the risk. And I remember Rajni Lallah played the grand piano so evocatively that day that we all wanted to climb right into it, our wine glasses and all. And it would only later turn out that maybe this collective form of publishing contributed towards saving me. Because a hundred people would already have a copy of the novel, when all hell would break loose, and they could read it.

This was in December, 1993.

Within days there was a whipped-up storm. The title, it was said, was blasphemous. At the same time as a handful of fundamentalists, political rather than religious men, threatened me with death, public rape, acid in the face and so on, the Prime Minister, Sir Aneerood Jugnauth, stood up in the National Assembly, accused me of blasphemy and set the police on me under the Criminal Code Section 206, a law to deal with cases of "Outrage Against Public and Religious Morality." It is dangerous in the extreme to be attacked by fundamentalists and by the State at the same time. So my friends put me into hiding for a few days, bought me a device that was a curiosity at the time: a mobile phone. So that I could start going around alone again after no more than a few days—with that little bit of technological support. And that was when I realized that everyone who knew me, loved me. Because when I took the risk and did go around all on my own in the face of those threats and of State repression, everyone—even people who I didn't know—showed, or rather had the chance to show, their care. But I only knew it because my friends, too, took the risk of encouraging me to move about freely, to assume it was only a handful of fundamentalists who were playing their political games, using me as an object in the games. While everyone else was nurturing me so that I could recover from the attack. Everyone but the most informed of people assumed I had been attacked by the State and the fundamentalists because I was a political opponent of the regime. Many thought I must have criticized someone high up in it. The idea that you could be threatened with death or prosecution for a mere story seemed incredible otherwise. People had no instinct to blame me. To hound me out. Even though I could have been hounded out as a foreigner, newly Mauritian through marriage.

Even as the calumny continued in some of the reactionary Press, even as threatening anonymous letters and phone calls continued, two senior Police Officers arrived at the Workers' Education print shop to arrange the confiscation of all the novels.

But the publishers and I had already in a joint communiqué announced the removal from circulation of the novel, in order to create time and space to listen to the objections people expressed to the title. Both Ram and I were also present, quite by chance. So, we sat down with the two police officers and explained that the law said that it was an offence to offer the publications for sale, and we were not offering them for sale, so they could not confiscate them. A protracted discussion took place, and the publishers and I firmly refused to hand the books over. I remember also the strange atmosphere of this encounter. When the State uses criminal law and proceedings against individuals for political reasons of any kind, it is my experience that it becomes unsure of itself. I asked the very senior police officer who was there, "Who is in this new 'Literary and Ecclesiastical Brigade' then?" He smiled and looked away. "Who was put in charge of reading my novel, before you were sent to confiscate it?" I persisted.

He hesitated, then replied, "I was," and this time looked at his boots. Being a writer, so often distanced from readers' reactions, I heard myself ask, "Did you like it?" There was a thoughtful silence and he said very quietly, "Yes, I did." And I asked, "What in particular did you like?" and he said, "The bits about the Police." So, the humanity of the Police officer came through. The novel is not kind to the police.

And more strange, the second in command, also a senior officer, towards the end of the bizarre landing kept asking his boss, "Are we finished yet?" And conversation would continue as to whether to confiscate the books or not. And finally, when it was all over, the second-in-command looked at Ram and said, "Do you remember me, Ram? Do you?" Ram said, "Yes, your face is familiar. From long ago?" And the police officer said, "We were in the same class at Brown Sequard Primary School. And I was hungry at school, we were so poor, and you would break your bread-roll in half and share it with me. I've never forgotten that." He had tears in his eyes when he said it. I did too.

So the Police went off to discuss in their bureaucracies whether to confiscate the books or not. Clearly they did not have orders to arrest me. They would have had to have had a woman officer in blue uniform present for that.

And then we took more risks, because the battle was not yet won. Worse, it wasn't even a draw. The book was withdrawn from circulation, stifled. Things were calm because we were, in a way, defeated.

Fundamentalists had meanwhile written in three-foot-high painted letters on a wall: "The Rape of Lindsey Collen," and we discussed this in the women's group I'm in. Some said, "We'll go paint over the words, they're too violent to leave there." But we decided to do something else. We went to the Police Station nearest the painted threat. There I made a formal complaint about unknown people having threatened me in writing. The police asked what action we wanted, and I requested two things: that the words be painted over by the Police and that those responsible be warned that it is illegal to threaten people. Then we said we would be waiting in the Police Station indefinitely. And proceeded to have a low-profile sit-in.

The Police officers were polite, and spent over an hour telephoning higher and higher-up men. Eventually, one of them got some form of go-ahead, and taking some petty cash from a drawer in his regulation desk, went out and bought a tin of black paint, and two or three policemen went to the offending wall, followed by us, the observers, and painted out the slogans. As a little motley crowd gathered, it was clear that the State had decided to offer me its protection instead of attacking me.

One or two newspapers continued to publish articles against me, and often against Ram and my brothers-in-law for not keeping order in their women-folk. Everyone in my husband's family stood by me. My lawyer, Jean-Claude Bibi, and I would go to the central Police with newspapers containing threats and defamatory calumny. We would ask them to warn the authors and publishers of these newspapers that it is illegal to defame and threaten people.

My friends and colleagues in the women's movement were tireless. They took copies of the novel in plain wrappers and offered them to writers, wives of politicians, artists, women activists, religious men. People would contribute their hundred rupees. "So that you know what the book is about, and can judge better," they would say. They would meet groups of women, groups of writers, groups of academics, groups of workers. The trade unions, no doubt loath to venture on a terrain as strange as literature, would support the Workers' Education publishers in other ways, in response to an open letter.

There was hardly a woman in the country who criticized me. Women seemed to feel strongly that rape was an issue that needed to be addressed. A taboo that had to be broken. For that they stood by me. And there was not a single artist who criticized me. All artists know how difficult it is to create, how risky, even without having the fear of being hounded out individually. Journalists and editors in all the major newspapers stood by me, again and again. Gradually more and more people stood up for free expression. Others went into the niceties of the contents of the book, thus taking the novel into the sphere of literary criticism.

Until eventually we felt strong enough for me to hold an open press conference, for me to take questions from anyone who wanted to ask them on any issues. Those who had hounded me out were absent.

And then three years of quiet work continued. And so it was that three years later and after *The Rape of Sita* had been awarded the Africa Region Commonwealth Writers' Prize, had been published in a new edition in the UK, and also in Dutch and German editions, that the book came out quietly on to the shelves in Mauritius. Without any fanfare. And it has stayed available.

Quite sharply from then on, rape became an issue on the political agenda in Mauritius. And political struggles followed. A woman who suffered two double-rapes on one night—as she escaped from one pair of rapists, she was raped by two of those who were "helping" her—spoke out on radio. The balance of forces had by then so changed that all four men were traced and charged. We, in the women's and political movement, meanwhile developed a fantastic demand, for which we struggled and which we won: "Rape Crisis Units" in all major hospitals. This way a victim doesn't have to go to police station anymore, to that most patriarchal, most hierarchical structure of them all, but can go instead to a place of healing, a free Government hospital. There, if she wants to give a statement, a woman officer comes to her and takes it in the caring environment of the hospital, after the woman has been given all the medical and psychological support immediately required. The police medical officers, people with a double identity as medical practitioners in the caring professions and as police officers in the repressive forces, now examine the woman in the hospital environment, rather than in the police environment.

And I, as a writer, have not had to change the title. I had considered it. "It's only a title, for godssake," I thought. And then, at one point, it became difficult even to think of changing it. In Mauritian editions, anyway. An old woman who can't read at all, but who had followed all that was being said, pushed her saree off her forehead back on to her long grey hair and said, "You must not change the title of your book, my daughter, because it is a title that allows women who have been wronged to walk with their heads held high. For the first time."

And that humbled me. For she had brought out a new meaning in the title. One that was only vaguely in my unconscious mind until then.

So, as always, I was reminded that as a writer, I learn from my readers. And in this case I learnt from someone who can't read or write.

Reminding me that it is people in the real world who respond to stories. Who link them with their own stories, their own thoughts.

PETER TURCHI

One Man's Risk

A few years ago, on an island off the coast of Norway, in the course of a casual hike, first my wife and then my son stepped from one bank of a narrow stream onto a concrete footing (what it was doing there, we never figured out), and from there to the far bank. The curious and, it turned out, troublesome aspect of this was that the stream bank was sheer, about a six-foot drop to cold, fast-moving water. The distance to the concrete footing was one longish stride; the top of the concrete pillar was too small to put both feet on, so the crossing required two quick steps.

I froze. And the longer I stood there, the more unlikely it seemed that I could avoid falling into the water. My concern was, as my wife and son pointed out, and I agreed, silly—but that made it no less paralyzing.

I could have found some other way around, but the physical block that had appeared without warning seemed both absurd and potentially crippling; so I stood there, willing my intellectual self to overcome my instinctual self. Our son offered to take my hand, but by then it seemed to me a perilous reach. He offered to come back across to demonstrate the technique, but the problem had nothing to do with understanding the necessary steps; it was a matter of overcoming a powerful and completely irrational fear. Finally—due to no particular urging or inspiration—I took the long first step, and plunged to my death.

Well, no; I made it across just fine, and we continued a perfectly pleasant mountainside stroll. The episode was so forgettable that I hadn't thought of it until today, as I considered the challenge of recognizing what is, for one person, a significant act of courage, but which might seem, to an onlooker, like a walk in the park. Specifically, I've been thinking of the wide range of risks writers take, from the physical to the intellectual to the emotional, and our inclination to value some kinds of risk over others.

When I started high school I was assigned to an afternoon Study Hall. After the first day, even I could tell Study Hall was a place where no studying would ever get done. I asked if I could take Journalism, which met at the same time, but which was normally reserved for upperclassmen. The teacher, Mrs. Lovell, agreed, but the other students—the editors and writers for the school paper—jealous of their territory, said they'd decide after I turned in a sample assignment. Reasonable as that sounded, it was in fact an excuse to get me to conduct an interview none of them wanted to do: someone needed to ask Coach Higgins about the upcoming football season.

I don't know that Coach Higgins taught classes; I certainly never saw him in a classroom. While everyone knew him as the football coach, he didn't look like a football player. For one thing, he was underweight. But he appeared to be made out of flexible metal, his face was worn and creased like an old baseball glove, and he had the voice of a man who smoked two packs a day before breakfast. He didn't so much speak as bark.

As a freshman and a decided non-athlete, it was intimidating enough to have to go down to the boys' locker room to find Coach Higgins's office. The locker room was seven stories underground, dimly lit by candles stuck into little niches in the stone walls. (I believe the candles were stuck in the skulls of boys who had failed to reach the top of the rope in PE, but I may be misremembering that part.) You had to wade through a swamp of old shower water and used towels and jock straps to get to the dim caves of the coaches' offices; and if you somehow talked your way past the lacrosse coach and the basketball coach and the various unidentified men who lived down there, you could finally get to see Kurtz—I mean, Coach Higgins.

Not only was I a freshman, but I didn't know how to interview anyone, and I wasn't entirely sure what my story was supposed to be about. So I mumbled something about being from the newspaper, and Coach Higgins barked, "What?" which I later came to realize didn't mean he hadn't heard you or understood you; it meant you had said something so dumb you should think again. I told him I was supposed to write an article about the football team, and he glowered and asked what *about* the football team, and I asked when the first game was, and he told somebody to hand me a schedule and I ran back to class. What resulted couldn't have been much of an article, but no one else wanted the job, so I was hired.

Over the next few years I became features editor of the newspaper and then editor in chief, but somehow I still had to interview Coach Higgins. He developed a knack of seeing me coming, so each time I got back to that dark and stinking office of his he'd come up behind me and bark, "Turchi!" just to see how high I'd jump.

I underwent a similar sort of hazing when I went to write for my college newspaper. This time the interview no one else wanted was with the college president, about his summer trip to India. His office was large and above ground, and even had windows; the problem with interviewing President McLain was that he was a year or two or five past what should have been his retirement, and he enjoyed nothing more than a captive audience. Getting the interview was easy; the problem was getting out. But again, I was a freshman, and I wanted the job, so I stayed in his office for a week or two as he talked about his summer trip, and his previous summer's trip, and anything else that crossed his mind, then got down on the floor and pulled out his old college yearbooks. Dr. McLain had not only taught at but been a student at the college; he had about 60 yearbooks. He went through them, year by year, showing me which students had married which other students. When he finally closed the last one, he pointed through the tall office windows to the quad and said, "When you go back outside, take a good luck at the girls you see. Odds are, you'll live with one of them the rest of your life."

I was 17; this was terrifying stuff.

But I stayed with it, and over the next few years interviewed the next president and a few deans and several trustees, got into the middle of disputes between the faculty and the administration, and in that way began to recognize the responsibilities of a serious journalist. Like any young person given authority, I misused mine at times; and seeing as how the things I wrote could seriously impact people's livelihoods, they did not hesitate to set me straight. When I grew tired of writing responsible news stories and high-minded editorials, I took over as editor of the underground newspaper, so I could attack myself. The low and high points came when I was nearly kicked out of school for something I published in the underground newspaper, yet awarded a citation of merit by the trustees for the overall excellence of the above-ground newspaper.

After a few more years of writing for an independent weekly, I drifted away from journalism to concentrate on writing fiction. In fact, to this point, I have devoted my professional life to writing fiction and teaching others how to write fiction. I take that work seriously, and believe it has value; but I've been forced to reconsider my choice by a series of books I've read recently. The books I'm thinking of are about the U.S. invasion of Iraq: Anne Garrels's *Naked in Baghdad,* Asne Seierstad's *101 Days,* Jon Lee Anderson's *The Fall of Baghdad,* and Thomas Ricks's *Fiasco.* Together, they reminded me how high the stakes of journalism can be. Garrels, an NPR correspondent, was one of a handful of American reporters who stayed in Baghdad after nearly all reporters were forced out just before the U.S. invasion; Seierstad, a freelancer, kept getting kicked out but kept re-entering the country, sometimes, necessarily, under false pretenses. They risked their lives to cover what they believed to be a story that could only be told first-hand; others, including their Iraqi translators and drivers, risked their lives to help them. Recognizing the potential power of the published word, ordinary citizens took enormous risks, in the weeks before the invasion, by daring to contradict the official propaganda in public. People in outdoor crowds would sometimes whisper to the writers in English, or a waiter would say something under his breath, knowing he could be abducted or killed.

Jon Lee Anderson developed relationships with Baathists, among others, who were in danger from both sides; and Thomas Ricks, the Pentagon reporter for the *Washington Post,* convinced men to risk their careers and reputations to expose a great deal of what went wrong in both Washington and Iraq before, during, and after the invasion.

As a writer, I am humbled to read those books, books that provide what feel like urgent messages. They make me reconsider what we mean when we talk about "taking risks" in writing. The risk of, say, self-exposure might seem inconsequential compared to the risk of death; yet I know serious men and women for whom writing honestly about events and emotions important to them in fiction and in poetry has required tremendous daring. And the stakes are real: we all know writers who have been ostracized by friends or family for making public what they consider to be private.

As the director of an MFA program whose students are adults (the average age is 37, and the majority have careers, or are raising families, or both), I have the opportunity to work with writers uniquely devoted to their education. The degree they receive will not get them a promotion, or an increase in salary, or even a job; the degree itself means very little to them compared to what they want to learn, which is of course as it should be. They make great sacrifices in terms of time and money—many of them not only use all their vacation time but take unpaid leave, they devote 25 hours a week for two solid years to their studies, and a large number take on a substantial amount of debt. Less easily quantifiable but no less significant is the fact that many of these writers devote those resources to their education even though the people around them—colleagues, friends, sometimes even their parents and spouses—don't understand why they feel compelled to do it or, worse, insist on telling them they shouldn't do it. Any given semester, at least one of our students sees his or her marriage dissolve.

On top of that are the personal, internal risks inherent in taking writing seriously. To work to improve one's writing (or painting, or piano playing, or dancing, if one of those activities is your life calling) is to dare to focus on what one doesn't (yet) do well, or well enough—to focus on what one is striving to achieve, as opposed to what one has achieved. This requires making oneself vulnerable, and to resist the daily temptation to return to what is familiar, or comfortable, or less threatening.

This seems like serious risk to me, even though, unlike Garrels and Seierstad and others like them, fiction writers and poets may not put their physical bodies in harm's way (though some do), and even though what they write may not influence world events (though it might). And I remind myself that the risks that nearly paralyze others may not seem like risks to me. For one writer, taking a great risk might mean writing about deeply personal family material despite the fact that people he loves might be angered, or hurt, by what he says; for someone else it may mean moving beyond the personal, to focus on the external, or the universal; for one person it might mean daring to break away from a strategy or approach that has served her well, but is paying smaller and smaller dividends; for another it might mean daring to do what others see as repetitive work because he knows he hasn't yet exhausted the material or the approach that haunts him. One writer might be taking a risk in daring to leave readers confused, or puzzled, or uncertain; another writer might take a risk by daring to drop a fashionable façade of obscurity, irony, or emotional distance.

In my early twenties, while I was in graduate school, my father had a multiple heart bypass. I flew from Arizona to Baltimore to be with him before, during, and after the surgery. Though some people I knew had died by then, none of them had awakened my sense of mortality the way my father's life-prolonging surgery did. I wrote an essay about the experience and showed it to my writer friends. They told me the essay was very bad, and I put it away. After some time had passed—a year or two—I wrote a short story about a man whose father had a heart bypass. The main character is not me, and the father is not my father, but the conflicted emotions the main character expresses toward his father are an exaggerated, or perhaps I should say simplified, variation of some of my feelings toward my father. The story was published as part of a collection that eventually earned me some money and attention.

My father was not a reader, or at least not a reader of literary fiction, but he was tremendously proud of me and my sister—so he was torn between his pride in what I had accomplished and his feeling that I had portrayed him in a very unflattering way. I can still picture quite clearly the evening fifteen years ago when he asked me to come outside and, sitting on the back steps of my house, asked me if the story expressed my "true" feelings toward him. I told him no, but probably not very convincingly. We never had much success communicating with each other—not happily or meaningfully, anyway—and I didn't know how to express the complex feelings I had about the story. I certainly couldn't tell him that I was struggling to express love and fear as well as frustration and anger. His feelings were badly hurt, but we never spoke of it again.

At least, we didn't speak of it for seven years, until he was back in the hospital, preparing for another heart bypass. This time my wife and son and I had planned to be in Baltimore to help my mother with his recovery. I was sitting in my office at school when my father said, over the phone, "Maybe you'll write a story this time, too. A nice one."

Probably there is some way I could have risen to the occasion; certainly I could have said something comforting and supportive and loving. But instead I stumbled over some attempt to say that his well-being was more important than any story. To be honest, I don't know what I said, but I know we were both unsatisfied. The next day, during surgery, he died.

As I said, my relationship with my father was full of miscommunication. I don't suffer from the delusion that I could have written a "nice" story for him, or that anything I wrote would have dramatically affected our relationship. That's not what fiction is for; that's what life is for. But my father's last gift to me—though I never thought of it as a gift until just now—was a reminder that this facility to tell stories, and to communicate with strangers, can be powerful and dangerous. I don't regret writing the story that hurt his feelings; but I do regret my failure to weigh sufficiently the story I wanted to tell on the page and the things I needed to say directly to him.

None of this should concern the reader of that story. When I sit down to write each day, my goal is simply to write something that interests me in a way that interests me, and to avoid repeating myself. Yet what I see as an important distinction from one piece to the next might be indistinguishable even to a sympathetic reader. Sometimes the risk is subtle, essentially private.

Other risks are more public. At our high school, there was a tradition of a senior class play, an original musical, the ticket sales for which provided funds for the senior prom. When I was a senior, I wrote the class play. It was a comic hodge-podge of famous characters and popular songs and local celebrities, and I'm very glad no one had video cameras in those days. But committing it to the page, combined with the cockiness of a high school senior in spring, gave me the courage to trot down those by-then-familiar steps, through the catacombs known as the boys' locker room, and confront Coach Higgins with the information that I had written a play, and there was a part in it for him. It was my retaliation, after four years, for all the times he had come up behind me and barked, "Turchi!"

Even though we were standing in his office, I knew I had him on my turf. Holding his gaze, I could see the doubt cross his face. Coach Higgins thought it over and, for reasons he never felt compelled to share, agreed. A few weeks later, knowing full well what was at stake, he stood alone on stage, in front of a thousand teenagers and colleagues, and sang. The result was quite possibly the most excruciating musical number in the history of high school theater; the coach got a standing ovation, and deserved it.

°°°

Writing Sucks

Writing sucks. Writing for anthologies that will benefit worthy causes sucks. Walking to work and seeing a flock of birds take flight and thinking "The Birds" and hoping you don't get splat on sucks. And wondering all the while what it is people want anyway. Immortality? Fame!

Waiting for your life to change.

Don't hold your breath.

Or maybe you are one of those people who stand naked and say: I have to write.

But is it a calling or a compulsion? And why? Did anyone ask you? Does anyone care? Why did you grab a notebook when you were eight and write down every indignity you suffered? And why as a middle-age mom with a good job and life that looks normal to the outside world, why do you still feel like such a freak and fall asleep at your computer . . . writing?

Yes, yes, writing is important for all the reasons we all know.

Dostoevsky wrote that everything important that needs to be said can fill two pages. Ha! Easy for him to say.

But it has "the ring of truth." That great golden ring. So if you only had two pages, what, my dear friend, would you say?

On the Line

When I was sixteen and considering writing as a career, I was told that becoming an author was just about the hardest thing one could try to do. That didn't bother me, though it should have. My only real concern was whether it would be adventure enough. I grew up in the suburbs of Southern California, so I didn't know even what I didn't know, but I could intimate that there was a world out there. I wanted to get into it. Not because I believed writers needed experiences to write about—I just wanted my life to be fun. And while writing struck me as the only appropriate response to life's central ontological mystery, the actual act seemed kind of dull.

It's probably a mistake to dump writers into categories of any kind, but I'm going to suggest a couple: those whose sensibility is based on experiences they consciously seek, and those who rely on a bed of memories encountered incidentally. Surely this fails in all kinds of ways, but I think it explains the difference between, say, Henry James and George Orwell. Actually, it was James I would need when I dealt with the material of my childhood in fiction. For James, a safe, static, sedentary life in a comfortable society was a problem that required a technical solution. Narrative ambiguity brought drama to scenarios that lacked the tension that could carry a story. Before I read James, my first attempts at writing goofed around with this, and after I found him I emulated it in a kind of auto-apprenticeship. It worked—but part of me was bored. I wanted to be George Orwell, shooting at elephants and fascists. I still do.

When I came out of graduate school, my MFA locked and loaded, there were no more dark continents and there were no wars worth fighting. Unless I could make a living as a short story writer—good luck—it looked like I would have to become a teacher. This is the basic predicament of thousands of writers now emerging from MFA programs every year.

Which is not to say that it's new. Melville had a suburban upbringing, too, first on Bleecker Street when Bleecker Street was considered a suburb, and later outside Albany when the family finances dissolved. He taught for a while—hated it—and went on his first voyage as a cabin boy. Back home, he tried teaching again, and might have stayed there forever had his school not folded. After that, he decided to risk it, and what we now know of Melville's life is best revealed in work that draws mostly on those experiences he had—his venture west, and the whalers—when he decided on a more adventurous course.

Somewhere I got the idea that my own adventurous course would be to move to Atlantic City and become a table games dealer.

Gambling is probably the coarsest form of risk we have. To me, it's insidious not because it's addictive but because it's a cheap way to battle the ennui attendant to affluence. It's a waste of time. But that wasn't what I believed then, and I admit that I thought of the job as a way to pay bills and indulge a side of myself I hadn't yet rejected. I didn't intend to write about it, and for the most part I haven't. The job would be an education, I reasoned, and for this I turned to Dostoevsky for rationale.

Dostoevsky was a gambler—he had some system for playing the columns in roulette and thought he had the game beat. He didn't. On various well-recorded gambling binges, he lost everything he had. In fact, he wrote *The Gambler* because he had busted again—he dictated it, married his amanuensis, and then kept gambling. My rationale was inside *The Gambler*. Dostoevsky claimed that in a casino people behaved in a crowd the way they did when they were alone. The endeavor had an anthropological quality. Much later, working on a book about William James, I found a description of a casino from 1905 which tackles the phenomenon from a number of directions. James wrote to his wife:

> I stopped over a couple hours at Monte Carlo to have a look at the famous casino. . . . The gambling was a curious sight—9 or 10 tables holding 40 sitters each, at it from morning till midnight, with a crowd behind, pressing in and on, and money changing hands without a minute's interruption all day long. You don't have to wait more than 30 seconds for your losses or gains to be "realized"—it is the spirit of "business" reduced to its absolute minimum of complication—the whole essence of the thing boiled down to its lowest terms—and the elimination of everything of accessory interest, of everything that isn't pure visible money gain or money loss, in the procedure, with the background of the luxurious palace, a vast Club into which anyone may enter by leaving his bare name, which swarms with servants & every luxury that Clubs afford, it all gave a kind of Satanic picture of human egoism enshrined—the absolute

quiet, rapidity, and deadly seriousness and absorption of it all in the one great human passion, set free of every usual obstruction, impressed the imagination greatly, and would have impressed it painfully save for the very simplification of the whole thing, which made it seem so trivially bare and void of substance that it became a sort of light joke.

The difference in the casino where I worked was that there were hundreds of tables instead of ten. And after a couple years—even a couple weeks—the joke was no longer amusing.

Dostoevsky made the point that different classes rubbed shoulders in casinos, and it's true. You can boil this analysis down to specific games. Craps is blue collar, blackjack is middle class, and baccarat is conspicuous consumption with risk as "bling." I didn't shoot any fascists, but I did watch a man die in a casino once. I didn't sail the world, but I worked alongside Vietnamese boat people and ghost-wrote asylum request narratives for refugees. To some extent my effort at self-education worked. I left a hunk of my soul there, but I'm glad I turned my back on teaching, like Melville, at least for a little while.

It turns out, however, that Melville's whaling experiences weren't as risky as the books make them seem. The industry was dangerous, but Melville's own career appears to have been uneventful. His actual experiences needed drama just as Henry James's did—he just found a different solution to the problem. In fact, the riskiest part of Melville's life appears to have been writing itself. One of his biographers claimed that "it was as though he needed to risk his life again and again, figuratively speaking . . . filling white paper with his ideas and wisdom, hiding them in his pockets." And much later his sister expressed concern about a return to the writing life after a trip that had done him good: "Were he to return to the sedentary life which that of an author writing for his support necessitates, he would risk the loss of all the benefit to his health which he has gained by his tour, & possibly become a confirmed invalid."

Looking back, the guy who told me that becoming a writer was hard didn't have it quite right. Implied in the way he put it—or in the way I heard it—was that once you got there and were a "writer," it wasn't hard any more. You'd made it. This seems to be a prevailing opinion, and just about everyone who "succeeds" experiences the various tiers of anticlimax—first it's publication, then it's a book, then it's a couple books, then it's the next book. Conceptually, success keeps receding.

For a metaphor to make sense of this, I can return to Dostoevsky and gambling. You'll know what I mean if I say that writing is a long-shot bet, but that's not quite accurate either. It still implies that you can win. Rather, writing is like a roll in craps: you come out on a number, back up your bet, and then you just keep rolling, rolling, with everything you've got on the line, and you never really win or lose. For Dostoevsky, this was both literal and workable material.

The Gambler wasn't one of his better books, but critics have argued that his struggle with gambling informed the spiritual crises of his best work. It seems that experiences like the ones I had and literature both are fairly risky endeavors, differing only in quality. Psychoanalyst Linda Scierse Leonard, writing about Dostoevsky in *Witness to the Fire: Creativity and the Veil of Addiction*, argues that "all creation is a *risk!* The difference between the risk of addiction and the risk of the creative process is that the former leads in the end only to slavery and self-destruction, while the latter opens up new worlds."

SARAH STONE

Politics and the Imagination

How to Get Away with Just about Anything (in Ten Not-So-Easy Lessons)

Defining the Problem

"I'm not interested in political fiction" seems at first like a completely baffling remark, not less so because it's a stance adopted by large numbers of people. Not interested in the ways people use their power over each other? Not interested in the ways we can, fatally, succumb to greed or the wide devastation that greed can cause? Not interested in the heroic—and occasionally successful—figure who turns against life-as-usual to fight for justice, freedom, peace, the future? And yet, we can imagine why a reader, picking up and setting down new novels based on their flap copy, might set aside one novel about human rights workers in San Salvador and instead take home the book about four college friends—whose lives have gone in very different directions—on a road trip to their 20th reunion. Maybe a reader doesn't want to be depressed, lectured, or made to feel helpless and stupid, but instead wishes to escape to Storyland, a delectable country of gossip, cat-fighting, self-revelation, sex, wit, and really good meals. Almost any one of us may find ourselves feeling like E. M. Forster's man on the golf course: ". . . I like a story to be a story, mind, and my wife's the same." Forster "destest[ed] and fear[ed]" that reader, but I think we could be a little more sympathetic than Forster to those who might only be willing to take on aesthetic and moral/intellectual challenges when there's something in it for them.

In political fiction, world events and societal conditions have a direct effect on the dramatic action and the characters' lives. The historical circumstances are more than just background noise ("During the Vietnam War, four college friends—whose lives have gone in very different directions . . ."). The characters may or may not be active contributors to their fates: an Argentine revolutionary in prison for his actions is in a different position from a woman born into slavery. In each case, though, their political circumstances are central to their stories. And we as readers, if given half a chance, will want to understand how human beings behave in extremity. We want to know more about heroism, betrayal, self-betrayal, and the high costs of living in the world.

Making political fiction delicious and fascinating is all about finding ways to evade the four horsemen of political writing: didacticism, self-righteousness, demonization of the other side, and subjection of plot/characters/language to the attempt to make a point. General rules don't seem particularly helpful (i.e., "Rule #1: Create vivid, living characters"—Hey, great idea! Why hasn't anyone thought of that before?). Instead, here are a few examples of methods used by writers who've gotten away with writing recklessly political fiction. Some of these writers get shelved under "Classics"; others use the techniques and approaches of post-modernism. What do they get away with? Making political speeches. Tackling the unthinkable head on. Wrestling with subjects bigger than any writer can legitimately handle. Writing about war, slavery, racism, oppression, class struggles, political prisoners, environmental degradation, and evisceration and making us want to read it.

A Few Basic and Not-So-Basic Strategies and Literary High-Wire Acts

1. Creating memorably anti-heroic, living, compromised, vulnerable characters in lieu of cartoon "heroes"

Not letting them have the last word, not letting them inspire others to action. Catching them in compromising circumstances. Displaying great ideals juxtaposed with human flaws, as with Astrov, the drunken, visionary doctor in *Uncle Vanya:*

> This is the map of the district as it is now. There are still bits of green here and there but only in small patches. The elks, the swans, and the capercaillies have disappeared. There's no trace left of the old settlements and farms and hermitages and water mills. It is, as a matter of fact, a picture of gradual and unmistakable degeneration, which, I suppose, will be complete in another ten or fifteen years. . . . *[coldly]* I can see from your face that this doesn't interest you.

Astrov's life is about helping others, but he's so cynical that he doesn't believe in his own goodness or in the possibility of a better future. We want to make *him* believe. Meanwhile, none of the other characters pay attention to his frighteningly accurate predictions of the future; when someone in Chekhov makes speeches about the destruction of the forests or human suffering, the other characters are defiantly unwilling to listen. They may stand in for the reader so that, instead of resisting these speeches, we are instead likely to wish that those in the story or play would *listen*. And Chekhov hasn't put in any mailing addresses or suggestions for action; whether or not the doctor is right, Chekhov isn't voting for him. Instead, he allows us to see how despair over the state of the world can wreck a life. Two women are in love with Astrov, and he can't listen to either; we're in love with him, too, and don't want to see him destroy himself. At the same time, the politics here are in the service of the story; even as Astrov delivers an environmental lecture, what we're paying attention to is what it means for his own relationships and future. The dramatic interest in this scene has to do with whether he's about to be drawn into an entanglement with the beautiful (and married) woman who doesn't listen because she doesn't share his deepest values, or whether he'll see the worth of the plain (and single) girl who values him for what he is at his best. He could avoid self-destruction, but he won't; his individual blindness echoes society's blindness, despite—ironically—his grand perspective.

Another way of sneaking heroes into political literature is to establish a world in which heroism is impossible, as in Jose Saramago's *Blindness*. Here, among all the (literally as well as metaphorically) blind, just one woman can see, and she uses her vision to make life a little more bearable for those around her. She's not unrealistically sweet, though: Saramago creates narrative tension by having her keep her vision secret, help her own spouse just more than the others, and let her compassion and protective role lead her into violence.

2. Breaking apart the form and language

With subjects too terrible to address head-on, writers sometimes dazzle us with the beauty and mystery of the style and arrangement of events. Theresa Hak Kyung Cha in *Dictée* keeps us off balance all the way through her collaged, intricate, mysterious book, divided into nine parts, each functioning in reference to one of the muses. The book uses poetry, maps, photographs, traditional Chinese medicine charts, lessons, memories, prayers, and history to evoke the complex tragedies of history—especially Korean history—and of Cha's own family. A book like this lets the reader be both partner and detective: how do these different pieces fit together? The right brain is engaged, along with the left, in making predictions and connections. The pleasure of the act of reading makes possible the pain of facing the history.

Toni Morrison's *Beloved,* one of the most passionately loved as well as one of the greatest of all novels, also uses the slow revelation of information, all in poetic prose, or even poetry, as in the voice/perceptions of the ghost baby. This book offers the pleasure of the puzzle, with Morrison doling out information a little at a time, employing the techniques of the mystery writer to make literature. The seriousness and majesty of the book are in no way undercut by the fascination of figuring out what has happened and why. Again and again, the gorgeous writing slams up against the horrors of slavery, as when Paul D. tells Sethe about a time when he needed to talk and couldn't because he had a bit in his mouth:

> He wants to tell me, she thought. He wants me to ask him about what it was like for him—about how offended the tongue is, held down by iron, how the need to spit is so deep you cry for it. She already knew about it, had seen it time after time in the place before Sweet Home. Men, boys, little girls, women. The wildness that shot up into the eyes the moment the lips were yanked back. Days after it was taken out, goose fat was rubbed on the corners of the mouth but nothing to soothe the tongue or take the wildness out of the eye.

The details help us come as close as we possibly can to a visceral understanding of the pain and the indignities of slavery, and the ways they permanently mark those who suffer through them. The "tree" of scar tissue from the whippings on Sethe's back is only the most visible reminder of ineradicable damage. There is a wildness that will never come out of her, including her belief that it would be better for a baby to die than to grow up to a life where she can have a bit forced into her mouth, as if she were an animal.

3. Using the pleasures of pattern, letting the reader recognize the repetitions and variations of images and events

There's an enormous pleasure in recognizing an image, idea, or theme presented in one way early on in the book and then in varying ways as the book progresses. These recurrences can also be of events that echo each other, as Charles Baxter points out in his essay "Rhyming Action." Michael Cunningham, in *Specimen Days*, gives us three different novellas with three permutations of the same characters, in the past, in an altered present, and in a distant future. In every case, the characters are in life-or-death situations; all the narratives are gripping, and every situation is political. Cunningham puts his characters at the mercy of crippling prejudices, exploitive labor practices, pervasive terrorism and frighteningly over-forceful responses, and the political choices that lead to apocalyptic futures. And yet, he has created a delicious, readable, exhilarating book. In part he does this through the vividness of the characters and language, but there is also a puzzle-solving delight in tracing the characters' changes, the transformation of objects, and even the different uses of lines of Walt Whitman's poetry.

Manuel Puig's *Kiss of the Spiderwoman*, told entirely in dialogue and footnotes, gives us the novel-as-tango, with Valentin imprisoned for his sexual orientation and Molina for his revolutionary activism. The plots of the movies Valentin recounts serve as an escape—for prisoners and readers—and echo each other in counterpoint to daily prison life. The routines of prison make a frame for the misunderstandings, suspicion, and increasingly complicated relationship between the two men. Much of the story unfolds through the slow revelation of their lives and circumstances and the way in which, as they form a personal connection, they come to understand each other's world views. In the beginning, Molina is full of prejudices and Valentin dangerously politically naïve, in ways that at first seem innocent, as in his romanticization of the Nazis in one of the films he describes:

> — . . . It takes place in Paris, a couple of months after the start of the German occupation. Nazi troops are filing through the Arch of Triumph. Flags with German swastikas, fluttering all over the place, on the Eiffel Tower and everywhere else. Soldiers parading past, totally blond, marvelous to look at, and the French women all applaud as they march by. Not far from there, one small group of soldiers make their way along a typical little side street and go into a butcher shop, where there's an old butcher, with a pointy head, and one of those tiny caps sitting on the back of his scalp.
> —Like a rabbi.
> —His face looks so ugly. And a horrible fear overtakes him the moment he sees the soldiers come into the shop and start to search the premises.

At this point in the novel, Valentin values beauty and style above everything else—better a marvelous-looking Nazi than a plain old Jew. The repetition and variation in the stories he tells Molina, as well as his increasingly tender care of Molina in bouts of sickness, show him changing, but it isn't until the real plot of betrayal and regret emerges that we understand the patterning and the echoes of the book.

4. Applying historical perspective

Distance adds layers and complications to contemporary/eternal issues. Novelists who explore past events often have a well of research to draw on, and, with the participants in those struggles long dead, it's possible—potentially—to be more objective. Writing about the past allows writers to depict political events without readers feeling as if someone is trying to force them to take direct action, or as if the novel is really a tract or advertisement for a particular view. The danger, of course, is that many readers have their own partisan views of these events, as well as a strong sense of historical fact and detail. Historical writers, therefore, have to be prepared to do more research than they ever imagined, not only in order to acquire facts, but also to develop their senses of perspective and understanding of the meanings of events. In all three of the works below, the beauty of the writing, the richness of the detail, and the sense of discovering an unknown and vanished world entice us in and keep us going. These books were each thought through over an extended period: the writers' commitment, research, and long, deep work gives them a weight that matches their subjects.

Edward P. Jones, in *The Known World,* gives every character—black, white, Native American, slave, free, exploited, exploiter, and exploited-exploiter—the dignity of a complete history in evoking the nightmarish, poisonous world of slavery. He knows his characters with a deep, magisterial compassion. Marilynne Robinson uses the form of a letter from a dying father in *Gilead* to tell a story of abolition and freedom, transgression and forgiveness. The novel is, at once, political/moral/religious/historical. In *The Air We Breathe,* Andrea Barrett shows the paranoia and inhumanity that can arise during wide-spread public catastrophe. The observer of this scene is Leo, surrounded by the effects of a polio epidemic in New York during the summer of 1916. Because he is suffering from a different disease—tuberculosis—and shunned for his own illness, he is hyperalert to the suspicions and dread he sees around him:

> In the shops, people turned away from each other, fingering the little bags of camphor and garlic hanging from their necks and embarrassed— had they been embarrassed?—not to be able to help each other for fear of infecting their own children. Everything had seemed infected. Bricks leapt from the roof of a building struck by lightning and hit the children walking below; a hammer glancing off a pipe at the oil-plant in Greenpoint set off an explosion; a subway excavation caved in and buried twenty workers. In Williamsburg, mothers carried into the clinics screaming babies who could no longer wave their arms or hold their bottles, while others hid from the nurses who knocked on doors. Rumors spread: that the doctors got a bonus for each child captured and taken to the hospital. That the children got sick from eating ice cream, which chilled their stomachs, and that stores sold them ice cream anyway. That gasoline fumes spread the disease (why were automobiles still allowed on the streets?), or commercial laundries (the germs moved in the sheets). That the mothers of stricken children shook their sleeves over the cans of purified milk at the milk stations, hoping other children might sicken as well.

The atmosphere here vividly re-creates the kinds of misunderstanding and distorted thinking that arise from fear, the desire for the regulation of catastrophe that can lead to oppressive laws and social policies. This is the moment where these laws start. The mothers of healthy children blaming the mothers of the sick, and the ways these mothers become demonized in the imaginations of their worried counterparts, pave the way for inhuman decisions, both personal and political.

5. *Making the reader a partner, using the layers of stories we already know*

Reinventing old stories/myths/sacred texts. Angela Carter and Tanith Lee are famous for revealing the complications of sexual politics by means of their often grim reworkings of fairy tales. Doris Lessing in her *Canopus in Argos* series uses the Judeo-Christian stories in such new ways that they are almost unrecognizable, and yet there's a resonance that comes from our sudden moments of recognition and from the importance of these stories in forming our imaginative understanding of the world. This allows Lessing to directly address questions of how we operate as political beings, and then to move into a more fantastic mode, as in *Shikasta*:

> All around the boundaries with Shikasta, on a certain level, crowd the avid ghosts, and not one of us enjoys contact with them.
>
> They are souls who were unable to break the links with Shikasta when they left it. Very often they are unaware they *have* left it, are like goldfish who find themselves inexplicably outside their bowl yearning in, not knowing how they got out or how to get back. Like hungry people at a feast: but while the food and festivities are real, they are not, dreams in a real world. These poor wraiths crowd around every part of Shikasta, as thick as bees. Some scenes, places, locations, attract them irresistibly. Around the proud and the power-loving, there they cluster, trying to partake of what they yearn for because in their lives they were powerful and proud and cannot stop themselves wanting that sweet food, or because they were beaten down and humiliated and wish now for revenge. Oh, the revengeful and bitter ghouls that surge all around the pomps and the powers of Shikasta!

Watching these wraiths, and their envy of the living, gives us a way of looking at our own world, our fixation on power, pleasure, and success—and serves as a reminder of the ways people beat down and humiliate others. Where there is pomp and power, this passage reminds us, there will be want and suffering. Lessing's vision of hell is of the souls excluded from life; they yearn desperately for everything they had and everything they didn't have, most especially the sweetness of power; they would do anything to get that power. Lessing could present the people and institutions we know, and has done so elsewhere in her work—but in the *Canopus in Argos* series she uses allegory as a way of waking up the reader and reminding us of what we forget as we go about our daily lives. Throughout her fiction, she uses the metaphor of being drugged to stand for the state of sinking into an acceptance of the unjust and bizarre aspects of reality.

6. Inventing something completely unlike anything we know, which sheds light on what we do know

These novels often give us future or alternate realities. Ursula K. LeGuin, in *The Left Hand of Darkness,* sends a human emissary to the cold, strange, enticing world known as Winter, in which the inhabitants share mutable genders—they enter *kemmer* and their sexual role changes in relation to current or available partners. In playing out a new anthropology of sex, its new and altered taboos on Winter, and how it might be to live without a fixed gender, LeGuin entices us into re-examining assumptions we may not even have realized we had. In *Never Let Me Go,* Kazuo Ishiguro creates a world that is almost like our own, and in which questions about cloning illuminate realities of class, privilege, and oppression. It's an enticing triangle of love, friendship, and power struggles—in a life-and-then-death situation. Ishiguro works by implication, a form of sentimental education. Octavia Butler's *Blood Child* complicates the relationship between humans—"convenient, big, warm-blooded animals"—and the alien masters who perpetuate themselves by laying their eggs in the particular humans they've adopted/enslaved. What the aliens do to the humans is hideous, but there is an almost-parental, almost-erotic, symbiotic bond between them which reveals something new and surprising about the workings of power in relationships.

7. Employing wit, usually biting, and/or playfulness

A sly appeal to the reader. It takes surprising courage for a literary writer, and one dealing with often grim subjects, to be funny. Sometimes writers worry that they're trivializing the circumstances with their jokes, or that they have somehow left the realm of the literary. Many people share the idea that a serious book must also be earnest. It might seem that some subjects—war, genocide—are impossible to treat in ways that involve humor. One way writers have managed it is to keep the humor as a minor, leavening element in a grim tale, neither letting it get out of proportion nor using it for its own sake. Marjane Satrapi's *Persepolis: The Story of a Childhood,* a graphic novel of stark black and white comic-book drawings with no grays, gives a complicated, shaded look—from the perspective of an Iranian child—at the Islamic Revolution and the war with Iraq. Like Art Spiegelman's *Maus,* the book intertwines political history with family troubles, making the unimaginable comprehensible. In both cases, the daily humor of family misunderstandings makes the political events even more tragic—we are reminded that these wars are happening to ordinary people, trying to live and grow despite the horrors around them. The visual images never let us forget the body count. The situation of children trying to find grown-ups to emulate in a world gone crazy adds additional pathos to both books.

Some subjects, like the often oppressive nature of the workplace and the abuses of power in the corporate world, lend themselves to a more openly biting sarcasm. George Saunders is one of the great exemplars of our world refracted bizarrely. He combines wild humor with surreal invention to produce a completely believable situation. We recognize the "cave-people" in *Pastoralia*: their dire family situations that keep them in a grim job, pretending to slaughter and skin goats, scratching themselves, faxing in their "Daily Partner Performance Evaluation Forms," and emptying their "Human Refuse" bags. In danger of being down-sized, our narrator is under pressure to betray his resistant work partner, as his boss comes to visit him and says:

> "I know it's hard to be objective about people we come to daily know, but in the big picture, who benefits when the truth is not told? Does Janet? How can Janet know she's not being her best self if someone doesn't tell her, then right away afterwards harshly discipline her? And with Janet not being her best self, is the organization healthier? And with the organization not being healthier, and the organization being that thing that ultimately puts the food in your face, you can easily see that, by lying about Janet's behavior, you are taking the food out of your own face. Who puts the cash in your hand to buy that food in your face? We do. What do we want of you? We want you to tell the truth. That's it. That is all."
>
> We sit a while in silence.
>
> "Very simple," he says. "A nonbrainer."

This speech mixes up diction as much as logic: corporate-speak with slang, the appearance of friendliness with a threat to the narrator's soul as well as his survival, the crazy logic of giving someone a warning and then immediately disciplining her with no chance for her to change, and the naked reminder of power. It's an unanswerable speech. The situation is anything but simple, and the boss's idea that it could be, along with the word "nonbrainer," reinforces our doubts about the intelligence of this genial thug.

8. *Giving way to the reckless pleasures of suspense*

Haruki Murakami, more unabashedly gripping than any half-dozen escapist genre writers, uses the strong pull of a narrative thread in *The Wind-Up Bird Chronicles*—the hunt for a missing wife—to weave together a range of stories and documents that take on war, compulsion, the nature of human evil, and the political and social situation in Japan during and after WW II. The wife is, we start to suspect, held captive and in danger of having her soul destroyed—at the same time, she seems to be a runaway. Did she go of her own volition or not? And what will happen to our increasingly less passive narrator in his magical, painful, continually surprising search for her? In *An Accidental Man*, Iris Murdoch, who more often grapples with characters' philosophical/moral predicaments than their politics, takes on the question of the draft and the Vietnam War. What duty does a man have to a war he doesn't believe in? As usual with Murdoch, it's the characters' social and erotic quagmires that propel the book forward.

9. Examining, in an intimate narrative, the story behind the news and what it's really like to live through extreme historical moments

A central question of fiction, as of psychology, is "What would make someone do such a thing? What could they have been thinking?" In other words, "What drives people to irrational acts?" Another question that we repeatedly need to have explained or embodied is "How can people survive in dreadful conditions?" In *A Man of the People,* Chinua Achebe dramatizes the Nigerian post-independence/pre-revolution conflicts through the creation of two opposing characters, the charismatic man of the people—now Minister of Culture—and the young intellectual who envies and despises him. The two men are romantic as well as political rivals, and the engine of the novel is driven by this rivalry and the revelations of the insidious workings of corruption. Achebe uses a fierce humor as well: political machinations, like corporate machinations, seem to lend themselves to this. Nadine Gordimer, in *Burger's Daughter,* explores political commitment across generations, what it means to be the daughter of an activist, whether one can flee one's own country struggles to a life of comfort elsewhere, and how we are formed by our historical circumstances.

10. Working with an enormous canvas

A novelist can depict so many different aspects and characters that it's impossible to take sides. Tolstoy in *War and Peace* lays out his entire theory of war, with dozens of characters in both Moscow and St. Petersburg. Meanwhile, the personal lives of his characters, their debts, their loves, their deceptions and self-deceptions, their family obligations and partialities, make this perhaps the most reread of all novels. Another top contender for novel-to-be-dropped-on-a-desert-island-with is George Eliot's *Middlemarch,* the story of an entire town, where the characters' intense desires—to create decent low-income housing (i.e. model cottages), build a new hospital, or cure infectious diseases—are derailed, temporarily or permanently, by their bad choices about love and money.

Gabriel Garcia Marquez, in *One Hundred Years of Solitude,* gives us a century in the life of the town of Macondo and its major family as they traverse an immense war-filled span of time. Marquez makes the story intimate by means of an exact observation of the eccentric and individual ways we form our beliefs, live our lives, and make the decisions that affect our own fates and that of the world around us. The book, combining history, mythology, and invention, is sad, humorous, full of vulnerable and vivid characters, inventive in language and pattern, suspenseful, and grand, all at once. It is never afraid to be ambitious, political, beautiful, imaginative, and even mundane. Along the way,

Marquez shows us the day-to-day interactions and moments that change history:

> "The Liberals will go to war," Aureliano said. Don Apolinar concentrated on his domino pieces. "If you're saying that because of the switch in ballots, they won't," he said. "We left a few red ones in so there wouldn't be any complaints." Aureliano understood the disadvantages of being in the opposition. "If I were a Liberal," he said, "I'd go to war because of those ballots." His father-in-law looked at him over his glasses.
>
> "Come now, Aurelito," he said, "if you were a Liberal, even though you're my son-in-law, you wouldn't have seen the switching of the ballots."
>
> What really caused indignation in the town was not the results of the elections but the fact that the soldiers had not returned the weapons. A group of women spoke with Aureliano so that he could obtain the return of their kitchen knives from his father-in-law. Don Apolinar Moscote explained to him, in strictest confidence, that the soldiers had taken the weapons off as proof that the Liberals were preparing for war. The cynicism of the remark alarmed him. He said nothing, but on a certain night when Gerinaldo Márquez and Magnífico Visbal were speaking with some other friends about the incident of the knives, they asked him if he was a Liberal or a Conservative. Aureliano did not hesitate.
>
> "If I have to be something I'll be a Liberal," he said, "because the Conservatives are tricky."

PART THREE

Where I Come From

NADINE GORDIMER

That Other World
That Was the World

More than three hundred years of the colonization of modem times (as distinct from the colonization of antiquity) have come to an end. This is the positive achievement of our twentieth century, in which so much has been negative, so much suffering and destruction has taken place. Colonization is passing into history, except for comparatively small pockets of the earth's surface where new conquest has taken a precarious hold and the conquered, far from being subdued into acquiescence, make life for the conquerors difficult and dangerous.

Surely the grand finale of the age of colonization took place in the three years, 1991 to 1994, when South Africa emerged amazingly, a great spectacle of human liberation, from double colonization.

For unlike other countries where the British, the French, the Portuguese and other European powers ruled the indigenous people and when these colonizers were defeated or withdrew, left the countries in indigenous hands, South Africa in the early twentieth century passed from colonization from without—Dutch, French, finally British—to perpetuated colonization within, in the form of white minority power over the black majority. All the features of colonization were retained: taxes and the appropriation of land by whites, so that blacks would have to come to town and provide cheap labour in order to survive; favoured status for the minority in civil rights, education, freedom of movement. Freed from British imperialism, South Africa was far from free; it was a police state based on the claim that the white skin of colonials was superior to black skin.

I think there is a definite distinction to be made, everywhere, between what were the first settlers, the so-called pioneers who fought their way into a country, killing Indians or blacks, and the people of later generations who were born into a society that had long established its ruling accommodation with the indigenous people: a society removed from all danger, that had made itself comfortable with injustice, in this case the theory that there are genetically inferior races with lower needs than others.

I emerged into this milieu with my birth in South Africa in the Twenties. I shall never write an autobiography—I'm much too jealous of my privacy, for that—but I begin to think that my experience as a product of this social phenomenon has relevance beyond the personal; it may be a modest part of alternative history if pieced together with the experience of other writers. And it has a conclusion I did not anticipate would be reached in my lifetime, even when I became aware of my situation.

We lived in a small gold-mining town thirty miles from Johannesburg, lost in the veld nearly 6,000 feet above sea level. The features of the landscape, its shapes and volumes, were made of waste. We were surrounded by yellow geometrical dumps of gold tailings and black hills of coal slag. I thought it ugly when I was a child brought up on English picture books of lush meadows and woods—but now I find the vast grassland beautiful and the memory of it an intimation to me, if I had known it then, that the horizons of existence are wide and that the eye and the mind could be carried on and on, from there.

My mother came from England when she was six years old. My father came from Latvia at thirteen. She had a solid, petty middle-class, piano-playing background, a father lured to emigration by the adventure of diamond prospecting rather than need. My father was sent away by his father to escape pogroms and poverty.

Perhaps because of their youth when they left, and because of this economic and social disparity, my parents kept no connections with the countries they emigrated from. They could not talk of a common "home" across the water, as many other whites in the town did. My father was ashamed of his lack of formal education and my mother did not disguise the fact that she felt she had demeaned herself by marrying him. There was a certain dour tact in not talking about where they had sprung from.

Though both Jewish, they did not take part in Jewish communal life in the town, or join the Zionist associations of the time; they did not belong to a synagogue—my mother was an agnostic and my father, who had had an orthodox childhood, could not withstand her gibes about the hypocrisy of organized religion.

In one of Albert Camus's novels, the child Jacques, born and living in Algeria, asks his mother: "Maman, qu'est que c'est la patrie?" And she replies, "Je ne sais pas. Non." And the child says, "C'est la France."

If I had been asked the question as a child, I probably would have said, "It's England." South Africa's British dominion status had ended the year after I was born, but South Africa was a "sovereign independent state" whose allegiance still was to the British Crown. At school we celebrated the Twenty-fifth Jubilee of "our" King, George V. The so-called mother country: that was the focus of inculcated loyalty, of allegiance, identification for English-speaking South Africans.

And yet it was so remote, that England, that Northern Hemisphere we learnt about in geography class. In the Twenties and Thirties it was four weeks away across the seas. We were at the bottom of the map; we did not count, had little sense of ourselves beyond the performance of daily life.

Italo Calvino was not a colonial but he knew the sense an imaginative child, living in a small town even in an integrated, Italian society, may have of living in an ante-room of life. He describes how, as a boy, passing the cinema where dubbed voices on the sound track of American films came through the projectionist's window, he could "sense the call of that other world that was the world."

This conveys perfectly, at a graver and more enduring—a damaging level— what was my sense of my own existence.

From a very early age I had the sense that that other world—the world of books I took from the library, the world of the cinema—was that other world that was the world. We lived outside it.

It called. Perhaps some day, if one were very lucky, very good, worked very hard, one might get to see it; and as I grew older that world took form, Dickens's and Virginia Woolf's London, Balzac's and Proust's Paris. As for America, I passed from Huck Finn to Faulkner and Eudora Welty; but America was not on the itinerary of the retired mine captains and shift bosses and their wives, my mother's friends, who saved all their lives to afford one trip "home" to England on retirement.

That other world that was the world.

For me, this was not merely a charming childish romanticism; I would not simply grow out of it, grow into my own world effortlessly, as Calvino would.

I had no lineal connection with the past around me, the dynasties of black people.

I had the most tenuous of connections with the present in which I was growing up.

My parents never talked politics; the only partisanship they displayed was during the war, when they wanted "la patrie," the British, to defeat the Germans. I was not even dimly aware of the preparation for the struggle for political power that was beginning between Afrikaners, who more than twenty years before my birth had lost the Boer War to the British, and English-speaking South African whites who were the victors.

I saw the bare-foot children of poor-white Afrikaners, victims of defeat and drought, selling newspapers, just as I saw black people, victims of a much greater defeat, the theft of their land and the loss of all rights over the conduct of their lives, sent back to their ghetto after the day's work serving the town.

Reading a biography of Marguerite Duras recently, I see in her colonial childhood in Indochina my own in South Africa. Her family "had the right not to be kept waiting at administration counters, and were served everywhere before the local Vietnamese. They benefited by the privileges reserved for the French colonials. Marguerite does not complain about this difference in treatment. The distinction between the races is a natural reality for her."

As it was for me.

What was my place? Could it know me?

On the one hand there was that other world that was the world, where Ginger Rogers and Fred Astaire danced in a cloudscape (I had ambitions to be a dancer, myself, as an entry to that world) and Maurice Chevalier sang about Paris. There were the moors where Heathcliff's Cathy wandered, and the London park where Mrs. Dalloway took her walks.

On the other hand, just outside the gate of our suburban house with its red-polished stoep and two bow-windows, there was the great continuous to-and-fro of life, the voice of it languages I didn't understand but that were part of my earliest aural awakening; the spectacle of it defined by my adult mentors as something nothing to do with me.

This totally surrounding, engulfing experience was removed from me not by land and sea but by law, custom and prejudice.

And fear. I was told by my mother to avoid passing, on my way to school, the mine compound where black miners lived; she did not explain why, but the reason seeped to me through adult innuendo: there was the idea that every black man was waiting to rape some toothy little white schoolgirl.

Many years later, my friend and fellow writer Es'kia Mphahlele told me he was instructed by his mother to turn his bicycle down another street if he saw he was going to pass white boys. He did not know why until, in the same way as I learned my fear of black men, he gathered that he must believe every white was only waiting for the opportunity to attack him.

There was certainly more substance behind the fear instilled in him than the fear instilled in me, since blacks were physically maltreated by some whites; but the extreme unlikelihood that he or I was in any danger in the manner anticipated was part of the paranoia of separation that prevailed, matched each to the colour of his or her skin.

Archbishop Desmond Tutu—he and I have discovered—as a child lived for some time in the black ghetto across the veld from the town where I, too, was growing up; there was as much chance of our meeting then as there was of a moon landing.

Did we pass one another, sometimes, on Saturday mornings when the white town and the black ghetto all stocked up for the weekend at the same shops? Did I pass him by when I went into the local library to change books, a library he was barred from because he was black?

Perhaps there were explanations for all this, but they were not evident at home, at school, or among the contemporaries who were chosen for me, to whom I was confined by law, so to speak. And if there were to be some explanations in that other world that was the world, over the seas, it was not open to me; you could not expect it to be bothered with us.

Albert Camus's unfinished, posthumously published novel, from which I quoted earlier, has what appears to be a puzzling title, *Le Premier Homme*; but this is not some Neanderthal romance. Jacques is a colonial boy born and growing up in Algiers. He's white, not Arab; therefore, as we have seen in his answer to his mother, he must be French. But he has never seen France. For fictional Jacques and for the child I was, the premise is: Colonial: that's the story of who I am.

The one who belongs nowhere.

The one who has no national mould.

As Jacques grows up he comes to the realization that he must *make himself*. The precept is: if he is not to be the dangling participle of imperialism, if he is not to be the outsider defined by Arabs—a being non-Arab—what is he? A negative. In this sense, he starts from zero. He is the constructor of his own consciousness. He is The First Man.

Let us not worry about the gender: I was to come to the same necessity; to *make myself*, in the metaphor of The First Man, without coherent references, up on his own two legs, no model on how to proceed.

Of course the realization of the necessity did not come quickly; one must not exaggerate, or rather one cannot exaggerate sufficiently the tendency of human beings to keep sipping the daily syrup of life in a cosy enclave.

Our place as whites outside that world that was the world, overseas, was suitably humble—what effrontery to think that we could write a poem or compose a song that would be "good enough," over there—but ours was a place secure and comfortable, so long as one kept to the simple rules, not walking by too close to the compound where the black miners lived. The ordinary components of childhood were mine, at least until the age of eleven when circumstances that have no relevance here put a curious end to it.

But with every adolescence there comes to everyone the inner tug of war— the need to break away, and the need to bond.

I had more passionate emotion for the first than courage to carry it out, but that would have resolved itself anyway, with time and confidence.

What was dismaying was the lack of discovery of what one might turn *to*, bond *with*.

Young white people in the town gathered in sports clubs and religious groups; they met the same people at tennis on Sunday as they had danced with on Saturday night. It was a prelude to going to one another's weddings, attending bridge afternoons and charity cake-sales (the white women) and meeting to exchange chaff in the club bar after golf (the white men). As Camus says, a life "with no other project but the immediate."

A life ordered, defined, circumscribed by the possession of a white skin. I did not know anything else, yet I knew I could not commit myself there; I felt it as a vague but menacing risk, bondage, not bonding. My reaction was to retreat, turn even further away from the reality of our life than the club life of colonials, which at least was an enclave within the life that swarmed around it.

That world that was the world, overseas, now lived my life as proxy for me; it was no longer the cloudscape of Fred Astaire and Ginger Rogers, but the world of literature. I ate and slept at home, but I had my essential being in books. Rilke roused and answered the emptiness in me where religious faith was missing. Chekhov and Dostoevsky opened for me the awesome mysteries of human behaviour. Proust taught me that sexual love, for which every adolescent yearns, is a painful and cruel affair as well as the temptation of bliss. Yeats made me understand there was such a thing as a passion for justice, quite as strong as sexual passion.

These and other writers were my mentors, out of whom I tried to make an artificial construct of myself. When young people are said to "live in books" rather than in themselves, this is regarded as an escape; it is more likely a search.

For me, of course, the search was not a success in terms of the unconscious purpose I had. I could not make myself out of the components of that other world, though I could and did appropriate it for my delight and enlightenment. What it could do for me, and did, was turn me to face a possibility; a possibility for myself. In my desire to write, in the writing that I was already doing out of my pathetically limited knowledge of the people and the country where I lived, was the means to find what my truth was, what was there to bond with, how I could manage to become my own First Man, woman-man, human being.

I had, in fact, been engaged with this possibility for some time, without understanding what I was doing.

An early story of mine harked back to a childhood impression I had thought forgotten.

On that same way to school when I avoided crossing the path of the black miners in the open veld, I would pass the row of "Concession" stores—trading concessions on mine property—which served the miners and had the intended effect of keeping them out of the town. I had taken my time, as children will dawdle, seeing through the shop doors every day how the miners were treated by the white shopkeepers, spoken to abusively, not allowed to linger in choice of purchases as we whites did. At the time, to me this was just another example of the way adult life was ordered; something accepted, not disturbing. But the images had fermented below the surface impressions of childhood as I developed the writer's questioning concentration.

What I was coming to understand, in writing that story, was one of the essential features of colonialism: the usefulness to the regime of the poor immigrant's opportunity, at last, to feel superior to someone, and thereby support the regime's policy of keeping the indigenous population decreed inferior.

My story's title was "The Defeated"; and it did not refer only to the black miners. They were despised, and bullied across the counter by white immigrants who themselves had a precarious economic and social footing: ill-educated, scarcely able to speak the two languages of the white community, carrying in their minds and bodies the humiliations and deprivation of pogroms and quotas they had fled in Eastern Europe.

In keeping with my ignorance at the time, the story makes too much of an equation between the defeated—the shopkeeper who relieves his feelings of inferiority within the white community by maltreating blacks, the black miners who are so stripped of every context of human dignity that they must submit to abuse even from someone at the lowest level in the white community.

For the shopkeeper and the black miner were, in fact, *not* in the same social pit.

I could have written a sequel set ten or twenty years on and the shopkeeper would have had a business in town and a son at a university, he would have been a naturalized full citizen with the vote—while the black miner still would have been drilling the rock-face or back in his rural home living on the meagre savings of a lifetime spent underground, and still without citizenship rights or the vote in the country of his birth and ancestry.

But if out of a muddled desire to juggle justice where there was none—a kind of reconciliatory conclusion I might have thought was the correct literary approach—I equated the measure of defeat in the lives of the two men, black and white, I did at least reveal in the story that important phenomenon whereby the balance of oppression is maintained not just by laws, but in every situation of social intercourse. I was learning that oppression thrives on all manner of prejudicial behaviour, is fostered by all kinds of insecurity.

With small beginnings such as this I started, tentatively, held back by the strictly controlled environment of the white enclave, to live in the country to which, until then, I had no claim but the fact of birth.

In my stories I was continuing to turn over, this way and that, events in the conduct of my narrow life that had seemed to have a single meaning. The only communal activity in which I'd taken part was amateur theatricals; the first uneasy stirrings of liberalism in the town came to be expressed in the mode the churches and individual consciences were accustomed to—charity. No one thought to petition the town council to open the library to blacks, but it was decided to take a play to the only public hall in the black ghetto.

The play was *The Importance of Being Earnest*, and I had the role of Gwendolen. I was twenty and had never been into a black township before; I believe none of us in the cast had. I believe that no one in the audience had ever seen a play before; how could they? The Town Hall, which doubled as a theatre, was closed to blacks. The audience started off close-kneed and hands folded but was soon laughing and exclaiming. We thought we had had a great success, and drank to it back-stage with our usual tipple, some gaudy liqueur.

When the scenes of that evening kept returning to me in aspects turned this way and that, and I began to write a piece of fiction, make a story out of them, what emerged was a satire—on us.

On the absurdity of taking what we imagined was bountiful cultural uplift, an Oscar Wilde play, to the ghetto the town had created. I came to the full appreciation that the audience, those people with drama, tragedy and comedy in their own lives about which we knew *nothing*, were laughing at us.

Not at the play, but us. They did not understand the play with its elaborate, facetious and ironic use of the language they half-knew, English; but they understood *us*, all right. And we in our pretensions, our idea of what we were "giving" them, were exquisitely funny. Oscar Wilde perhaps would have been amused to think that his play became doubly a satire, functioning as such far from Lady Bracknell's drawing-room.

I think I have been fortunate in that I was born into the decadence of the colonial period.

It has been ravelling out during my lifetime. This is so, even though the mid-century saw the hardening of South African racism in huge forced removals of the black population in order to satisfy white separatism and economic greed, the outlawing of all opposition to these policies as subversion, and for millions the suffering of imprisonment and exile. These were the ghastly paroxysms of a monstrous regime thrashing about in death throes.

The reaction of the white community to strikes and mass demonstrations was to raise the drawbridges over which blacks might commingle with whites. Sexual relations between black and white became a criminal offence, no mixed membership of political parties was allowed, even ambulances were segregated so that an accident victim might lie by the roadside until the vehicle mandated to the appropriate skin colour could be summoned.

A larger and larger army and police force were deployed to keep blacks out of white lives, and all the devices of bugging, opening mail, infiltrating, trapping, spying were gratefully tolerated by the white community within itself for what it believed was its own safety. For, of course, there were dissidents among whites who actively supported blacks against discrimination, and who, going about undetected in their white skin, could be hunted out only in this way.

But no piling-up of restrictive laws, no recruitment of professional liars, stool-pigeons and psychopath interrogators, no population removals could stop the historical process of unravelling. The population removals brought more and more people illegally into the cities, since they could not subsist in the barren areas they were banished to. Arrested, sent away, they came back again. No console of listening and watching devices discouraged dissidents in the white community; merely sharpened their skills at, in turn, evading detection of their communications and contacts, at home, with the banned black liberation movement, and with its supporters abroad. No bans on the mixing of black and white could stop the reaction to the ultimate in inhuman segregation that we were living: there was the violent urge to separation, and the counter urge it set up: the urge to move towards blacks, not alone as a matter of justice, but as a human imperative.

When I had longed to get out of the small town which did not know me, my perceptions of it setting me apart, I had envisaged this as a move that would bring me closer to that other world that was the world—European ideas, mores. Johannesburg, the city, was surely at least the local representative of that world. But by the time I made the move to Johannesburg it was to bring me closer not to Europe, but to the discovery of what could be my own country; closer to the appropriation that was all that I rightfully could begin to lay claim to. As whites, we had moved away officially from the claim of a "mother country" across the seas—we were even to leave the British Commonwealth in the 1960s. I could now speak of "my country," and mean South Africa.

But it was not possible for me to say "my people." That I began to understand.

The whites were not my people because everything they lived by—their claimed racial superiority and the methods they were satisfied to use to maintain it as if it were truth—was the stuff of my refusal. And they did not recognize refusal as a valid position. Refusal was treason.

The blacks were not "my people" because all through my childhood and adolescence they had scarcely entered my consciousness. *I had been absent.* Absent from them.

Could one, in fact, make the claim, "my country" if one could not also say "my people"?

The breaches and interstices that the ravelling-out of apartheid colonialism produced, even while it fanatically shored itself up, were being rapidly invaded. The African National Congress, which since its founding in 1912 had gone through the revolutionary evolution from a self-help ethic to mass passive resistance campaigns, and finally the 1961 decision to take up armed struggle, went Underground when it was banned. From there it tunnelled beneath successive white governments. So did the other banned liberation movements, the Pan Africanist Congress, and the South African Communist Party, which was also part of the command of the African National Congress's military wing, Umkhonto we Sizwe, "Spear of the Nation."

While this political revolution was taking place despite—indeed, because of the treason trials, bannings and banishments with which the State tried literally to shoot it down—there were other, insidious, invasions penetrating the security system into which whites had withdrawn their bodies and minds.

In the Fifties when I came to live in Johannesburg, one of the points of entry was Bohemianism. A quaint, outdated import from the Europe of several generations back, yes, but serving a different purpose, in South Africa's largest city.

We were not starving artists living in garrets and defying the bourgeois values of some integrated society. We were young people starved of contact with one another by innumerable barriers of law and custom and fear. We did not know how to go about putting our country, ourselves, together—that was the half-understood motive. We broke the easiest taboos first. Black musicians, teachers, journalists, aspirant writers met their white counterparts to talk, drink and dance—the two latter rituals standard as the preparation for many different kinds of human intercourse. We gathered in old factory premises clandestinely decked out as clubs; in whites' houses, where blacks were forbidden to be except as servants; and in the black shebeens hidden in the city.

The blacks came from the ghettoes of Soweto and Alexandra and from the streets of the old mining camp quarters of the city where people of all colours once had lived, and which were being bulldozed to establish white occupation only. The whites were young men and women like myself. The mild risks we took, of discovery and prosecution, were our adventure: a prelude to commitment to revolution.

Of course, there were white people who were dedicated revolutionaries in the South African Communist Party and other, minor, Left groupings, and who became the hunted when all liberation movements were outlawed. The Communist Party had members of all colours; the African National Congress did not openly have white membership, but a devoted group of whites, growing over the years, worked within it.

I did not join or commit myself formally to a liberation movement in that period, no doubt out of fear—a new fear in a way of life new to me, then; still there was the lingering colonial conditioning that revolution was the blacks' affair. But at the same time, in mixing more and more with blacks, sharing with them as aspirant writers, painters and actors the sense of *learning how to think* outside the way our society was ordered, I was going through a personal revolution that had no other issue but to lead me into theirs; to find myself, there.

Where there is the necessity, through historical circumstance of time, place and birth, to "make oneself" many processes take place at once. Because I had turned out to be a writer, because I was just that, because it was my fundament beneath all that had been done to condition my being, all my confusions, my false consciousness—because I was a writer, my principal means of "making myself" was my writing.

Only through the writer's explorations could I have begun to discover the human dynamism of the place I was born to and the time in which it was to be enacted. Only in the prescient dimension of the imagination could I bring together what had been deliberately broken and fragmented; fit together the shapes of living experience, my own and that of others, without which a whole consciousness is not attainable. I had to be part of the *transformation of my place* in order for it to know me.

This does not mean that I saw my way as a crusader, writing to expose injustice, a polemicist and propagandist. My comprehension of life had been kept so narrow, everything in it painted white—white morality, white customs, white habits, white values; once free of that, I had the writer's healthy selfish instinct to keep open the multiple vision that the fly's eye of the writer had brought me.

There were so many human drives and emotions that had been unknown to me, because life sheltered in the white enclave did not have, or did not see the necessity to take on, the situations which brought these forth. What did I know about courage? It was something associated with illness—"borne courageously"—or war; in the small town I had left behind me there were men with medals. But in the life of clandestine involvement with black men and women, one found that courage was a daily commodity.

A black had to have courage to risk arrest for being in the streets after curfew or leaving a town to find work in another; the courage to get up at three in the morning every day to travel from some distant ghetto to work in the city; the courage to go back to school after spending years at menial labour so that a brother or sister might have a spell of education; the courage to live without privacy, to create self-respect without personal space, the terrible ordeal of slum living.

And out of this taken-for-granted courage came a capacity to live life through to the full that I had not known among whites. This vitality, informing my writing because I was now open to it, affirmed in fiction—the truth that is in fiction—the reality that was rising beneath the repression. The expression in art of *what really exists* beneath the surface is part of the transformation of a society. What is written, painted, sung, cannot remain ignored.

And where was that other world that was the world, during that period? Came the day when that other world that was the world sought *us* out.

Of course, they had been here before: "discovered" natural features and places by giving European names to what already had been named by people who had lived here since antiquity. Those of us who were white were even descended from these explorers: we'd never have been here if they had not opened a way. But this time when they came it was not to plant flags or name, neither was it to see Table Mountain and the wild-life parks.

It was to tour *us*. Our lives were the artifacts they took home: to recount, to display in discourse, as previous tourists would have hung masks and bead-work. Just as there is now ecological tourism, there was in the Sixties, Seventies and Eighties revolutionary tourism. Come and see the banned, the restricted, in their own habitat.

Without my making any display of political commitment, my writing became the "essential gesture" of the writer to her or his society of which Roland Barthes speaks. It was with my stories and novels, my offering of what I was learning about the life within me and around me, that I entered the commonality of my country.

As a consequence, some of my books were banned. Of course, that was not enough; I was a citizen as well as a writer, I was white and living in the privilege decreed by my skin. If I were to "live to the full" this contradiction of my time it was necessary for me to act, as well, in forms other than writing.

Personal friendships that ignored the taboos of colour were only the beginning of taking responsibility for what was being done in the name of white skin; what was implied was the obligation to oppose and destroy the power of racism in its seat of government. The party was over—the happy defiance in drinking and dancing; there came the need to hide people from the police, to help people flee over the border—both treasonable offences—to forget the old white middle-class guilt about lying—what was their petty standard of truth when the entire platform of their life was the lie of superiority?

There was the need to forget that so-called morality and learn to live devi-ously for the survival of others, and oneself.

For years I did these things, always conscious that what I did was not enough. I became a small component in the vast movement where millions, shunted about the country, imprisoned, banned, cast into exile, tear-gassed and shot, yet trudged towards the end of colonialism in its final avatar, South African racism.

And still I was aware that although I could say "my country"—blacks did not dispute the claim of birthright—I could not say "my people."

Until every law that set me aside from black people was abolished, until we were all to be born and pursue our lives everywhere in the same right, governed by the free choice of all the people, my place would not know me. No matter how I and others like me conducted ourselves, we were held in the categories of the past. The laws that provided that more money be spent on a white child's edu-cation than on a black's, that a white worker be paid more than a black worker, that black people could be transported like livestock to exist where whites decreed—all this had to go.

The exiles had to come back to their rightful home; the prisoners of conscience had to be received on the mainland from Robben Island, and to walk out of Pollsmoor prison; those who had been harried and cast out had to take up the seats of power where their persecutors had ruled so long.

It came to pass.

It is not only in a religious sense that one may be born again. In 1994 the struggle, the final process of decolonization was achieved, after decades when the end receded again and again. In April 1994 all South Africans of all colours went to the polls and voted into power their own government, for the first time. There are now no overlords and underlings in the eyes of the law. What this means to our millions is something beyond price or reckoning that we know we shall have to work to put into practice, just as we worked for liberation. We know we have to perform what Flaubert called "the most difficult and least glamorous of all tasks: transition." This is the reality of freedom. This is the great matter.

I am a small matter; but for myself there is something immediate, extraordinary, of strong personal meaning. That other world that was the world is no longer the world. My country is the world, whole, a synthesis. I am no longer a colonial. I may now speak of "my people."

JAMES MCPHERSON

Melodious Chimes

Now that Rachel, my daughter, has taken up residence in Barcelona, Spain as a teacher, I have begun to use her old bedroom in this house as an extension of my own living quarters. Each evening I sit on the edge of her bed and watch the evening news. No matter how tragic the news is (bombings in the Middle East, hurricanes and the damages they inflict, the dying economy), whenever I leave the room and turn off the overhead light a tune flows out of an attachment to the light switch, one which I installed when Rachel was a child. The unit contains the melodies of cheerful childhood songs, played on chimes. Among them are "Whistle While You Work," "When You Wish Upon a Star," "Hi Ho, Hi Ho," . . . "It's a Small World After All," "M-I-C-K-E-Y, M-O-U-S-E" . . . and others. In recent months I have come to realize that these old tunes provided a very cheerful balance for us each night when we were going through very painful times.

In recent years divorce has become a rather mundane rite of passage, but in 1981, when I was being divorced, the trend was just beginning. My own divorce took place in Charlottesville, Virginia during a period of increasing racial antagonism. I had already won a Pulitzer Prize, and during the custody hearing, I was selected as a MacArthur Fellow. This development did not sit easily with the presiding judge. He observed in his custody decree that, without any inspection, my house was "inferior" to the house of Rachel's mother. After reading the decree, I wrote on the back of it my resignation from the University of Virginia and moved to Iowa City, Iowa.

"Hi ho, hi ho—It's off to work we go. . . ."

Now that Rachel, my daughter, has taken up residency in Barcelona, working as a teacher, I have begun to think back on the emotional experiences we shared. Beginning in 1981 the MacArthur money was used to rent an apartment in

Charlottesville, to provide transportation between Charlottesville and Iowa City, back and forth over the years, for the two of us. When the money was exhausted I earned extra money by teaching summer school. I was able to pay Rachel's college tuition and much of her living expenses during her time in Boston. During the summers and during some of her Christmas breaks she lived in this house, sleeping in her bedroom. Her daily exits from her bedroom sounded happiness throughout this house.

"When you wish upon a star. . . ."

I learned from this heartbreaking experience that one's emotional health is saved from tragic circumstances only if one is able to locate a source of optimism, no matter how slight it may seem. The music hidden in Rachel's light switch now cautions me to not fear the darkness of the tragic nightly news which pours from her television.

My move from the entire South to Iowa City shocked my family and friends. *"What about Rachel?" they asked. "At such a distance how will you maintain an emotional bond with her? You can't escape racism. It exists in every part of this country. . . . Boy, you are sick. You are an uncaring father to require her to fly through winter snow storms. You are a coward to run away from the mess you made. . . . You got that MacArthur Fellowship so you could take time to write, not to be a babysitter. . . . "*

"It's a small world, after all. . . ."

These days the cheerful chimes from the light switch continue to comfort me and to keep my spirits refreshed. A friend, an elderly woman, called me recently to express her fears about the state of the economy. "We're doomed, doomed, *Doomed!*" she lamented. I tried to comfort her with humor. Another friend here, a man I have known since 1968, was recently fired from his position as Vice President for Student Affairs. He called me recently, asking for help in writing a paper detailing the circumstances of his ordeal. I agreed to help him. Friends here tell me that I am unable to say, "No," and tend to respond to every request, even selfish ones. But from my own point of view, I have known great pain and have grown much more sensitive to the pain of others. I believe now that I was *not* dehumanized by the inhuman treatment which I received. I want to believe that the tragic experience has made me much more human.

Rescued by Junkies

I was maybe sixteen and out with my stoned, amoral, largely lackluster friends, looking for a party, riding in a Dodge Dart so old as to have pushbutton transmission and yet so soothingly quiet as to be a slight embarrassment: "Engine by Singer," we used to say.

My friend Clam at the wheel took instructions from the rest of us. That he had even this tenuous station among our crowd was my doing. An odd fellow, Clam, smart and socially inept, so fucked-up-in-the-head that he was unwilling to eat anything but cold cereal and baked potatoes, an undeniable loser who I alone got along with, so desperate for attention he made wide-eyed clown faces and shouted unfunny non-witticisms, and—let's face it—when stoned, his head was so far up his ass he could see behind him.

Clam was my responsibility, and I felt the weight of his egregious awkward self and his wimpy rust-spotted car. I rode shotgun with him while my other pals sulked in the back. Yet whenever I recognized pleasure mixed into the bitter outbursts directed at me by my resentful-of-Clam backseat pals, I took it as evidence of their deep understanding that I just might have a future, while they assuredly had none.

I was *that* stoned.

"Turn here," my buddy Penis Eyes said, leaning forward, pointing, aiming us at a Taco Bell beside a bank with a green lawn, an odd place for a teen hangout, but maybe twenty kids already draped their bodies along the bank's grass or slinked in the shadows of the drive-through wing to exchange bills for baggies the approximate size of newborn lungs and with the same promise of the spanking new as the squalling oxygen of the recently birthed.

They were dressed so carefully bad, that crowd of kids on that spit of grass, in just-ratty-enough jeans and tee shirts, worn Converse high-tops, the girls demonstrating their braless breasts like that overeager salesman at Sears who thrusts a battery-operated screwdriver at a hapless screw every time you pass his aisle. I climbed from the car tugging conspicuously on my long manly curls, staring at the Phillips-tips of desire beneath the cropped, cotton, midriff-exposing tees on the lounging females, my cock sending the "Full Alert & at the Ready" signal—a redundancy given the 24/7 Code Red I lived under in those days.

A guy I'll call Osvaldo stopped me with a sharp but friendly fist to the chest, then lowered the fist and dropped two red capsules in my hand. "We're even, man," he said, and I nodded my agreement, having no idea what debt he'd repaid. I swallowed them both without asking name or nomenclature, a sip of lukewarm Bud washing the submarines down.

For a while a hunkering and haphazard nothing transpired, until R. M., a friend and fellow long-hair who a few years later would try to woo my future ex-wife from my clutches, appeared in drug-addled caricature cackling at my shoulder. He had a line on some heroin. Penis Eyes, who's dead now, got the details. "A dime a piece," he told me, adding up the bills we thrust his way. R. M. said that he, like me, would just sniff the powder through a Taco Bell straw, the fear-of-needles rather than the desire-to-live guiding our actions. My cowardice encouraged the others. None of us was going to shoot up—a chicken-shit snort crew.

We decided Clam couldn't have any.

"You're driving," I said, as if that had ever stopped any of us from ingesting anything. No one wanted to see what Clam would do on heroin. "Horse," we called it unselfconsciously, the stupidity of our night's metaphors thus destined: "That's good giddy-up." "Don't fuck with my gallop." "Wanna pony up again?"

Clam wanted to know why he had to put in ten bucks for the horse if he didn't get to ride. "Because we need your money," Penis Eyes told him. Actually Clam seemed relieved to be left out while the rest of us tooted the white stuff.

The night soon became disconnected from the chronological, and I kept coming to—without ever passing out—in different places. First, in the backseat of the Dart at the drive-in theater, my hand in the cut-off shorts of this girl who sat behind me in Math Analysis, the stretch waist of her plaid blouse pushed up to her shoulders, her tiny nipples the color of plums, Steve McQueen leaning on the giant screen to peek through the windshield at us, my buddies giving us privacy by slipping off to throw up in the toilet. "You remember that time you asked me for help?" she said while I tugged at her panties. She was talking about a math problem.

Then I found myself at Burger Chef, where Suzie, a beautiful brown-haired junkie who lived down my very street, agreed to meet us (by which she meant *me*) after work, her lips scissoring across her teeth in the ineluctable language of sex, while her supervisor in his white-paper chef-hat glared at me and the gangly crowd counting their change behind me, boys stinking of testosterone, who would (he was sure) eat his burgers and suck his shakes without paying a penny if he didn't keep a righteous eye.

"How," Penis Eyes wanted to know, the crowd of us in the Men's, peeing in anything porcelain, "did you get *her* interested in *you?*"

"She just digs me," I said, a line so transparently inadequate that even Clam, deep in my debt and (unlike the rest of us) stone-cold sober by now, laughed out loud. I fessed up. Suzie had a fucknut brother, an idiot annoyance of such magnitude that I avoided their house (missing her for fear of being stuck with him). It was often my job to get rid of him, and I had dismissed him one night bearing a message: "Tell your sister I want to fuck her." He announced the message in his family's living room in front of their parents. Somehow, she managed to overlook the tawdry predictability of the line while also miraculously crediting me with the boldness of making the claim before her mom and dad.

"In other words," Penis Eyes summarized, "sometimes being a dipshit works out."

Who was I to argue?

Suzie had a fat bag of burgers ready for us when we came out, grease windowing through the white paper, her boss on some errand in the back. We slipped out the swinging door without paying one penny. "I get off at midnight," she called to remind me, and then somehow we were in Mexico, fifteen miles away, at a bar with a crowd of well-dressed Mexican teenagers I had never seen before, and I was speaking something like Spanish to a dark-haired girl whose lipstick had to have been imported from 1953, and she was telling me about her sister and maybe a car or a beloved pet. My Spanish sucked, so I kissed her, and she kissed me back, and shoving suddenly ensued, initiated by a brother and/or boyfriend, and Clam took a smack in the jaw . . . and then we were behind a cantaloupe packing shed, back in the U.S.A., drinking bottled beer and staring out at the empty furrowed fields, no girls whatsoever in the landscape, and I looked at my watch and saw it was 1:15. "We forgot to get Suzie," I said, which caused an eruption of laughter.

I woke that morning in a strange house and unfamiliar bed that had been stripped to the mattress pad. I was naked and lying beside a grown woman, who was also naked, her wide hips and white buttocks seeming now and again to levitate from the sheets and gesture at me. They were very animated buttocks. It struck me as a come-on offered from some deep region of her slumber. And I with my morning hard-on accommodated her, climbing on, no idea where I was, who she was, or how I was getting home, pushing aside her almost-golden hair only after I'd entered her. She was pretty in a dissipated and distracted way, thirty-something, a complete stranger, who smiled at my entry and squeezed my thigh and said soft, incomprehensible words of amusement and encouragement, and never quite opened her eyes or came fully to.

A minute or so later, I was done and in my Levis, wandering the house—the hardwood floors had been painted and were flaking blue in some rooms, green in others—finding nobody until, pissing in the toilet, I noticed a vaguely human shape behind the pale shower curtain. I pushed the curtain aside, still pissing, to discover a passed-out girl, naked from the tank-top down, a roll of tummy fat that seemed to me oddly sexy. She had her bare feet on the chest of this guy we had nicknamed "the Flirge" because he lied about girls and never chipped in for dope. He had his pants on but was bare-footed and bare-chested, and there were purple marks around his nipples, which reminded me of the drive-in and the girl from Math Analysis, which seemed like years ago, and made me wonder where she'd gone, and for that matter, where everyone else had gone—Clam and Penis Eyes and the other guys I'd been out with. I wasn't entirely sure what day it was.

I called the Flirge by his real name, and he came to, fluttering his eyes vamp-like and mock-yawning. He had to've been faking it to wake up as quickly and theatrically as he did, but the girl was really out and didn't stir, even as he jostled his way out of the tub.

"You get laid?" he asked me.

"You watching me pee?" I replied, still peeing.

"No," he said, affronted and still watching.

"Where are we?" I asked.

He shrugged. "Have you looked around?"

We woke no one. I stole a green tee shirt and climbed barefoot into the Flirge's car, a sun-bleached Pontiac with bad upholstery, parked with two tires on the curb and the bumper up against a yellow fire hydrant. That was how I'd later identify the house one day as I was driving around my little sister—the yellow fire hydrant.

There had been a party, the Flirge explained, and then another party that my friends hadn't wanted to go to. Evidently, I had. A party full of adults, the Flirge had warned, and no one else had been up for it. The party had been as advertised—martinis, the Flirge claimed, women in dresses, men wearing ties, all several sheets to a powerful wind. "You told everyone you'd snorted heroin and weren't responsible," he said. "You got away with murder."

For the next year or so, I kept hearing about that night, the things I'd done and said. "Skag puts you *down*, man," witnesses would patiently explain to me, shaking their heads with amused resignation. "You're supposed to get *mellow*," they'd admonish, as if I'd gotten it all wrong and somehow ruined the drug's reputation. I tried to explain about the speed Osvaldo had slipped me before I snorted the H, but no one was interested enough for facts.

As it turned out, except for the brothers of the Mexican girl (none of whom I ever saw again), no one was mad at me. The girl from Math Analysis even invited me to spend the night with her when her parents were in Greenland or Iceland or some other remote cold land. I didn't do it, but I appreciated the invitation. Suzie—she's dead now, too; the predictable overdose—forgave me for standing her up. She wanted me to shoot up with her, and I realized that I'd told her in Burger Chef about the horse, fudging on the needle factor. I, of course, just wanted to fuck her. Neither wish came true, but we became friends.

And Clam, it turns out, had taken everyone home that night and then headed for the party—the grown-up party the Flirge and I had gone to—thinking I needed, I don't know, a *hand,* I guess, some kind of help. "You were wasted," he kept telling me. "You weren't even wearing shoes." His reasoning: high among a crowd of adults, I'd get arrested.

I was already gone by the time he arrived, knocking on a door he would show me later—a square brass knocker on a wide door of a slightly-larger-than-average ranch-style house. A middle-aged woman in a nightgown told him I had gone off with "a responsible party"—the agreeable woman whose bed I shared and tee shirt I stole.

Clam and I are still pals. The others are shadowy presences in my fiction, but otherwise out of my life. What I think I understand now is this: that night was the ideal of the existence I was making for myself at the time, a night when the important things fell into place, when the high actually made me happy and lively, when some part of me could slip to the surface and laugh in a manner that let the women who wanted to love me just go ahead. Nights like that you have to acknowledge, even if the way you see the world has changed, and the people who used to populate the adventure are mostly dead.

We made a life of stupid and uncalculated risk, guzzling drugs and fucking strangers, driving too fast and flying too low, and those of us who survived recall certain of those nights with a middle-aged awe at the wicked fun we had.

As for those of our gang who didn't survive, they paid the price for the rest of us, heroes who threw their bodies in front of streaking hypodermics aimed right at our hearts, who crashed their cars into dangerous ditches to make bridges for us to cross, who fell out of truck beds to make us wear seat belts, who sank beneath a pool's artificial water to advertise the danger of drunk diving, who tumbled facedown on a pool table with cue in hand and the whole world spinning to a tune he could never quite make out in order to end another wretchedly beautiful night before the rest of us killed ourselves. They redeemed us, those lost children, dying not for the sweet and mindless thrill of a good ride but to provide warning and the cold comfort of survival for their friends.

I prefer to think of it that way.

Rescued by Junkies: put that on my tombstone.

Oh *Jesus,* what a pure and clarified dumbfuck I was, saved by a phobia and those braver souls who lit their veins with kerosene so the stragglers could see the safer path.

So yeah, I still take risks, at my keyboard, writing my stories and this essay, reminding our generals about the legions of the dead.

<><><><><><><><><><><><><><><><><><><><><><><><><><><><><><><><><><><><><><><><><><><><><><><><>

The Prozac Variations

In Susan Sontag's essay on Roland Barthes she writes that "his late writing . . . was organized in serial rather than linear form. Straight essay writing was reserved for the literary good deed." So I've decided to take a risk. Rather than writing an essay, I've arranged in serial form, and edited, the journal I kept when I wasn't able to write, between the years 1995–1996. The journal contains my reflections on literature, my life as a writer, my doubts about myself as a writer, my depression, the drug I took to overcome it, and how the drug affected my life as a writer, which is the only identity that's ever mattered to me, which in itself is a risk. No one should judge him or herself so exclusively, but I do. Ibsen wrote, being a writer means that you sit down every day to judge yourself. I believe that's true. And Flaubert wrote, "We work in the dark, our passion is our task, we give what we can. The rest is the madness of art." I believe that, too. The journal arose this way: twelve years ago I awoke in the middle of the night, convinced I was wanted for crimes I hadn't committed. I was teaching at the Iowa Writers' Workshop. I'd just finished my third novel, *City of God*, and would shortly turn forty. I remember feeling briefly happy at the beginning of that summer, but also slightly puzzled. On the trip to Iowa City, I found myself floating in a motel pool, looking up at the sky as the interstate traffic washed past, and thinking, how did I get here? I experienced, I suppose, what V. S. Naipaul calls "the enigma of arrival." Weeks later, my paranoia and delusions started. For the first time in over a decade I was unable to write fiction. After several months of sleeplessness, anxiety, waiting to be arrested, and wondering how I'd survive in prison—of course, I thought, I'll have all that time to write, and read; I'd even tutor other prisoners, who, rather than regularly assaulting me, would wind up calling me "teach"—that's when I began to take Prozac for, according to my psychiatrist, "major depression with an obsessive feature." My primary concern was: how would this drug, and this illness, which runs in my family, affect my life as a writer? Would it change me? And if my obsessive nature receded, would my desire to lock myself in a room three to four hours a day to obsess over invented characters, and the clarity and music of my sentences? He didn't know. So taking the drug presented me with a risk. Refuse to take it and fall into a deeper depression—which ultimately turned out to be manic-depression? Or take it and hope it didn't change the chemistry that made me a writer? When the delusions and paranoia became too intense and relentless to live with, I said, I'll take the pill. And since I couldn't write fiction, I wrote what follows, beginning with my fear of seeing my life as a writer come to an end.

2/12/1995: Reading Jung reassured me that I have not dried up creatively. The last book was dark, the new one needs to be light, perhaps, and I just haven't been able to see my way to it. Told my editor my next book was going to be "happy." He said, "You don't do happy." Maybe I need to link the dark with the light for it to work.

2/14: *City of God* seemed to work out my death dread, making death seem less, or somewhat less, judgmental, individual, terrifying. With this fear somewhat alleviated, am I free to look at my life now and discover that I'm actually afraid of being here? If I "locate" my "identity" (my shrink's words), will my need for personas and masks—hence my writing—vanish? (Jung says no.) I find the entire notion of "identity" fuzzy. I don't understand this solid, unchanging thing underneath all the personas. Is it synergistic, the sum of all personas *plus something?* Or is it separate, which is, I would think, impossible.

2/17: Is it possible my fear of death has taken on this other guise? I have, at times, considered that my delusions about being guilty of committing a crime (imagined, one I'm not responsible for, Kafkaesque) and being imprisoned for it a kind of moral theater, acting out the basic problems of sin, judgment and death.

2/25: Picked up Jung's Collected Works # 9, which deals with archetypes, and also with fairy tales, which is the/a direction I feel my work should go in once it begins again. And I feel as if it is beginning, as part of this reorientation via depression/analysis/and pills. Of course, this could just be my new persona, too—the dutiful productive patient.

3/8: Am really wondering about going back to writing, full of doubt about the worth of it all. The entire culture is moving away from it into mindlessness, so am I *morally* obligated *not* to go in this direction? Does it make a difference? I can't, at the moment, distinguish between moral purpose (subjective) and narcissistic satisfaction (also subjective). But sitting here, writing, with headphones and good music on, this act of thinking and making language seems whole again, for the first time in a year.

3/9: Less frustrated today, but still ambivalent about writing, its value, going back to it. Max Apple says writing is a luxury, and it is.

3/20: I *may*, may even have begun a new novel. And, maybe not so coincidentally, it's a wicked voice, one that breaks rules, challenges, taunts, and *hopefully* seduces. That will be the trick. There's also rage. So, we'll see. Having just scribbled a few pages, I feel as if I've let the id out of its proverbial cage. (False start though. Went nowhere.)

3/28: I see that what I like about writing novels is the way they completely consume me for a year or two at a stretch. Then the world isn't boring, it's an interruption or a source of frustration. Inside *I'm* alive around the clock.

4/6: I can't get the energy together to begin a new book. I feel like, what's the point? This is my life now. If Prozac helps, it will be synthetic help.

5/9: Spoke with a student who's had trouble writing since he went on Zoloft. Worry that Prozac has taken my "edge" off, my drive and aggression when it comes to writing.

5/12: Committed to going ahead with new novel, even began work on it.

5/23: Writing is finally beginning to kick in on new book. Interesting thing, at bottom—delusional or not, hung-over or not—my true voice is always the same, the core is always there.

6/4: Wrote well, I think. Several pages, surprisingly. Dreamt I met David Foster Wallace and he liked me.

6/11: In Iowa and back to writing again. Pages I had left off at were rough. Slower pace, but still went back in fairly easily. Maybe too easily. Either Prozac helps my writing, or the book is ready to be written so it's coming fast at first. Or, it's coming fast because it's no good.

7/12: Talked to a friend about "the end of the book." Don't know how many readers are left. NEA study said 18–30 age group of readers dropping precipitously and certain to continue in this direction. So why am I writing a new book? Is it "the" last novel, or my last novel? My friend said, everything dies.

7/18: *City of God* coming out. Having to read in public leaves me restless and depressed. I now see writing the way Glenn Gould sees music, as private ecstasy. I hate publishing books. I wish I could vanish for the release period. I like people reading books, I just hate the intersection of writer and publishing, which is different than writer and reader.

7/21: Review coming in *Philadelphia Inquirer*. Dreamt that *Times* reviewed *COG*—full page—but in the Children's Section.

8/3: Read Kay Jamison on manic-depression and artistic temperament. Jamison talked about hypo-manic moods lasting two weeks. Jamison shows marked increase in productivity among artists from May–August, steep decline in fall. End of winter always the most difficult writing time for me. The slide during the fall is one reason I'm inclined to stay on Prozac.

8/4: One year of obsessive-depressive business. Prozac is working and body is probably naturally recovering. My loss of anger is the most marked change. Jody [my wife] says I shouldn't have to go through agony to write well, *COG* being almost impossibly hard. I like the feel of the new book, though this is always a tough call (about whether it's any good or not). Feels right, constantly surprising, not false and forced.

8/31: Read *New Yorker* fiction issue, the journal excerpts. We're all nuts.

9/10: Put novel aside. After three books I feel no *compulsion* to write (Prozac probably contributing to this). The *world* just does not need a new novel from me every two to three years. No one has time to read everything. So, say only what's absolutely necessary. Never thought I'd be an exquisite-ist, but saying only what is demanded as simply as possible is proving alluring after all my years as someone who had words to burn. But moving from expansiveness to crystalline distillation and elegance is perhaps "natural," or at least warranted.

9/11: Vonnegut said this week that "TV killed literature." He doesn't have much energy for writing any more since it doesn't matter. TV rules. Literature has to adjust in terms of depth, range, relevance, and *beauty*. It has to move people at a level nothing else in the culture can. Am I trying to convince myself?

9/12: Listening to John Hurt read Van Gogh's letters reminded me of the pleasures of this journal. Artifice is unnecessary. I don't have to compose and construct a world capable of sustaining certain truths, which is both the beauty and limitation of fiction. Virtually anything can happen in the "real" world, hence its beauty is diminished. None of art's inevitability is behind it. Life is a lottery, one thing can happen as well as another. No limits, fleeting beauty. *Fiction limits*—it creates a world in which not *everything* is possible, only a few key things—which makes fiction capable of expressing beauty, discovering it. A few things illuminated until they take on the radiance (to copy from Joyce) of the eternal. Van Gogh talked about painting being religious. What else could have sustained him? The trick is never to believe art's about anything else.

9/17: Finished rereading Van Gogh's letters. They're brilliant, funny, sad, excruciatingly so near the end. Would we have "Starry Night" if there had been Prozac? And what would his work have been like after his "attacks," which I now fully understand? Also, how when the attacks lifted, they were gone. But when they descended, they were, as he says, "no joke." Wonder how my work will change, if at all, in the long run. Quote from Flaubert via Van Gogh: "Talent is long patience, and originality an effort of will and of intense observation."

9/28: What I think I realized last night is that my guilt, my need to produce books, my doubts about actually having a choice, depends on whether I want to do a book or not (which I find unfathomable—me having a choice, a *desire*). Behind this all is an emptiness that nothing can fill. My psychiatrist said I'm brilliant at adapting masks, inhabiting voices and characters. But take them away—presto! Nothing! Or only the shape shifter, the thing that slips from mask to mask.

10/11: Ambiguous sounding message on machine from Henry [my agent], which led me to believe the worst. Gallimard withdrew offer, savage review of *COG* in the *Times,* and, of course, the authorities were looking for me and contacted my agent first. Actually, it turned out, he'd read excerpt from my new novel. Said he found it "incredibly sad." I said, "Now you know why I don't write autobiography."

10/15: Reread *The Stranger.* Great closing paragraph. Best in the small details where he finds both the pointlessness and beauty of existence. The mundane is tedious and ecstatic. All depends on your point of view. Camus's vision of universal indifference is chilling and comforting. Last stage of Romanticism, the exaltation of the individual in an absurd universe. Think the fundamentalist fervor we're experiencing worldwide, the personalizing of "Jesus," is post-Romantic thinking. Personalizing Christ is a regression from the mystery Camus faced up to. The *tension* of faith is gone.

10/16: Reading Heidegger. He points out why polemical essays fail. They're not about beauty, they're not a dialogue; they're position papers, they set up a value system—like capitalism. They're concerned with being "right," rather than "true," which is measured not by ideas but by beauty.

10/18: Heidegger says thinking is a form of saying thanks (the two words share similar Old English root—thinc/thanc). Thanks for being. Memory is ultimately devotion. So, in an age of public memory loss, due to the glut and surge of information, is it impossible to give thanks? Where's the *voice* in the whirlwind?

10/20: Reading new Kundera essay (*Testaments Betrayed*). Will literature return? What in human history bears out such a regression in terms of media? Things go forward. And the more they do, the more capable they are of doing so. Technology makes better technology. Literature, by comparison, moves at a nearly imperceptible pace. Our story form spans 2000 years. Computers double speed and memory every two years.

10/30: Rereading *The Inferno*. The Christian mythos is beautiful and absurd. God, who abhors sin, created Man anyway, knowing he'd sin. Pagans are in hell because they didn't know any better. They didn't follow the "one true religion," which of course didn't exist yet. So, Aristotle's out of luck. There's no suffering in the philosopher's zone, though, but no hope either. Only reason. Dante can't hold a candle to Shakespeare. Beside him, Dante's two-dimensional. But Shakespeare had the benefit of the Renaissance, and better quills.

11/4: Had lunch with Joseph Brodsky, we talked about whether or not we're "conscious" at the cellular level. He agreed. Said we're made out of elements like carbon. We're really elements "recognizing" elements. That's the origin of consciousness. All the bookstores are gone from New York, he said. The rare bookstore, the Phoenix, near where I used to live on Jones Street is gone. Meeting Brodsky was a joy. Brodsky genuinely, *passionately* loves ideas, talk. Told that he had to leave, he seemed truly sad to go. He said goodbye with real feeling, not just to me, but to the place, to the moment, as if he knew every implication of the fact that he was leaving it all behind forever. Henry called. New novel not going well. I wondered if I've "shot my artistic load." Maybe I'm done. I wondered if Prozac has taken my edge off, or if my depression and obsessive breakdown fractured or shattered me in some way, or else ended the period of crazed creation. Brodsky talked about free verse's authenticity. He said being authentic, honest, is good and virtuous in human relations, but not the highest good in art. More is required—music. I don't know, maybe I need to begin all over again.

11/6: Spoke with Charlie [D'Ambrosio] on the phone yesterday. Said he thinks I'm leaving behind a certain form as a novelist, the realistic autobiographical novel, for something I can't quite describe. Something I can't quite get at via a traditional novel. A kind of language that Heidegger speaks of as "beyond yes and no."

11/11: Sometimes I feel like a jerk for writing novels. But reading a piece on Rupert Murdoch last night reminded me of why I write novels. It's a way of working against power. The moral equivocation of "it's just business" is now used to rationalize every form of totalitarianism.

11/20: Watched Bellow interview. Interesting things to say about how Enlightenment writers used mockery to separate man from his religious sensibility. This ties in with birth of the novel and its spirit of humor, according to Kundera. Bellow also spoke of the "destabilization" of the individual after the 19th century, we're more fractured. The individual was a product of the Enlightenment; image, which is a product of technology, has replaced the individual. So, again, novels are dead things. A few works per century matter or last. The rest is just typing.

12/12: Paul Auster says, via Celine, that great works spring from a moment of rage. Prozac seems to have smoothed out my rage, hence my difficulty finding the stamina or juice for fiction.

12/19: Read Woody Allen interview in the *Paris Review*. He talks about wanting to be a novelist. He should only know. Want to give up Prozac and go back to drinking and maniacally writing. Don't know about continuing with "New Dark Ages" essay. Essays are easy to dismiss. Your opinion is equal to the essayist's opinion. With fiction, character has authority. You can't simply accept or reject a character's beliefs, you can only acknowledge whether you like them or not. You have to acknowledge their absolute existence. They *are,* rather than are right or wrong. Essays qualify, fiction exists.

12/24: Boy, was I crazy a year ago.

12/27: Read Frank Kermode's *A Sense of the Ending.* Endings are hard. One of the dichotomies of realism is that what it aspires to in detail and representation it betrays in neat endings and resolutions, which are contrivance. Reading Martin Amis collection. In one piece, Updike says he hasn't read the new Bellow book because, "I can't bring myself to fork over the twenty bucks." If Updike won't, why expect citizens to! Why bother? Had a dream that the Eudora Welty conference I'm supposed to do in May listed me on the program among the "unknowns," then charged me to go to the writers ball. Some fucking help Prozac is!

1/9/1996: Re: Kermode's *Sense of the Ending.* Describes movement (in Western literature) from myth to tragedy to the absurd. The absurd is now commonplace, literal. The absurd originally contrasted pre-God-is-dead meaning with

post-God-is-dead meaninglessness. But now the absurd's lost its power of revelation. Denis Johnson's work descends from Kafka's and Beckett's Molloy.
Johnson's guys, particularly Fuckhead in *Jesus' Son*, are barely even aware of their
isolation. The condition is so natural to them they aren't even aware of their
absurdity. The *fractured* meaninglessness of their world precludes meaning.
Fuckhead is ready for revelation, but ill-equipped to understand it as any expli-
cable sign of redemption. The "melo-tragic" mode of Roth's *sabbath's theater* is
hollow because Lear is a pre-absurd sensibility. The individual railing against
the meaninglessness of the world is an exhausted cry, after Beckett. In the post-
absurd world, revelations still "descend" on characters, but they're fractured,
there's no language to describe them. There's no sense of rational understanding. Just an apprehension. Like "seeing" transcendent reality and having it turn
out to be a Pollock painting.

2/11: Novels can be used, should be used, to pose alternative worlds as models
for our own—without the bonds of verisimilitude, but with the grace of
enchantment. Lying awake last night, I recalled finding my voice for *Stone [of the
Heart]* back in the slum on the Cape. I was drunk and bored, so I started writing.
And when I reached the point where I'd normally begin to invent some idyllic,
"literary" childhood for myself, I went in the opposite direction, a kind of attack
that clawed at the apprehension of some emotional truth. I realize that lately
everything I've written has been too responsible. The gloss of literary decorum,
a kind of false voice and vision, afflicts each piece. Thought again about
Celine's notion that all art begins in a moment of rage. Perhaps a rage against
whatever's false, a rage for the truth, even if it's horrible. Prozac may have taken
this edge away from me. Or perhaps I'm simply seeing and feeling the world in
a new, somewhat synthetic way because of it, and unconsciously transferring
this semi-placidity into my work. Maybe I'm too concerned with writing
"literature," the way I was sixteen years ago when I began *Stone*. Feeling that
"literature" was outside my "experience," I invented rather than sought out and
examined. So concerns about writing a memoir have vanished. If I'm only writing about myself, who cares? Maybe I just need to give myself permission to
write a memoir and not feel it's inferior work. Or maybe I'm just getting lazy and
self-indulgent.

2/24: Everything looks and feels dead. The emptiness of things isn't dulled or
blunted (by Prozac). I just feel half-alive.

2/25: Wondering if I have writer's block. Or if Prozac keeps me from applying
as much pressure to the work as necessary. I seem to lack the stamina and drive
on the one hand, and think "logically" on the other. Do I want to work hard
3–4 hours a day, seven days a week, to produce another unread novel? I feel

completely empty and without anything to strive for. The "New Dark Ages" essay didn't work, so who knows what I can do any longer. I understand how everything can suddenly feel very much like nothing.

2/26: Noticed that without a project to write, I feel completely empty, nothing to *be*.

2/27: I just don't have the faith in novels at the moment to sustain me through one. The juice simply isn't there. True, I could focus all my energy on a book. But why? The books I buy from Daedalus are all hardcover first editions. Looking up novels for my fall classes yesterday, I noticed that Richard Ford has only two books in print, *Wildlife* and *Rock Springs*. Richard Ford! Read piece in *Times* by Susan Sontag about the death of the love for cinema, which she claims is at its end as an art form. So it isn't only novels that are gone. As Kundera says, it's art.

3/23: Thinking about J. Franzen's despairing memoir about being a novelist in this month's *Harper's*, I recalled Max Apple saying that to write at all is the greatest luxury. Although, as I write right now, I notice how it calms me, anchors me, stops some of the spacey-ness and drift I feel. Anyway, the novelist's or writer's desire to be read is not vanity. At its deepest, it's a longing to connect what's seemingly personal and singular with others. A student said to me last night that the stuff I read (at a reading) was so close to my private thoughts that listening to it was almost "chilling." So to write only for oneself, as Franzen finally decides, is where all work always begins. But the desire to connect, to make the reader feel that connection, this desire will always be inseparable from the great works. Lose the desire to connect and you lose the grace and power of the attempt. You lose sight of the sublime, at which we all aim.

4/7: Went to hear Martin Amis read. He said that if he couldn't write, life would just be one thing after another. It is. Watching our new house being built, I think, it's just another thing. Never for an instant has it come close to the buzz I get off a good day on the page. The juice of connection and transcendence, that high, comes only in the writing itself. Not in publication, reviews, etc. That's what I miss right now, being at work.

4/11: Saw Allen Ginsberg documentary last night. His mother was deeply paranoid, died in an institution. Made me grateful for Prozac. A nice improvement over straightjackets, shock therapy and lobotomies, which she wound up having.

6/29: Really been holed up, haven't seen anyone in a month. Stopped Prozac altogether three days ago. Oddly, it doesn't seem to affect my writing. Low mood, though. Guess I'm just a dysthymic guy (minor, chronic depressive). Dysthymia Man, the Apathetic Superhero.

8/21: I feel like my spirit and energy are somewhere outside of me, just beyond reach. *Need to slow down and go back to sentences.* May go back to novel. May not write at all. Pointlessness sure feels concrete these days.

8/22: I read a newspaper article stating that a new, more selective generation of anti-depressants, which will target specific serotonin receptors in the brain that control mood, will be on the market within five years. "The dream," one neuro-scientist said, "is to prevent psychiatric disease altogether."

The back page of the newspaper section is taken up by a green and white ad, the same shades of green and white as Prozac capsules. The green section proclaims, "In the future, new forms of technology will make life easier." The white section below the fold ads, "Good news. The future starts soon."

Flipped through the new Daedalus catalog. Harold Bloom's *The Western Canon* ($29.95 hardcover) is available for $3.98. In the book, Bloom notes that modern "thinking" or "personality" began with Shakespeare and Cervantes, who created characters capable of internal change. Quixote and Sancho Panza "change by listening to each another. In Shakespeare change comes from self-overhearing and from pondering the implications of what one has heard." He concludes elegiacally, and predicts the dawning of a new theocratic age in which people will again listen to and heed only the voice of God (or Prozac?), instead of each other or oneself. I looked back at the green and white ad page, which is anonymous, no company name spelled out in type like a commandment. At the bottom of the page there was a graphic design. Black ink on white paper. Just a few splashes, enough to form one upright line with sort of a head at the top, and six lines extending from it like dead flower petals. It's a Rorschach, sure. But, and maybe this is just me, I couldn't help thinking that it looked like a happy crucifixion. A Prozacian crucifixion.

A flower to commemorate the end of meaning.

8/23: A federal anti-violence program toyed with the idea of testing violent kids on serotonin-raising drugs to see if their violent behavior receded once their serotonin levels and, in tandem, their self-esteem was sufficiently boosted. Our definition of human personality has shifted from a moral to a biological one. The fading echo of Enlightenment voices are replaced by the voices of psychopharmacology.

Some medical ethicists insist that Prozac disconnects users from reality, and possibly from their own humanity. Harvard psychiatrist Richard Schwartz "fears that mood brighteners have the capacity to reinforce oppressive cultural expectations." Even losing the dystopian spin, Prozac and other SSRIs still cut individuals off from the personal myth-making that once went into the creation of a self. The personal myths that make up our pasts no longer count. We're only the sum of the pills we take.

8/24: Kafka's K is still faintly aware of his connection to a collective moral existence, caught between dream and hallucination, and engaged in a desperate search for the moral compass he suspects he once had. But Kafka's novels are incomplete because there is no way back to man's antiquated sense of moral order.

8/25: Liturgy: "Go in peace."   Nike: "Just do it!"

8/26: When personality comes in tablet form and genes are engineered, "Man's" consciousness is a product of technology. Hereafter, all transcendent experiences will be synthetic.

On 8/28, this journal ended when I heard a voice and began what became the novel *Will@epicqwest.com*. Its first and last lines are: "Granted, I've been wildly medicated."

JOHN BENSKO

∞∞

Our Side of the Tracks

First thing you see that woman
Going to her trunk on that other woman.

Gets out the sawed-off and props it
On her hip that's swung out, props it

To say, *come closer to me & this gun*
And I won't even need this gun.

Second thing, it's night and a coyote
Walks stiff-legged down the sidewalk. The coyote

Steps into the street and stops
To look each way. Just like the moon stops

Sometimes so bright
Even in the city that the shadows seem bright

And fall on the grass with an immensity
That makes us forget we need immensity.

We mow the lawn, eat, sleep, die.
The moon makes us want to lie down beneath it and die.

First published in *Prairie Schooner*.

In May, the trees drop their seeds
In puffs like dingy cotton. Seeds

That gather in balls across the yard. Our children
Are frightened. We never want them to act like children.

The drive-bys so often while they're playing
Catch them playing.

The House Fire

Living in Memphis, as in most large cities, leads to choices that balance safety against other concerns. For the poor, you can bake in a 120-degree house with no air conditioning in the summer or leave your windows open and risk an attack from an intruder. With money, you might move to the suburbs where you can at least hope that you're more insulated from home-invasion robberies and drive-by shootings. My wife and I have the money for the suburbs, but we don't like them. It's not just the long commute; it's the lack of character in the houses and the neighborhoods. We chose an older part of town, where the houses were run-down enough so that we could afford a large fixer-upper on the salaries that teachers make. It's convenient to downtown, to the river, and to the university where we teach. When we moved in, water was standing in the basement with a dead rat floating in it. The electrical wiring had so much jackleg work over the years that we faced a fuse box hanging by its wires from the rafters and over-heated aluminum wiring that hung in long loops through the crawl space, nearly reaching the ground with its crumbling insulation almost gone. At night, occasionally, we hear gunfire close enough to wake us. Anything of value left visible in a parked car guarantees a smashed window.

It has been said that good fiction depends on trouble. Is it the same for a good life? We have old saws to fall back on when things go bad: "What doesn't kill us makes us stronger." We speak of experiences that "build character," as if the world's vagaries might have some underlying plot, designed to make us more attractive to a reader. Robert Frost once said that a poem is only as good as it is dramatic. Like Frost, I've concluded that poems come alive through their tensions. They need not necessarily grow from dramatic or narrative conflict, although that narrow interpretation of Frost does apply. Instead, the stresses may be very subtle and have more to do with tensions of sound, of form, of various meanings of words that play against each other, of themes and attitudes that have complexities that do not allow them to organize themselves into an easy resolution. Poems have to risk flying apart before their unity, before their safety, can become powerful.

There are several experiences behind the poem, "Our Side of the Tracks," that led to my writing it. The first was a piece of language I overheard one day in a store when two women, one of them dressed very fashionably, got into a heated argument. The well-dressed one, reaching a rage, shouted into the other's face, "Don't you make me go to my trunk on you!" My first thought was a steamer trunk full of clothes. Was it to be a contest of high-toned dressing? Then, of course, I realized she meant the trunk of her car. For what? A tire iron? During the next week or so, it seemed an uncanny coincidence that every shooting I'd read about in the paper involved an argument where someone then went outside and retrieved a gun from the trunk of the car, returning to shoot the victim—or, more likely, some bystander—for it seemed that those who were targets were also highly adept at getting out of the way, leaving hapless and slowfooted witnesses like myself to catch a bullet. That year, I was also deeply troubled by repeated incidents of gang members shooting at each other after school and instead killing or wounding innocent children walking home. But it was one event in particular that precipitated the poem, and oddly enough that dramatic occurrence doesn't even appear in it.

Behind our back yard was an empty house that was gradually taken over by street people. We complained to the police, tried to contact the out-of-state owners with no success, and gradually learned to live with the pizza boxes, cardboard sleeping pallets, and stolen shopping carts strewn over the yard. Then one evening I was upstairs reading when I heard some very loud pops, like tree limbs cracking. I looked out the window and flames were shooting about thirty feet over the vacant house. I spent the next hour or so in our yard with a pitifully inadequate garden hose, trying to keep flaming balls of debris from setting fire to our house as they fell from the sky. Later, talking to the firemen, we learned that for the last few weeks there had been many such fires across the city. It was a new form of gang initiation to torch a house.

Why did this event lead to the poem, when reading of worse in the paper had not? And why did events in the paper make it into the poem while the fire did not? My guess is that the fire was too spectacular and too close to home. It was too immediate for me to write about it that soon, but it did unlock a larger set of anxieties that were in me, that were more complexly human than the fire. The fire seemed like the outburst of all the tragedies I had heard about, the pictures of children who'd been shot, the on-camera interviews with devastated relatives and friends of victims. It was the culmination of years of worrying about the house behind us, once a beautiful old place like ours, that had been broken into, looted, made a stopping place for drunks and prostitutes and drug addicts, and then finally turned into evidence of gangs potentially taking over the neighborhood. Dragged into it were more ridiculous anxieties like the aggressive raccoons that had moved into our porch roof, and the armadillo that had been tearing up a neighbor's yard. Coyotes, and even bobcats, had been seen within the city limits. Where were we living? Things were out of control, but not in the way the fire was. The struggles were mostly distant, quiet and ultimately for me, interior. The fire itself was immense, its flames eventually reaching almost a hundred feet in the air, its crashing walls, its flood of flaming cinders whirling into the sky. It was too much, too unreal and overwhelming to write about directly.

My first surprise in writing the poem, and perhaps its greatest risk, was that I found myself writing in couplets, and not only with full rhymes but complete repetition of words. I often tell my students that it's very hard to write a serious poem these days in couplets because the form has been so often used for witty turns of phrase, and it's so overt as a form that it can easily weaken a poem's sense of emotional immediacy and authenticity. And yet, there I was, using a risky tactic and feeling that it was right, that the poem needed the control of the repeated words, that the closure of the couplets was an important tension against the chaos that the poem was talking about. The certainty in the return of the words became increasingly ironic for me, because the reassurance of it was like hope and yet the determinism of it was like fate.

Wordsworth talked about poetry having its origins in powerful emotions recollected in tranquility. The fire was too close to be a direct subject, but it could be a catalyst. Like Wordsworth, I've learned that I need distance on things before I can write about them well. The immediate and terrible events of our lives are too close at first for us to comprehend them in any well-formed way. They have to sink into the swamp of other memories, fears, hopes, hatreds, loves, and desires, to percolate there. Wordsworth, who along with Coleridge formed an idea of the poetic imagination as the part of us that pulls chaos into order and reveals what is transcendent in both the ordinary and mundane as well as the extraordinary and dramatic, might have said that tranquility itself is a catalyst. What the fire taught me, though, was first that violence, like its opposite, tranquility, can draw up unexpected wonders from the depths of our being, and that poetry has its origins there too. And secondly, it showed me that the powerful emotion that leads to poetry does not have to be the emotion that the poem ends up expressing. When asked why she had so much violence in her fiction, Flannery O'Connor said that it was necessary to break her characters out of their ruts in life. It is one of life's ironies that both a meditation within tranquility and an act of violence might lead in the same direction, to transport us from our everyday concerns toward a world closer to poetry, a poetry that at its greatest may calm and reassure us, while it also touches our deepest fears.

JIMMY SANTIAGO BACA

The Risk of Deadness

We have the finest athletes in the world streaming into Beijing and as they train for the Olympics, they complain their lungs and heart hurt. Too much pollution, too much black smoke, and I'd venture to say much more than that—all kinds of nameless toxic-merging of poisons in the air, water and soil, passed on to foods, the clothes they wear, the words they use to speak with—polluted air does not isolate itself from our emotions; eventually our words make room to accommodate our corruption. Any politician can attest to that.

But bringing that consciousness back home to America, I look around and shake my head very slightly. I don't want too many people to see that I disagree with much. At first my disagreements were kept to myself, had little impact on my living, but then they grew worse and worse until what I saw had the pallor and menace of impending disaster. For instance: when my two boys were in high school, I noticed a certain deadness of spirit and emotion in the faces of students when I dropped my sons off at school in the morning. Gabe was just starting the 9th grade, and when he told me he wanted to quit I said sure, not a problem. After all, almost every single friend of his was quickly losing their center and spiraling into drugs or mental illness and I thought it was because of the meaninglessness of their lives. And it was true. No one knew how to cry from joy and sadness; it always held back and kept inside one's heart to turn gangrenous and vengeful. When they smoked weed in the downstairs bedroom, when they went out late at night, Gabe and his friends, they did things to get lost, tracking through the city's concrete flood channels at night, a band of urban tribal kids on the search for ritual, and finding none from adults, inventing their own. It was serious. My oldest son chose the way of pot-heads, firing blunt after blunt and living in a permanent haze, anything to dismiss and elude this nightmare we call reality. I'd find all kinds of pipes and rolling papers and his room smelled of high-grade bud.

I was learning what life was like for my two young teenagers and I wasn't alarmed or shocked or frenzied in the O-my-gawd how could this be happening. What I saw around me had a sequential source or origin in our societal inclination to ignore the wart on our nose. In other words, we all know education isn't working; we know that right after kids leave school they hit the line coke rail on biology book and snort; they whip out the glass pipes of meth and inhale meth crystals; they smoke up; they drop acid and chew peyote—anyone who doesn't know this is happening this very moment with a majority of kids in high school is comatose—sleep-walking on Mars. It's like some padlocked-brain woman from San Antonio who reviewed a book of mine wrote, "Mormons don't drink, and because they don't drink it makes your whole short story a failure."

I thought, well, they're not supposed to drink, but I've known some who do. And like the rest of society, presidents are not supposed to be stupid and we have one now that shattered the world record for ignorance. Athletes are not supposed to be in motel rooms smoking crack and screwing whores; oil companies are not supposed to advertise on Charlie Rose and NPR advocating environmental harmony as they destroy the earth and air forever. Engineers are not supposed to create phony levees that break and kill hundreds; lawyers are not supposed to use deception and downright lies to free the rich to wreak havoc on our society; bureaucrats are supposed to help, not obscure and send away the needy; there are a lot of things people are not supposed to be doing that they do. Preachers molesting children. Wasn't there a minister in Denver smoking meth and getting laid by a gym instructor? The list of maddening crimes we commit against our future and our children's future is endless.

So knowing most of this, I told my son get your GED, do what drives your passion, what you love to do, do. Likewise with my oldest. And I am happy to announce, years later, they are both doing great in their lives—happy, fulfilled, and paying the rent on time. It's lovely to see what they've done through courage and faith.

Which brings me to the fulcrum of this piece—why I decided for the last thirty years to teach marginalized populations—barrio kids, rez skins, trailer whites, ghetto brothers, prisoners, d-home kids, gang-bangers, etc. It's because they were not institutionalized or caged birds who had forgotten what the morning felt like, flying in trees and gardens and over neighborhoods. I really feel terrible for kids and adults who have been educated. The educated ones have justified torture, have systematized racism, have polluted the waters with oil spills; an educated one killed Lenin, and a Yale graduate started two wars and brought America to its knees and the distinction of being the most hated country on the globe.

So what did I risk? My two older boys' lives by allowing them to follow their hearts; they could have been miserable failures and drug addicts. But they are not—the lawyers and judges and dentists are the drug addicts. But again, after thirty years of teaching free spirits and having great success, I am in the cycle again. I just brought my five-year-old to school; he's starting kindergarten and I'm sitting off in a corner writing this as the teacher is encouraging the kids to make farting sounds with their mouths. I see my son Esai smile. I also remember that Heidi Patton, a poet from Denver who once was a student of mine in my prison writing workshop, is driving down this weekend so I can interview her— she's getting her first book of poetry published and is a major part of a documentary to be aired on PBS.

The teacher is not forcing my son to sing rhyme songs; there is no enforcement—only engagement and encouragement. I like that. I like the fact that Heidi is not formally educated. I like it too that my sons and daughters never had Jordans and Nike wear and gold chains and nice cars—I couldn't afford it. Every time a university offered me tenure, and over the years there's been twelve lucrative offers, I took none, because I didn't want to teach people forced to be present—no teaching can ever happen when duress is an integral application in the process. The person has to want to learn and I feel especially privileged and fortunate to have taught thirty years, sharing with people society has thrown away. Thank you Creator for the throw-aways; they have made my life worthwhile.

So instead of teaching and training minds to run and condition their bodies to compete in a country that supports genocide, ignoring the black dust they inhale, I teach them no medal or certifications are needed to find their path, no A's are needed to walk up to the mountains, and meditate in deserts and meadows and listen, be thankful, and part of living as a human being.

I have risked it all, my career, my writing, my family and myself on an instinct that as a human being there must be a better way to learn and live. As I said, I have been teaching social castaways for thirty years—some of them now run bookstores; many of them have published their own books; others have returned to their barrios and projects and rezes to serve the oppressed and deprived. It's been so nourishing for my soul and I believe, truly believe, has permitted me to live on earth this long and do what I love to do—make movies, documentaries, write poetry, novels and prose.

What bothers me most is the deadness in the eyes I see in those who are educated. Deadness that believes poetry can be learned in classrooms, deadness that believes prisons rehabilitate. It is a deadness deeper that drug addiction, a controlled deadness and enforced death traded against life for a degree.

I will never play it safe.

The Risk of Consciousness

The ocean in this place was dark and not a place you would want to enter or swim or even wade. I stayed as the only guest. It wasn't a hotel, so much as cabins without doors, only shutters. It was Jamaica during political turmoil. I didn't know it. I didn't even know the location. I was dropped off by a kindly tour bus driver who was taking a group to a fenced-in tourist hotel. After a time, I suspected the owners were selling drugs, or passing them through. I would go to breakfast and be the only person sitting out on the tiles, eating fruit, drinking coffee, looking at the dark sea. And for dinner, I was the only person, sitting, wondering why no one else came.

Each night, a man came and stood by a tree outside my room to fish. He was silent. I would walk to my room, looking at the trees painted white around the base, say "Hello" to him and go to bed with only the shutters between us. Yet he seemed kind and so I began to accept his presence as if he were a deer or some other life that belonged to the earth.

In Jamaica at that time, and perhaps still, the people hated Americans for the overthrow of the government. There were acts of terrorism, all unknown by me. They were now off of the International Monetary Fund. And the British and Americans had mined in this world, deforested this world, grown tomatoes for ketchup, grown rich off black labor.

I wanted to go to Kingston and meet with some of the other writers, especially a poet, Beulah Brown, but there wasn't a way to go there and finally the owner of the shuttered rooms let me borrow his black man, for a price. The man would drive me there and care for the Russian car like it was "his baby."

At first I stayed at the University, but it was behind so many walls, behind gates, the entire place fortressed. I had to use three keys to go to the room and looking outside seemed impossible for the many bars and other protections. I called the name of one of the writers and her husband came. In spite of the fact that I had paid to stay, I left, quickly, anxiously, more afraid of the building and being closed in than I was of whatever harm was outside.

I traveled alone. I still would if I had the time and money. I discovered that single women, if they want to go somewhere, they usually go alone because friends will say, Yes, I will come, but they don't. So, suddenly being taken into a home with the comfort and safety of a family was a blessing to me until the father of the family told me about being held by terrorists the previous week and how they held a gun to his mother's and daughter's heads, but I needn't worry now because they'd hired guards and had dogs. They were mixed-blood like me and able to pass for white and I didn't know if it was race or class or both.

He drove me to the city that evening to meet with Beulah and I looked at the shanty towns and the lack of food, the way tires were beds or sofas, the lack of space and clean water, the poverty all around me and I wondered how many tourists had seen this, the men with no work, the people with not enough food, and I knew that the hotel owner's black man, ironically called "Bigger," lived there and wondered what he had done with the car to keep that "baby" safe.

Beulah and I had no time to really talk because my host returned early and said the police were there and we had to go. Beulah's brother walked me past the police and I was so aware that I was not a black woman and that I was in a place where I was not supposed to be.

Later, after I returned to the shuttered room, I went walking through a field and into the next town and saw a cave. At the door was a hand-written invitation, a tourist attraction. I am a cave person and I wanted to go. There were two men at the door and I paid them for a tour of the cave. Light was a bottle of kerosene with a rag in it. Along the way, the young man and I talked and he told me about the role of America in their country because I asked and he was as grateful for our open conversation as I was. We went downward, down into the earth where there were blind fish and white crickets. And as we did, our shadows were on the walls but I was more interested in our conversation than in the waters at the bottom of this earth.

There is more. But in spite of all this which now sounds like an excerpt from a suspense story, it wasn't a risk. I was never afraid. Horrified by our country and Britain, yes. Hating the conditions humans have to live within, yes. But I never felt fear, only that moment of claustrophobia, only a few doubts, like was the man outside my door safe, but looking at him I knew he was. This wasn't my risk.

Nor was my risk getting on a horse, even purchasing a horse, after having been severely injured in a horse accident, broken, having a brain injury that changed my life. At the first opportunity I adopted a horse rescue mare, then a mustang. My family was shaken. "Why?" my mother wanted to know. I couldn't help it. I loved horses.

So the one risk I took, the step in my life that most frightened me was coming from a background of poverty and going to school.

I began working at fifteen as a nurse's aide. This is not a "poor me" story. I loved working with the elderly and often the younger people who came through. There were wonderful patients, and I was young and didn't mind lifting or bedpans or changing diapers or feeding by spoon the bird mouth of an old woman who needed compassion and kindness, or letting a man think I would return to bed after I checked on the children before I left his lonely room. I thought, if I only had money, I would become an LPN. And then I was fired. I was fired because I found out the others were making more money than I was and I went to the owners and asked if I could make the same amount.

Then, my step up in the world. I landed a job as a dental assistant. I did it by calling Dr. Pitcher every Friday until finally someone quit. I don't know why I called him and not some other dentist. But eventually, he hired me and I was excited and I learned from him, x-rays, lab work, etc. At the same time I had aspirations to become an ice-skater so I took lessons with my money, which was still rather paltry. I became good. I could jump, spin, and began to also do dance. Then I paid for five-thirty in the morning patch sessions where I practiced only figures in silence or with my coach. But I loved my job as a dental assistant, too. And he said I was intelligent. Yet I had a little dream that I would become a great skater even starting at an older age. I could see the words, Olympian started as an adult.

I bought a Volkswagen. It was red and cute and brand new. And I left my job and went to California, looking toward two things, a job that paid more, and the audition with the Ice Capades. I knew I could do it. Either one and I would have been happy.

Instead, I stayed with my aunt and uncle. My father was a Chickasaw and my mother was white. I stayed with my father's brother's family and they took me in, my aunt so kind to me, more than I had ever known. My cousin, Sakej, was in the University. He invited me to a party. Suddenly I was with people of a kind I had never known. They said things I didn't understand. I am not sure but I believe I became drunk out of embarrassment and acted as if I was from someplace like New York. It was so long ago. I probably even tried to fake an accent I had never heard. All I knew was I didn't belong. I didn't fit. I was not one. So I'd try to be something, anything. We were so many worlds apart that I felt I would not ever know their world. I had never known anyone who went to college or, in my history, never even heard the word "professor."

And so, while working as a dental assistant by day, I worked in a nursing home at night to save money. I skated when I could, half-preparing for the audition. Then, on my nights off I took classes in reading, vocabulary. And then, one day, I left and went to Colorado to go to school. It was the first year of

Colorado Mountain College in Leadville. My brother was a miner, my brother-in-law was a miner so I'd be near my sister. I thought this would be the right place. I passed. I worked in the credit union by day. I received good grades, but it wasn't yet interesting and my mind had not yet developed. In Colorado Springs I went finally to the University of Colorado branch and remember my first day and the fear, the tables set up for registration, the teachers available to answer questions. I wanted to offer something to the world. I wanted to learn biology because plants and animals interested me. I could only go at night because I had to work. It ruled out Biology because all the labs were in the daytime. So I went up to Dr. Nichols. He was the father of John Nichols, the writer. And I asked about his class. He said, Are you smart? What could I say but, Yes, knowing it wasn't the truth. But I ended up in Comparative Psychology. Maybe I still do it as a writer. Maybe it was his generosity to me, finding me jobs at the school, helping to pay for books, then helping me get funding as a Native American. But it began a long journey that ended up with me writing my way into consciousness. I have had to keep up with my own writing. I do not know where it comes from. It is a mystical process. It takes me to new places. I love doing it, as much as gliding over ice. It has opened a world.

Sakej is now the head of the Native Law Center in Saskatoon and on the U.N. Indigenous People's Working Group. I have worked with him a few times in Native Science Dialogues and have myself been an indigenous writer speaking at the U.N. I continue to unfold and make new leaps into the international world where I know what is happening. I would go to countries that may be unsafe. But both times I went back to school; later in Literature, I was scared to death. I was not one of them. Nevertheless, I had compassion and a consciousness of earth and life and how sacred it is, and how we could have peace. I had something I will never know so I call it my ancestors because my Native blood gives me a different education even in the same system. And I still want to feed the hungry mouths of the world and take people away from pain and to use words that will make change happen in this world where we are so beautiful and have so much potential and yet find ways and ways to do harm. I do not stand for it. I stand up for this world and its life. Maybe that is the ultimate risk.

High Noon at Midnight

My marriage had collapsed and I was adrift and alone. I tried alcohol but that was the curse of my family and better avoided. At midnight I planted a chair in the middle of the kitchen and dared the demons to come. In various forms they came: priests, teachers, old girlfriends. They howled. They told me what a despicable man I was, a failure as son, brother, husband, father. I agreed, Oh, yes, yes, you're right, till a long solemn comforting face appeared in their midst: Gary Cooper.

In the movie *High Noon,* Sheriff Gary Cooper has just married Grace Kelly. They are packing and waiting for the train that will take them on their honeymoon.

But there's disturbing news: on that same train the bad guys are coming to town.

Can you blame Sheriff Cooper if he says, "Waal, this is my honeymoon and I've done enough for this town and I deserve this one happy moment in my life"?

Of course it depends on who you are, your values, your sense of community responsibility, your romantic or ideological soul, your morality—if you want to call it that.

Can you blame Coop if he ducks the coming menace, skips the train and lights out for the wide-open spaces on horse and buggy, Grace smiling by his side, Grace thinking of intimacies to come, babies gurgling?

No, it is not to be, not yet anyway. Coop has to do the right thing and that is to wait, secure that badge on his vest, sling on those guns, and face the bad guys. Grace is not pleased.

Would you?

Be pleased, that is?

Grace Kelly is exquisitely beautiful and I often wondered what she was doing in that desolation of a town anyway. Why wasn't she back east serving high tea on Fifth Avenue? She was so desirable you couldn't blame the Sheriff for entertaining thoughts of flight—or did he? No, sir. No, ma'am. Sorry, Grace, but he knew what he had to do. No Hamlet he. The bad guys had to be dealt with—and there was only one Sheriff in town.

The theme song broke my adolescent heart:

> Do not forsake me, oh, my darling,
> On this our wedding day . . . ay.

I was forced to take sides, Grace or Coop. No fence straddling, lad. I pushed it as far as my teen mind would go. Hitch up that old buckboard and head out, man. To hell with the town and citizens who wouldn't give a damn anyway if you were shot to bits on your wedding day. Take what you have and go. At least you have Grace and a future. It's risky either way.

If you leave, what will she be thinking? Years down the road will she tell the children how their daddy threw his badge in a drawer, unbuckled his gunbelt, and put the town behind him?

That was the part that often made me, the Coop stand-in, feel uneasy—what Grace might be thinking. Would there be respect as we rode the buckboard and I giddy-upped the horse? Would she cast me the occasional loving glance? You could never say, "Grace, honey, I did it for you, turned tail and ran." She'd assure you that you did the right thing but . . . but you would never know. Never.

Yes, yes, you knew you loved Grace, but there's something else in the world and what the hell is it? The bad guys are coming, dictating the course of your life. Bad guys are always coming and you have to stay, badgeless and gunless, and face them. You can dodge, you can run, but where and for how long?

I didn't know it at the time but I was beginning to listen to the still small voice within, the Coop conscience, and I was troubled. In Ireland no one had encouraged me or my generation to think for ourselves. Before confessing our sins we were told to examine our conscience, and that was simply a list of sins—not the small voice. I hadn't discovered yet the truth of that fine old platitude, "A man's gotta do what a man's gotta do." The dictum from the church was "A man's gotta do what the church tells him or risk eternal damnation." Ay, there was the rub, there the risk. To think for yourself, to feel for yourself, was as dangerous as waiting for the bad guys. Examine your conscience—but not too much. Stay within the churchly parameters. There be dragons—and bad guys—and if you're not careful, you're riding a buckboard to hell.

I can't say I was Coop, can't say I was a hero, but after dodging and running I heeded the still small voice in my head. I squirmed on that kitchen chair and let the demons come. They screeched and squawked around my head but I out-lasted them. I out-Cooped them.

You can't bargain with bad guys and demons and they don't give a damn about your gun or your badge or your lovely Grace. You learn from *High Noon* you have to go it alone.

That is the risk you have to take.

Recipe

My father taught us to love a snack. One of his favorites was crackers with peanut butter and horseradish, slice of sweet bread-and-butter pickle optional, about twelve crackers at a time, stacked precariously six-by-six on your palm on the way to the TV room. Or a whole celery stalk salted hard and filled with peanut butter, or cottage cheese, or anything, really, to add some fat to the vegetable. You never ate a little dainty triangle of watermelon, but cut the whole beast into halves, then quarters, and ate a full quarter melon no matter how big—with salt. Toastie pies required a toastie-pie maker, which was a clamp, basically, two long handles both ending in a large scallop shell. You buttered this copiously, put a piece of white bread on each shell, pressed the bread into the mold, filled the resulting depression with jelly (the exact amount for perfection being an art learned with practice, about four tablespoons), then clamped the thing shut and lay it over a burner on the stove long enough to brown both sides and seal the bread slices together.

Dad loved breakfast, and made us love it, too. Breakfast was how you got the energy to start the day and then make it all the way to lunch. Pancakes, heated syrup (never the expensive maple stuff, but A&P brand), bacon or sausage links or both, scrapple when you could get it. Scrapple is a Pennsylvania Dutch specialty, multiple pig scraps, nicely seasoned. It came in a pound block like butter or lard and wasn't far from those. My dad would slice it, dredge it in flour, drop it into a spider pan (as he called a cast-iron skillet) sizzling with old bacon fat (plenty of bacon fat—we kept a supply in a coffee can by the stove always).

I kept a coffee can full of bacon fat by the stove through college, but at some point realized I never used it, partly because it was astoundingly disgusting, but also because I'd lost the art. But my dad—Depression-era guy—Dad used it for everything. One of his favorite breakfast items was biscuits and gravy. The biscuits were just flour and baking soda and a little salt with as many tablespoons of the bacon fat as practicable mixed into the batter. The gravy was the bacon fat, again, this time cooked down and thickened with flour, seasoned with a great deal of salt. This was pretty good alone, but with four or five or six eggs, well, wow.

My dad's hash browns were elegant, too. You grated raw potatoes into an enormous pile after peeling them. While you peeled them, you told stories about KP duty in the navy: mountains of potatoes to be peeled before you could go back to your hammock, the cook bombed on gallons of vanilla extract he'd ordered to get around the shipboard alcohol ban. Then onions, one for every four potatoes. Maybe peppers, if you had 'em, but only enough for a little color, and never the hot kind. And heat up a cup or so of the bacon fat, get it so hot it spits, drop the potatoes in a little at a time. More fat was always good as you went along, fry 'em till they're brown, ketchup optional.

And why eat toast when you could have French toast so easily? Simply dredge whatever stale bread you've got in beaten eggs—soak it good—a little cinnamon, a lot of sugar, bacon fat in that same spider pan, presto. Pie was good for breakfast, too, and when you ate it for breakfast, it wasn't dessert, so didn't count against any diet some doctor might have put the Old Man on. Once during one of those diets we kids looked out the kitchen window a floor above the driveway where Dad was vacuuming the VW beetle we had at the time. It was funny to see his bald head from above, and then funnier to see right down through the windshield as he slid a full-size Table Talk pie out from under the passenger seat, ate it whole with his hands. We called Mom. Dad was *busted*. Under the VW seat we found his stash—two more pies, and two- or three-dozen empty boxes, blueberry, cherry, apple, Boston creme.

When we were done with any meal—five kids, remember—we all passed our plates up to the head of the table where Pop finished every bite we missed, pushing three hundred pounds. After breakfast, you discussed what you'd have for lunch and possibly dinner, got all the day's eating straight.

And in fact we ate pretty well for the time—which was the late 50s through the 60s—very little restaurant food, very little fast food, tons of vegetables (many from our gardens). But every meal was big, very big. Seconds, thirds, fourths. Always dessert. My dad had been an only child in a house without much love, in a house where only food could fill the void, where food, in fact, was as close as you'd come to a hug, food offered in aggressive mountains. And in our house, too, love was measured like data are now, in bites, mega-bites, gigabytes.

In high school I thought I was fat at times, but that couldn't have been true: I remember clearly the weight listed on my draft card (I burned it during an anti-Vietnam War rally in 1972): 140. By college I definitely had a beer belly started, from my habit of drinking a six pack or two of beer every night and sometimes a few tots of whisky, too. Talk about love! I played piano in bands and my Wurlitzer electronic would have a forest of bottles on it, end of the night. My girlfriend Robin excoriating me for my nascent beer gut—it couldn't have been much—and I remember how I lost it: she left me. I stopped eating for a couple of months, or ate only desultorily. All calories came from alcohol, a handful of Fritos here and there. I lost my beer gut and more, got that waifish appearance, long hair, scraggly beard, ethereal eyes. Friends said I looked great. I called it the broken-heart diet.

But I liked to smoke pot, too, and not even the broken-heart diet could hold up in the face of the munchies. I avoided the Ithaca College dining hall with its institutional blobs of watery plant and animal remnants steeped in Crisco (college dining has changed dramatically everywhere, I'm here to tell you, and certainly at IC). My nostaligo-geographical memory of Ithaca, New York, includes several diners (the State, the Rosebud, the Aurora), also several sub shops. I'd still love to order an MBC, which is a meatball cheese grinder, hot, but I avoid such things now. But in those heady days decades before my dad's triple bypass and its hints and warnings of awful death, everything was game. You'd go in with a friend and get the giant for two bucks, cut it in half and share it. Then down to the Pine Tavern for Drunk Night: twenty-five-cent shots! Two bucks and you were chiffoned, as we liked to say.

I smoked like four packs a day.

Gradually my heart got unbroken and by the time I finished college I weighed in at 185 pounds, still five-ten. The only fat thing about me was my belly. My legs were hard and athletic as ever. It did get into my face and neck, giving me a jolly, harmless look that kept me out of fights.

A year or so later, I got fired from the Daily Planet Band and adventured to Nebraska to help my Uncle Carl develop a cattle operation he'd started in retirement. In Nebraska we ate beef, my cousin's beloved 4-H calf, whose name had been Pucky. Uncle Carl and his family loved Pucky well done. I never thought the meat was much good till I got put in charge of the barbecue one night and was able to cook my own meat rare. As it turned out, Pucky was the best meat I'd ever eaten, grass-fed, beloved. Along with the beef (about two pounds each) my aunt served my cousins and uncle and me Jell-O salad and huge mounds of mashed potatoes and rolls (fresh rolls every day), and gravy made from the morning's bacon, and peas, always peas, dressed with butter. Lunch was the same, but brought to you in the field, big wedges of cake for dessert, and ice cream.

Breakfast was dozen-egg omelets and bacon, more and more bacon.

And I worked sixteen-hour days, much of many of them on horseback. I thought I'd lose weight but did not, instead reached 190 pounds, all while losing every pocket of fat on my body. My shoulders grew wide, my back grew strong, my belly was flat as the Nebraska plain, rippled like armor. I was buff, and there wasn't a girl in sight.

This is the Amish Diet: eat all and whatever you want but work your ass off.

Back home I resumed the Drinking Man's Diet—there was in fact such a thing, a popular book in the 60s, which basically said drink very heavily if it suits you, just don't eat, and don't forget to walk around and stuff. And went to New York City, where I was lonely but played in pretty good (if destitute) cutting-edge bands and worked as a kitchen-and-bathroom contractor. I'd eat a mountainous breakfast—all the familiar stuff—at one diner, a voluminous lunch at another: triple hamburger deluxe, double fries, nothing else, every single day. I used my muscles all day, danced on stage behind my piano all night, stayed buff. Dinner was the same as lunch, or maybe a steak, or maybe the greasiest possible Chinese food, which I regarded as healthy eating.

And that's how it went in those years.

I got to be thirty, then thirty-three. In that portentous year, two things happened. One, I quit smoking. Two, I went back to school. The Grad School Diet involved no changes at all except a complete cessation of physical activity. Suddenly, I was a library worm and a desk fixture. After a year I'd lost five pounds or so. Sounds good, but I'd lost all muscle tone, as well. And then the numbers started going up. I hit 200 for the first time, not a happy milestone, kept going. At a friend's wedding I put on my old surf jams and joined the party at the hotel swimming pool, and everyone laughed, jeered. Strange thing about our culture: you can laugh at men when they're suddenly fat, but not women. No, no, no. The very slim bride-to-be balanced her margarita on my belly as I floated around the pool. Pretty soon I looked like a coffee table in a frat house, everyone's old beer bottle and a couple of ashtrays on my prodigious self. I laughed with the crowd, why not? At least I wasn't smoking.

Back in New York after the weekend I went to the somewhat less-than-excellent health service there at Columbia University. The doctor said, and I quote, "You aren't young any more." He thought I should lose 30 pounds. Thirty pounds! He drew blood. My cholesterol was over 300, nearly all the bad kind. My blood pressure was up. I sucked in my gut for the EKG nurse and she scowled, stuck sensors to my ample bosom.

That summer in Colorado I got down to a svelte 169 pounds by eating little but trout and by hiking hundreds of miles, got back into my 32-inch-waist Levi's. But that didn't last, because you can't catch trout in Manhattan (though I've caught a few PCB-laced striped bass off the piers there), and because I was back at my desk.

In 2000 my daughter was born. A week later, my mother had a massive heart attack, but lived, now hooked to oxygen. My father took over all the cooking, and he really did try to follow the sheets and sheets of suggestions and dietary commands that the hospital had handed him on the way out. I arrived for a visit one night and found him all jolly in front of a bubbling huge pot. "You'll love this," he said. "I'm making Weight Watchers for your mother and me."

"Weight Watchers!" I said. A miracle!

"These frozen thingees. Only 500 calories each!"

"Why the huge pot?" I said, just curious.

He didn't answer.

So I peeked in: more than two frozen dinners in there. More than three. There were fourteen, in all, seven apiece. You do the math.

Dad had some chest pain a couple years later and was sent immediately for the triple bypass I've mentioned. Funny, he was in the same ICU room as my mother had been. The surgeons cracked open his chest, dug veins from his legs, replaced clogged arteries just like that. But don't think and don't let anyone tell you it's routine surgery: it's not. It's devastating, and my dad was all but dead in his telemetry bed when I first got to see him. When he woke he ranted and sputtered. There were complications, but in the end, and now after a pacemaker, everything has come out all right.

Sight of him *in extremis* like that made me take a self-centered vow, and I have mostly kept it, become a vegetarian almost entirely. I don't add salt to anything, eat tubs of hummus on airplane trips, pop vitamins every morning, gobble tomatoes and cucumbers at my desk—whatever my doctor says!—an 81 mg aspirin a day, exercise, exercise, and more exercise: miles of Nordic skiing in winter, big hikes the rest of the year, bicycling, swimming, a trundling brand of tennis, wood-chopping, brush-hauling, dog-wrangling, extreme parenting, big-time gardening, athletic Viagra-fueled sex with my new young girlfriend, Lolly (at least it's athletic for her!). Despite all, I still can't seem to break 190. But my cholesterol is down below 200, lots of the good kind, and my blood pressure has dipped back down below the borderline of danger. My heart pounds rhythmically.

Still, as Thomas Lynch, poet and essayist and undertaker, reminds us, my risk of dying, either sooner or later, is 100%, and I guess that has to be acceptable.

Risk

I find golf so metaphorical about all aspects of life that when thoughts about risk-taking arise it's natural that I focus first on risk as it applies to the game. And I'm reminded of those times when I hit the ball awry, and instead of a fairway found the woods. There have been times when I have been so jailed by trees that getting out in a forward way would constitute an impossible shot and I had to chip the ball sideways out into the fairway, wasting a stroke. But my favorite times are when there's a slight opening, where the loft of a perfectly struck iron will lift the ball just high enough to clear one branch but not so high that the ball will hit another. I find myself becoming more intrigued and focused as I imagine the clubface meeting the ball, then the flight of the shot as it avoids obstructions, and finally how and where it will land. A good kind of nervousness sets in, an excitement and somewhat queasy sense of daring that is part of the allure of all sports. And a high percentage of those shots actually play out just the way I planned them. The higher intensity of focus, the anxiety, the adrenaline rush, and the otherwise forgotten lessons often combine to produce something exceptional that would be beyond us in ordinary circumstances.

I recall watching a University of Southern California football game on television when John Robinson was their coach. It was very late in the game, less than a minute left, and third down with something like four yards to go, and USC desperately needed a score. Coach Robinson called a time out and went over the play with the quarterback as the suspense built up. But then he looked up with a changed expression and smiled at the quarterback and enthusiastically said, "You've gotta love this, don't you?" The quarterback seemed a little surprised, but agreed, and with his tension replaced by the joy of challenge he went back out and got the winning touchdown.

Risk, no matter the field, is all about that challenge, that imagination, that purposeful narrowing of options, that striving for the exceptional in spite of the odds. But it is not really gambling in the sense of the hopeful dependence on luck. Effort beyond our abilities is foolhardiness. Risk is bravely attempting the difficult and even the seemingly impossible, knowing that it will try our skills and talents to the utmost and with the recognition that because of our human imperfections we could fail.

I heard of a test conducted on unsuspecting job applicants. Entering a large and all but empty room with an overhead camera recording their actions, each was instructed to throw a child's basketball into the wastepaper basket. Simply that. Each complied. Nothing else happened, so they understood that they were to continue tossing the ball. Some stood very close to the basket for easy accomplishments, some tried to make shots from enormous distances and continually missed, and some stayed far enough away that their shots were not guaranteed to go in, but had at least the likelihood of occasional success. The applicants in the last group were the ones hired. The company wanted people who chose to stay right at the edge of their limitations, but not go crazily beyond them.

New Zealand short story writer Katherine Mansfield urged others to "Risk! Risk anything! Care no more for the opinion of others, for those voices. Do the hardest thing on earth for you. Act for yourself. Face the truth."

I find that last sentence intriguing in its relationship to risk. Mansfield seems to be saying that truth is liminal, a kind of boundary or doorway, and only by exposing or extending ourselves, by hazarding, adventuring, chancing, and calling upon ourselves to give a task or contest everything we have, will we ever find the truth of our own natures and that of the world.

In a dramatic monologue imagining the thoughts of the Italian painter Andrea del Sarto, the British poet Robert Browning included the famous line, "Ah, but a man's reach should exceed his grasp, or what's a heaven for?"

The yearning, he's saying, is God-given. And caution and timidity about overreaching is just a way of denying ourselves the pleasures and risk of grace.

PART FOUR

Creating Change

Taking Risks

It is almost laughable to compare the risks I have taken to those taken by hundreds and hundreds of refugees and war survivors I have met while living and working in Africa over the last quarter century. I think of it more as taking less traveled roads throughout my life, creating paths marked by adventure, danger, tragedy, and—ultimately—meaning.

The first less traveled road I took was around the age of twenty, when I decided after seeing some footage of famine-stricken Ethiopia that I must go to Africa and see for myself what could be done to ease the suffering of the people there. It was an innocent impulse, full of chutzpah and naïveté given that I knew no one on the entire continent of Africa and had never read a book or taken a course about the place.

I was humbled by what I found: by a gracious people in the midst of deprivation; by the fact that my country was often more a part of the problem than of the solution. I knew from the moment I began to learn about the root causes of the crises there in Africa that I was in for life. This wasn't like fixing a traffic light or passing a Congressional resolution. This was about changing the entire way we as the most powerful nation in the world relate to the continent with the least political and economic power in the world.

A second less traveled road I took was a few years later, when I decided to go to Washington, D.C., and work for a group that was dedicated to ending world hunger, Bread for the World. They could only offer me a stipended internship, for which I received $8,000 per year. I lived in a condemned building and did landscaping jobs on the weekends, payable in cash so I could eat enough to provide the fuel for keeping me out on the basketball courts at night.

I look back on those days wistfully, as my jump shot has slowly, steadily abandoned me over the years.

A third less traveled road I took was about a decade later, when I decided to leave behind the inescapable poverty of loveable self-righteousness of the non-governmental world and go to work directly for the American people in the Clinton White House. Never before had I had such direct access to helping craft the kinds of changes to which I had committed my life. And though we had some successes, a lot of things were left undone.

After leaving government courtesy of W, I worked for a while writing in-depth reports about the peace processes and policies that I had worked on while in government and before. Soon, though, frustrated by a lack of impact, I took a fourth less traveled road. This road emerged from a realization that unless there is a politically potent, organized constituency of people throughout the United States and beyond who are willing to fight against genocide and mass atrocity crimes, and who are willing to work for peace in the deadliest war zones in the world, then our government would never do it on its own. Our elected officials need to be pushed, pulled, cajoled, pressured, sweet-talked, embarrassed and whatever else it takes so that they will not stand idly by when our brothers and sisters halfway around the world are targeted on the basis of their ethnicity, raped on the basis of their gender, or pressed into military service on the basis of their age.

This last road less traveled may be the road on which I travel for the remainder of my life. We need to build a permanent constituency of people who will stand up and demand action in the face of the world's worst crimes against humanity. Those of us on this road collectively have a dream that some day we will wake up in a world in which genocide and crimes against humanity are no more, and that the end of impunity for war crimes has arrived. We have seen great movements produce huge changes over the last century: the women's movement, the civil rights movement, the environmental movement, the labor movement, and the anti-apartheid movement to name a few.

It is time to build the movement to end genocide and crimes against humanity. The risk of joining in this movement is that we will fail. But if enough of us join, if enough of us make the commitment, a new and different future is possible.

But only if we try. No matter how great the risk, no matter how high the costs, we must try.

JANE ARMSTRONG

Spinning

I have these world globes on top of my bookcase. I started collecting them years ago, when I bought a wobbly tin cast-off in a yard sale. The dented sphere reminded me of a game I played when I was a little girl. I had a similar globe—a cheap educational model. I'd spin the globe hard, close my eyes, and stop it with my index finger. Wherever my finger pointed would be the homeland of my one true love. I conjured romantic dreamboys from faraway places with exotic names I couldn't pronounce.

My grown-up romance with globes is purely decorative, each chosen for its size, stand design, or geographical color scheme. On one, a turquoise Tasman Sea laps at a Pepto-pink New Zealand. On another, the parchment beige Atlantic buffets the tangerine divots of the Falklands.

Lately, I've been taking the globes down from the shelf, to study the shifting political topography of the world. I begin with America, trace the United States from New York, over to Pennsylvania, then down to Washington D.C., incredulous that wounds deep enough to justify wars don't register on the smooth landscape beneath my hand. I move across the continent, eventually inch my way along the Himalayas, cross the tip of India into Pakistan and stop at the fine red line that separates it from Afghanistan.

I wonder if each cartographer, in arrogance or in optimism, thought that his depiction of the world would be the last.

I turn one globe slowly, run my hands from pole to pole, touching all coordinates from east to west. I try to picture how the surface will be drawn years from now. What will be renamed? Whose land will be erased?

I spin the globe hard, listen to it whir on its axis. I watch the blurred bands of moving color. As the rotations slow, I see stretches of blue, patches of green, flashes of light. The red lines disappear.

And there, between revolutions, spins a world without borders, remote and fanciful, like a childhood dream.

Girls and Guns

I am afraid a man will shoot me. This fear has nothing to do with my personality, psyche, or romantic history. The man who might shoot me has no face, no name, and no motive. His desire to shoot me will come from someplace other than the hidden room of resentments we all carry within us. I am afraid a man will shoot me because one, I am a woman, and women are often the targets of men with guns, and, two, I live in a part of the country where men have guns, where they display them, and where they use them. In other words, a man will shoot me not out of rage but out of opportunity.

I. Girls

I was once a girl, and, for the most part, I was raised without guns, but when I was ten, my father came home from work with a pistol. This was the first real gun I had ever seen. It lay on the kitchen table with a clip and a box of bullets. My father told me he bought the pistol for protection. He wanted me to hold it. It was much heavier than it looked. It was silver, streamlined, like the kind of guns crooks used in the movies. My father was uncharacteristically cheery, watching with a smile as I held the gun. A painfully shy man, my father was an unlikely gun owner. I think now that he must have been proud. The pistol must have distanced my father from my mother and me; it allowed him to play a stronger role with us, and it gave him a persona he could never have created on his own.

Years later, after my father died, my mother found the pistol hidden in a basement closet. She had forgotten about it, so she didn't hesitate for a minute before she gave it away (it was unregistered) to my father's brother. That same brother also got a rifle my mother found in the basement, which she brought up the same day as the pistol, the stock clutched in her arthritic hands.

The one direct confrontation with a man and his gun I had in my youth was, like all stories in which firearms serve as the centerpiece, a memory glazed with the taste of myth. It is the late 1960s. My mother and I are waiting in our idling car in the alley behind my grandfather's house. My father is in the backyard next door with my grandfather and a neighbor. Across the alley, a man comes out of his house to empty the trash. He stops and stares at my mother and me sitting in the car. He looks angry. My mother reassures me: That's just old Crane, she tells me; he was some playmate of your father's who was always crazy, even when he was a kid. After a protracted stare, Crane goes inside, but soon he's back, charging out his door, trotting down his porch steps, and racing to our car. He lifts his hand and I see a gun. He taps on the driver's side window with the barrel. I have a second during which I miss my father's presence more than I ever have before. I'm sitting closest to the window outside of which Buckets waits, gun in hand. My mother sighs. "Roll down the window, honey," she says, "and see what he wants."

II. Guns

That's what you're supposed to do: Bring in the gun, create some tension, put it in the hands of someone who's likely to fire it. However, in real life, as in the case of crazy Crane, guns can be present and never go off, and in their cocked silence they're more frightening.

I moved to western Washington—to the New West—in the early 1990s. Soon after I arrived, big money flowed in. Huge, cheap-looking houses sprouted up, and BMWs and Mercedes wove through traffic along I-5. The once ubiquitous pick-up trucks with gun racks seemed to disappear overnight. Only when I took my dog to the kennel out in rural Pierce County did I see pro-gun bumper stickers. Out there in the country, my dog sitter's boyfriend could put a sticker on his picture window that read, "Protected by Smith and Wesson."

This *was* technically the West, so there were vestiges of the gun culture and Western myth caught in a kind of lazy stubbornness. People here didn't like laws and rules, or anything that seemed to prohibit personal freedom. I guess I shouldn't have been surprised that busy Sunday morning I waited in line at Starbucks behind a prosperous-looking young man and his woman friend. This being the West, I shouldn't have been surprised that when the man dropped his money and bent down to get it, his leather jacket lifted up in the back to reveal an enormous handgun stuck in the waistband of his pants. That was the first time I felt that aphasic blurring of reality and fiction that the presence of guns often inspires. For days—even years—afterwards, I tried to understand why anyone in his right mind would walk to a coffee shop with his girlfriend on a Sunday morning and bring a gun. This was Old West meets New West, a gun-carrying man in a tiny Starbucks outpost. People didn't get mugged in our neighborhood, and this guy didn't look like he needed money. The only conclusion I could come to was both simplistic and chilling: the man at Starbucks owned a gun, so he carried it around. The laws allowed him to. Pure opportunity.

After almost a decade in Washington, I moved to Colorado. Here men were definitely carrying. I saw truck gun racks galore. I saw a bumper sticker with a picture of a blazing pistol that read, "I DON'T Call 911." I saw the extensive display of weapons magazines at my local Barnes and Noble. I saw, when I drove to the county dump to recycle my cardboard boxes, signs directing me to Office Paper, Glass, Aluminum, and Shooting Range. Apparently you could carry to the dump, too, and squeeze off a few rounds after you had discarded your old issues of *Newsweek*.

Men were carrying in my city, only you couldn't see it. In 2003, Colorado joined the rest of the West and became a "shall-issue" concealed weapon carry state. That means that anyone who meets the criteria for gun ownership and applies for a concealed weapons permit will get one. Most states in the U.S. have some kind of provision for their residents to carry concealed weapons; the differences in laws seem to concern reciprocity, or whether a state will honor other states' permits for concealed weapons. Over the past several years, more states have adopted "total reciprocity," which means they allow any resident of any concealed weapon state to cross state lines with a hidden gun. I can't help but imagine men inside streams of vehicles crisscrossing the West, handguns and rifles stashed in their cars and strapped onto their calves, risk at their fingertips. I imagine each one of these men as an individual army, looking right and left at potential enemies.

Soon after moving to Colorado, I began to question how much of my understanding of the gun culture came from Western myth, from historical accounts, or the movies, TV shows, and cowboy stories I'd seen or read. For help I turned to a Western gun culture magazine called *Guns of the Old West*. In *Guns of the Old West*, I learned which rifles the buffalo hunters used, which reproductions of antique guns are most effective, which gun Frank James used to rob trains. I saw photos from Wild West events in which white men in authentic western wear shot blanks at "Indians"—white men in face paint. I learned that men in the West (and Western-loving men elsewhere) were still brandishing six-shooters and muskets and even practicing precision knife throwing. They were keeping alive a tradition that was never in any danger of dying.

New or Old West, one thing I learned from *Guns of the Old West* and from *American Handgunner*, *Gun World*, *Concealed Carry Magazine*, and other publications I consulted, was that by moving to the West I had moved to the land of men. It finally didn't matter to me that within this realization lay the fiction that you *cannot* be a man in the West unless you carry a gun. Or, if you prefer the flipside: You *will* carry a gun *because* you are a man in the West. What makes me uncomfortable as a new resident of Colorado is that this realization bumps up against a belief I've held for most of my life, and that is: Unless you are in a war zone, unless battle is raging all around you, or unless someone is directly threatening you with harm, you do not need a gun. If you are a man walking around in the New West, and, say, you're walking to Starbucks on a Sunday morning with your sweetheart, or, say, you're taking your trash to the dump, you do not need a gun.

III. Girls and Guns

I am afraid a man will shoot me. After reading some statistics, I'd call myself lucky. In 2004, according to the most recent study available from the Violence Policy Center, 1,807 women in the United States were killed by men in single-offender/single-victim murders. Forty-nine percent of those women were killed by firearms. In 2002, homicide was the leading cause of death for pregnant women, and the second leading cause of workplace death for women. How does the gun industry respond to this level of violence, given the fact that most of these women were killed by husbands, boyfriends, or relatives? They talk about "firearms feminism," and encourage women to arm themselves. In other words, gun advocates ignore the fact that the real gun violence threat a woman faces probably lives right inside her home, and no matter how many firearms training classes a woman takes, she's never going to be ready or able to protect herself from that danger. In fact, in a home with more than one gun, where, perhaps both a woman and a man own guns, a woman is seven times more likely to be killed by a spouse, relative, or intimate acquaintance than she is in a home without guns. And as a study by the Centers for Disease Control and Prevention found, women who are killed by relatives and intimate acquaintances are more likely to be murdered with a firearm than by all other means combined. Gun violence against women is not confined to any particular area of the country, but it does give me pause to know that in 2003, out of the ten states in the country with the highest female homicide rate per 100,000 people, five were in the West.

When I look at the photos in gun magazines of somber men standing behind the barrels of pistols or even AK-47s or when I see my townsmen driving out to the shooting range or when I pass by yet another sculpture or painting depicting a cowboy shooting his guns, I am struck once again by the chasm between the myth of gun ownership in the West and the reality of it, especially as it relates to women. I think of it this way: if a man shoots a woman, his act will almost certainly be on purpose, his victim will almost certainly be someone he knows well, and the shooting will not be an act suffused with honor, an echo of the West's legacy, or the demonstration of a freedom worth defending.

I'm not suggesting that the West is the nation's epicenter for gun violence. But here the horizon is wide open, a welcome place for wild souls; here there's a lot of room for animals to run and people to travel, and a vast landscape at which to fire weapons. The West is a place where one can exercise a kind of Manifest Destiny of violence. There's a geographical promise here that has worked against women's safety. Even though I recognize that I'm not living in a battlefield, I am a woman who resides in a part of the country that passionately celebrates guns and gun ownership. Whether the Old West really was "won" with a gun or not, a pervasive attitude here insists that it was, and that's coupled with a belief that the New West needs some of that same rough treatment. I love my part of Colorado, the spread of land, the vista of possibility, the history I see in every street that dead-ends at the foothills on the edge of town. But I'm edgy and nervous sometimes, and I wonder how many men, steeped in some everlasting myth, are carrying weapons, and why. I think there's a callous permissiveness in the land I love, in its open blue sky and rising plains and hills, its old and new residents, all of it—and us—held out like an invitation, like a target.

From Individual Despair to Collective Risk Taking

Stopping the Corporate Bullies

I don't remember the day I took my first risk, but I am pretty sure it was before I was five, when I stood up to my abusive father by refusing to cry as he repeatedly slapped me hard across the face. He wanted to see tears, but I knew somewhere inside my soul, that if I gave him what he wanted, it was all over for me. What followed for years was intermittent beatings, a small price to pay for keeping my inner self intact. Like most oppressors, my father wanted me to crumble in the face of the overwhelming odds stacked against me. Well today, I am still facing overwhelming odds, as indeed is the majority of the world's population. Our physical, emotional, economic and spiritual survival is under threat from bullies who will exploit anything or anybody to maximize profit.

In a society of plenty, such as the United States, risky behavior has come to mean doing too much; too much drinking, too much drugging or too much indiscriminate sex. The slew of prevention programs that have grown up are all about moderation, calling for us to set limits in what is increasingly becoming a society without limits. But when faced with an environmental, cultural and economic crisis, surely we should begin to think of risky behavior as doing nothing; the less we resist, the more the corporate bullies will plunder. If we are to have any chance of creating a world worth living in, then we need to see our resistance as having no limits. Drastic times call for drastic risk taking. But for those of us who have spent our lives taking risks, we know that on an individual level, such risks are like drops in an ocean.

When I refused to capitulate to my father, I was isolated in the family, as no one else wanted to risk taking on the patriarchal bully. It was the isolation, not the physical abuse, that led me to years of despair. Now as an adult who continually resists corporate patriarchal bullies, it is not despair that I feel, but an overwhelming sense of being alive, because my resistance takes place within the radical feminist movement. The day I discovered radical feminism (as an undergraduate student who stumbled on Robin Morgan's *Sisterhood is Powerful*) is the day my life changed forever. Although I was sitting alone in the library, I was catapulted into a community of radical women who, just like me, had come to the profound realization that giving in to patriarchal bullies was a sure path to destruction. By joining the radical feminist movement, I relinquished my isolation, and instead of feeling out of place in the world, I found my sense of place.

Engaging in resistant behavior is indeed risky if done alone. The psychologist Judith Herman, in her work on trauma, makes the point over and over again that the isolation caused by trauma is often more unbearable than the abuse itself. On a political level, we live in a society that is one big perpetrator. The unequal distribution of wealth, the mind-numbing work inherent in capitalism, the fear of becoming poor, the lack of access to life-giving resources and, of course, the physical, emotional and sexual violence that so many people, especially women and children, suffer on some level turns the majority of us into victims of trauma. We walk around with our own PTSD, thinking that something is wrong with us rather than understanding that PTSD is a normal state in an abusive world.

In her remarkable book, *Medicine Stories*, Aurora Levins Morales talks about individual and collective healing, and echoes Herman's argument that rebuilding the self after trauma requires collective political activism. This message does not bode well for us in the United States, where individualism is the religion and self-help is the gospel. The risks we have to take today to wrestle the world away from the global perpetrators require acts of unbelievable bravery as they have to be uncompromising in their aims and unflinching in their defiance. Stopping environmental destruction is not about buying a fuel-efficient car; it is about organizing to end the capitalist society that is based on over-production of useless status symbols. Fighting for economic equality is not simply about organizing unions; it is about ending an economic system where inequality is inherent, not an unfortunate by-product. Stopping the destruction of our culture is not about calling for more stringent FCC rules; it is about ending the corporate control of media. And none of these changes will ever occur if we don't tackle that which few progressive movements will risk to even mention: men.

At the heart of all of our problems is a death-loving masculinity that devours anything and everything in its path. To see the world's problems outside of a gender analysis is like trying to fight pollution by eating organic food. In a word, useless. Masculinity, as it has been constructed and as it is reproduced through every single social institution, is about control, colonization and destruction. We socialize our boys to become men, real men, whose "healthy" development depends upon the eradication of emotion, empathy, intimacy and connection. Clearly, not every man lives up to this ideal of masculinity, but patriarchy as a system has the horrible tendency to elevate the very worst of men to the very top. The rest, refusing to risk their "manliness," conform to varying degrees. The solution is not to make men more caring and empathetic, but to get rid of masculinity and, of course, its handmaiden, femininity.

If we refuse to risk looking at the overwhelming enormity of the problems facing us, then we risk losing everything. We may very well slouch along for a while, believing that some new politician with a good bumper sticker speech is our savior and that the pendulum always swings back and forth. If, however, we engage in the riskiest of behavior possible, a continuing refusal to acknowledge that we are on a collision course with disaster, then all is lost and men like my father ultimately will have won. He did not draw tears from my five-year-old eyes, but his patriarchal brothers, if allowed to win, will draw enough tears to drown us all.

STEVE ALMOND

ᴑᴑᴑ

Angels or Apes?

An Inquiry into the Nature of Modern Sadism and the Optional Extinction of Our Species

Back in 1986, when the Reagan Revolution was still in full swing, an Arizona Senator by the name of John McCain decided to uncork a little of that famous conservative wit. Addressing a crowd in our nation's capital, he allegedly told the following joke:

> Did you hear the one about the woman who is attacked on the street by a gorilla, beaten senseless, raped repeatedly and left to die? When she finally regains consciousness and tries to speak, her doctor leans over to hear her sigh contently and to feebly ask, "Where is that marvelous ape?"

Twelve years later, McCain regaled fellow Republicans with another wisecrack. "Why is Chelsea Clinton so ugly?" he asked. "Because her father is Janet Reno." Chelsea Clinton was eighteen years old at the time.

More recently, he entertained a crowd by singing the refrain "bomb bomb Iran" to the tune of the Beach Boys' sunny hit "Barbara Ann."

And just this month (I am writing in July of 2008), McCain responded to a reporter's question about illegal U.S. cigarette exports to Iran by quipping, "Maybe that's a way of killing them."

The McCain team has not denied he made any of these comments. While noting that the candidate has done and said things in the past that "he regrets," spokesman Brian Rodgers observed that the American people "want somebody who's authentic and this kind of stuff is a good example of McCain being McCain."

My point is not to criticize McCain for having a lousy sense of humor. I've laughed at enough potty humor over the years to keep a couple of lesser cable channels in business. No, what amazes me about all this is that McCain can make jokes that clearly indulge in sadistic fantasies—rape, bombing foreigners, sexual humiliation—and not run any sort of political risk.

The public expression of sadism, in other words, the pleasure of inflicting pain on others (or imagining it) has become entirely acceptable in the America of 2008. You can run for the highest office in the land as a registered Sadist. Never mind an apology, just get yourself a press agent.

The American tradition of regeneration through violence has been around since the war that granted us independence. It's what made the federal army's systematic destruction of the Native Americans so gratifying.

So it shouldn't shock anyone that the American populace managed to render the airborne murders of September, 2001, not as an occasion for mourning and reflection, but an opportunity to reawaken our heroic killing spirit. This is why, within months of that attack, you saw people cheering with great vigor for events in which thousands of people—innocent or otherwise—were killed. Which is to say, for the two subsequent wars.

Those were publicly sanctioned acts of sadism, carried out in defense of the homeland. Less frequently discussed were the capture and imprisonment of thousands of suspects who continue to be tortured.

By tortured, I mean that American citizens beat their bodies until they are on the verge of death, hook them to overhead manacles, sexually humiliate them, force them to defecate themselves, and prevent them from sleeping—blaring noises, strobe lights, John McCain comedy routines—until they go mad. Most famously, these American citizens pour water down the throats of suspects and into their lungs, which is to say they are drowned, but not to death. These acts are carried out on a military base in Guantánamo Bay and in Iraq prisons and in various black sites in Egypt and elsewhere.

Most Americans are only vaguely aware of these sadistic behaviors, which are disavowed, for the most part, by the politicians who order them to be carried out. They are rarely written about by the free press whose job it is to cover the affairs of state.

This is not to say that Americans are unfamiliar with the mechanics of sadism, because many of our most popular films and television shows include scenes of simulated sadism. (Many of our most popular sporting events and reality TV programs contain *actual* sadism.)

What makes all of this even more interesting at the current historical moment is the blurring of the line between entertainment and government policy. Note this snippet from Jane Mayer's perfectly terrifying 2008 book *The Dark Side*, in which she reveals that top officials at Guantánamo were gathering ideas about how to torture suspects from, among other sources, the hit television program *24*.

There are any number of experts—people whose lives are devoted to gathering data about the efficacy of torture—who will tell you that beating someone senseless, or drowning them half to death, does not produce good intelligence. It turns out people lie when subjected to extreme pain. (Full disclosure: I lie when subjected to mild discomfort.)

But again, my central concern isn't whether torture works or not. What worries me is that overt sadism has become an acceptable form of conduct in our culture.

People may not be seeing the real-life consequences of that sadism; the media has, for the most part, happily consented to censor the worst of the violence carried out in our names. And yet our pop culture has managed to fill in the blanks with a dizzying variety of entertainments—video games, movies, records—whose most salient feature is a reliance on sadism. I would refer you to the game Mortal Kombat, in which opponents fight to the death, with the winner granted the opportunity to tear the still-beating heart from the chest of the loser. It is routinely played by children.

Let me add that it has become something of a sport amongst distressed liberals and moderates (and some conservatives) to lament the failings of the George W. Bush administration. They tend to argue that Bush is incompetent, incurious, and/or corrupt.

These are comforting myths, compared to the alternative: that he's terribly anxious and frightened, in precisely the same way as an unsupervised child, and that he manages these feelings through acts of sadism. As a child, he tortured animals. As an adult, he oversees the torture of human beings.

What has any of this to do with risk?

Precisely this: sadism can be seen as an abdication of our capacity for sympathy, which encompasses the central risk of human consciousness. What else separates us from the animals? From the pitiless sharks and tigers, the voracious insects and marauding apes?

The modern world, with its routine pleasures and anxieties, has insulated most of us from the physical risks of our forebears. For those of us living in the convenient precincts, where the lower reaches of the Maslovian scale are assumed, the suffering of others counts as the big peril.

If we start to consider the bad news of starvation and displacement and war and poverty, if we start to see the victims of atrocity as entirely human, well then, we start to feel responsible. We start to feel that perhaps we have to *do something*.

Our survival as a species hangs on this very simple question: will we take moral responsibility for the suffering of others? Will we accept this risk?

This is the larger context into which we must place the notion of a presidential candidate who jokes about rape, or one who devises rationalizations to torture, or citizens who cheer for war, or those of us who allow such sadistic behaviors to speak for us.

The rise of evil in the world, the great machines of evil—from the Biblical tyrants to the inquisitors to the Nazis—have relied on populations who are essentially risk-averse, who will keep their mouths shut in the face of sadism, as their standards of humanity are methodically dismantled.

We find ourselves now in an unprecedented crisis. Our way of life is crumbling under its own absurd abundance. The cheap oil era is drawing to a close, and the creep of climate change—even if admitted to and addressed—may soon give way to upheaval. At the same time, the tools of violence are more abundant than ever. There is no end to the martyrs willing to kill themselves for a divine cause. The corporations obey no law but profit. And ten-year-old soldiers in African countries carry high-caliber rifles.

We can certainly debate what political or economic measures might be most effective in fighting these risks. And there is some good to be done by these larger manipulations of our remaining resources.

But there is only one abiding cure to this human disease: the risk of love in our time on earth, and the acts of generosity and forgiveness such love promises. There's nothing bigger or deeper, more painful or worthy of our hearts.

CHRISTOPHER L. DOYLE

Reclaiming the Self

Pain and Risk in the Pursuit of Our Best

We give up parts of ourselves to make our way in the world. What if we renounce the best parts? How might we reclaim them? Would we even be able to recognize if something had gone badly amiss?[1]

These questions have come to define much of my experience as a parent, teacher, academic historian, and voter. Lately, they recur with increasing urgency. Maybe we have arrived at a moment when they matter especially. When my friend Luke Reynolds asked me to write on "creative risk taking," I saw an opportunity to crystallize my thinking about them and to probe why they keep surfacing. I also saw in Luke's offer a chance to provide practical examples, past and present, of how "ordinary" people tackle difficult existential problems. Readers looking for Hollywood-style inspiration may be disappointed, because my trio of creative risk takers reclaim themselves by wandering into caves, stumbling around in the dark, scaring themselves witless, and refusing easy exits. They offer all the messiness of authenticity.

One of my twelfth-grade students showed me this not too long ago. Ashley came into my "Humanities" class in fall 2004. Smart, hardworking, infectious laugh, she got good grades, waited tables at a pizzeria, and undoubtedly earned great tips. She loved chatting with the older diners and told me once how moved she was by an elderly couple, regulars, who still held hands under the table. Attractive, athletic, with a devoted boyfriend, Ashley had a bright future. She seemed to be sailing through senior year.

In late fall, I asked Ashley and her classmates to do something that I thought would be easy: identify a personal interest and study it until it became more meaningful. I envisioned the assignment as an avenue to self-knowledge. Students could also engage creative faculties by describing their intellectual journey in whatever medium seemed most appealing—an essay, poem, film, portrait, or song. I was open to just about any form they wanted.

I was stunned when Ashley foundered. I watched her in the library alternating between frantic motion and inertia. She ran through topic after topic. I wanted to help but insisted she define her own subject. Three weeks later, amid cold morning light and stacks of books, the problem surfaced.

"I still haven't decided on anything."

"Why do you think this is so hard for you?"

"I don't know." She looked beyond the blank space on the library computer search engine and the incessantly winking cursor. "We don't ever get assignments like this." Silence, and then startlingly, she burst into tears. "I don't even know what I'm interested in! How pathetic is that?" She sobbed for an uncomfortably long time.

I have come to interpret Ashley's response as a rare, brave step. She could have dipped into the popular culture, pulled out one of dozens of hot topics, aced the assignment and moved on. Instead, she decided to confront her self-censor. When she did, she began wrestling against a culture that can be brutal and insidious. She lived in an affluent community and attended a "good" school, but growing up and winning approval in such an environment require immense sacrifices.

Across many disciplines, scholars paint a picture of coming of age in middle-class America that shows unequivocally how adults direct, supervise, and manipulate children to a degree unheard of even a generation ago. Never, historically, have children possessed so little free time; they are even losing the capacity to "know how" to play. Never before have we segregated children so narrowly by age, class, and our often-premature judgments of their academic and athletic ability. "Standards" have come to define educational experiences; we test their "mastery" at unprecedented length and foster the impression that the stakes in exam results have never been higher. Advertisers pitch to children earlier, more determinedly, and more systematically than ever before. We medicate children who deviate from the fast track at record and rapidly escalating rates. In such a world, Ashley discovered profound irony. She has been encouraged to imagine existence as a series of free "lifestyle" choices, yet she operated in educational, familial, and social milieus that prescribe "success" and proscribe "failure" down to minute levels of thought and performance.[2] It is easy to lose oneself in this environment.

As a female, Ashley faced especially severe threats to self-realization. Our society particularly encourages girls to please others. We teach girls to displace anger and not to challenge authority directly. Perhaps even more than we do to males, we train females to seek external measures of validation. The costs of such upbringings have been made abundantly clear by scholars of gender, psychology, pedagogy, and sociology. Literature and autobiography have confirmed and deepened the work of the social scientists.[3] Ashley's anger, fear, sense of helplessness, and stress are norms of female experience today; so are feelings of inadequacy and neuroses.

Ashley stands out because she confronted and voiced her frustration instead of displacing it. In the aftermath of her realization, I did what I could. I asked if she remembered ever pursuing her own interests and if she ever got so caught up in doing something that she lost track of time. I suggested books that might give context to her feelings (some are cited here). I also tried to draw on insights gleaned from discussions with my wife, a physician and wonderfully perceptive about the problems of growing up female. Later, when Ashley said she was contemplating a career in medicine, I thought that a role model might help and so put her in touch with my wife. Still, most of my interaction with Ashley took place in forty-two-minute intervals, with about twenty other students, five days a week. Ultimately, she found her own solutions. Defining a problem was half the battle.

She came to visit last fall. She is a sophomore in college, majors in health sciences, is deeply concerned with women's health issues in Latin America, and spoke briefly and eloquently to my students about college life, her recent work in El Salvador, and community service. When I asked her recently about that moment in the library, Ashley described it as part of a larger "identity crisis." She claimed she felt caught between a personal desire to excel and many external expectations. My sense is that she is finding better and truer parts of herself.

I turn to history to provide my two other exemplar responses, because people long dead offer advantages of perspective: we know how their lives turned out. Yet, trained as an academic, I confess to wariness about using the past cavalierly as a guide for conduct now. When teaching, I stress the unique modes of thinking and acting that past cultures produced in individuals, and I avoid facile nostrums about how "those who forget the past are condemned to repeat it." Repetition assumes a fixed set of circumstances and responses. What the past presents, in fact, is variety and novelty. My students hear *ad nauseam* about the dangers of projecting motives and beliefs anachronistically into the past. Nevertheless, I find the following examples irresistible and useful studies of how individuals can find the best parts of self when their culture stacks the deck against them.

Nearly everything in Robert Pyle's world suggested that slavery was a benevolent institution. Around the dawn of the eighteenth century, Philadelphia had become a prosperous trade hub dominated by Quaker merchants. Some 2,200 souls lived crowded around bustling wharves on the Delaware River, and the population was growing rapidly. The merchants profited by sending their ships out on the triangular routes that linked the corners of the Atlantic world. They traded grain, flour, and lumber for Caribbean sugar and molasses, European iron and luxuries, and Africans. Some of the wealthiest Philadelphia Quakers had emigrated directly from the slave-killing sugar plantations on Barbados and Jamaica. Building fine brick townhouses on Second Street, administering the burgeoning population, and amassing fortunes, Pyle and his fellow Pennsylvanians had little reason to question the ethical under-pinnings of their wealth.[4]

There was no strain of thought at the time, 1698, that would qualify as abo-litionist. In the 1670s Quaker founder George Fox had expressed misgivings about compelling blacks to labor. However, Fox never suggested that enslaving Africans was antithetical to being a good Quaker. John Locke included a brief denunciation of slavery in his *Second Treatise of Government* in 1689–90, but he was in England, far removed from the realities of trade on the margins of empire. Philadelphians did hear, in the 1690s, from a schismatic schoolmaster named George Keith; he criticized the slave trade and much else about Quaker society, but he was soon run out of the colony. Much more typical were the one in ten Philadelphians who owned slaves, including founder and Proprietor William Penn himself.[5]

So when Pyle considered purchasing a slave, he was powerfully taken aback by a dream he recorded. "I saw myself and a friend going on a road, and by the roadside I saw a black pott. I took it up. . . ." Proceeding down the road, the dreaming Pyle encountered "a great ladder standing exact upright, reaching up to heaven up which I must go to heaven." But the black pot in his hand pre-vented him from gripping the rungs of the ladder and ascending. For Pyle, a pious Quaker, this dream qualified as a nightmare. Reflecting on it, he con-cluded that his slave-coveting "self must bee left behind, and to let black negroes or potts alone."[6]

But Pyle went beyond merely renouncing the potential slaveholder in him-self. He devised an emancipation plan and tried to convince fellow Quakers to go along with it by freeing their slaves. Thus, in the face of all cultural norms, he attempted to reclaim the most principled part of himself.

We can only guess why Pyle had the dream and how he reached his inter-pretive conclusions. Maybe he had read Locke's or Fox's criticisms of slavery. Perhaps he had heard Keith speak out or witnessed Africans debarking after the Middle Passage, a sight even callous slaveholders found unsettling. Pyle seems not very different from many people, past or present, who have undefined feel-ings that the moral order has been violated. Neither is he unique in connecting his dreams to a conscious sense of injustice. Pyle's creative risk was acting on his dream. Refusing to purchase a laborsaving symbol of wealth and status, Pyle hazarded conflict with and alienation from his slaveholding brethren. Maybe he concluded that the only way to challenge the unassailable was by appealing to dreams.

In essence, Pyle became subversive. He defined the origins of his subver-sion as undercutting parts of "self" which "must bee left behind." Then, the process extended into the Quaker meeting he attended, where he argued for freedom. In his lifetime, Pyle's success was merely personal, not societal. But he planted a seed.

Afterward, in Quaker Philadelphia the unspeakable became a subject of public discourse. In the 1720s, merchant Ralph Sandiford was expelled from the sect for publishing an antislavery letter. At about the same time, Benjamin Lay set himself up as the public conscience of Philadelphia, refusing to meet with slave owners and staging acts of civil disobedience to protest the trade in Africans. The Society of Friends expelled Lay, too, in 1738.[7] Questioning a vital source of Philadelphian wealth was still anathema, but Pyle had moved the subject firmly beyond the realm of dreams.

Born into this culture of subversive antislavery in 1720, John Woolman felt it work on him. A well-off Quaker, Woolman grew up full of ambivalence about Africans and their enslavement. His family owned slaves, he profited directly from their labor, and he kept a journal that charted his long-term battle with conscience. In it, Woolman described several dreams involving slaves and slavery. As he approached middle age, the pangs of guilt grew more frequent and the dreams more graphic.

In the 1760s, Woolman went on a kind of pilgrimage. He walked, the mode of transport slaves used, to meet with Quakers and their slaves in the South, in New Jersey, and Rhode Island. At the same time, he published two tracts arguing that slavery was incompatible with being a good Quaker. Yet, he was careful to vet the pamphlets with Quaker elders before releasing them. In 1770, he dreamed that "an old Negro man" was killed and sacrificed to a monster creature that to Woolman represented the "cunning" and "vain delights" that went along with catching and exploiting slave labor. Woolman continued to agitate Quakers to abolish slavery. Historian Mechal Sobel has called Woolman "*the archetypal figure of a moral antislavery activist in the second half of the eighteenth century.*"[8] In the last two years of his life, Woolman assumed his most strident antislavery activism. Alternating between profound depression and acute joy, he died without realizing the fruit of his labors. Validation came four years after his death in 1772. In the year of the *Declaration of Independence*, Philadelphia Quakers condemned slavery as a sin and decided to expel any brethren who continued to keep slaves.

What do Woolman and Pyle have in common with my student Ashley? Like all of us, they were shaped by a socializing mechanism that historian Norbert Elias calls "the civilizing process." Elias points out that in Western culture this process is particularly hard on the individual. It goes far beyond the constraints to self necessary for societal harmony, or rules of behavior that existed before modern times. Refined over the last five hundred years, the civilizing process reflects and advances dominant power: capitalism, bureaucracy, the state. It does so, as Elias describes it, by forcing "Each man, [to] confront himself. He 'conceals his passions,' 'disavows his heart,' 'acts against his feelings.' "[9] Thus, we internalize the ironic dilemma that Ashley detected. We accept that the path to "freedom," what today we interchangeably call "success," lay in self discipline, and finally self-renunciation. In the face of this irony, it can become difficult to articulate, or even remember, our passion, heart, and feelings.

Today we would describe Pyle and Woolman as heroes, but they ran the risk of being outcasts and pariahs in their own time. Ashley ran similar risks of disappointing her parents, teachers, and peers by challenging outside expectations for her success and trying to locate internal sources of meaning. Their creative risk involved finding a language to describe and reclaim their best selves. For all three, the risk involved pain, and it was often a quiet, internal struggle instead of a dramatic and sensational one. We now face profound, unprecedented, and overlapping external pressures to direct and shape individual thought. We, too, will have to find the courage to admit when we have lost ourselves, to reject dominant images of what we should be, to search our dreams for clues as to whom we might become, and to risk the strain and alienation that go along with realizing our best selves.

NOTES

1. The exact phrasing of the questions is mine, but the areas of inquiry are hardly original. Michel Foucault's way of putting it influenced me: "What must one know about oneself in order to renounce anything?" From "Technologies of the Self," in *The Essential Foucault: Selections from Essential Works of Foucault, 1954–1984*, ed. Paul Rabinow and Nicholas Rose (New York, 2003), 146.

2. On economic segregation of children, see Jonathan Kozol, *The Shame of the Nation: The Restoration of Apartheid Schooling in America* (Pittsburgh, 2006). On the standardization of education and its detriments, see Alfie Kohn, *What Does It Mean to Be Well Educated? And More Essays on Standards, Grading, and Other Follies* (Boston, 2004); and Deborah Meier and George Wood, eds., *Many Children Left Behind: How the No Child Left Behind Act Is Damaging Our Children and Schools* (Boston, 2004). For a disturbing set of case studies on what the pursuit of test results does to the brightest students, see Denise Clark Pope, *"Doing School": How We Are Creating a Generation of Stressed Out, Materialistic, and Miseducated Students* (New Haven, 2001), especially chapters 2, 3, and 7. On the demise of play, see David Elkind, *The Hurried Child: Growing Up Too Fast, Too Soon*, 3d ed. (Cambridge, Mass., 2001). On advertising to children, see Juliet B. Schor, *Born to Buy: The Commercialized Child and the New Consumer Culture*, (New York, 2004); for a historical context, see Steven Mintz, *Huck's Raft: A History of American Childhood* (Cambridge, Mass., 2004). Mintz notes that today "intergenerational contact is increasingly confined to relationships between children and parents, teachers, and service providers. More fully integrated into the consumer economy than ever before, and at a much earlier age, the young are, at the same time, more segregated than ever in a peer culture. Kids have more space in their own homes, but less space outside to call their own" (381). On increasing rates of medication, see "Checklist for Camp: Bug Spray, Sunscreen, Pills," *New York Times*, 16 July 2006; and "Sleeping Pill Use by Youth Soars, Study Says," *New York Times*, 19 October 2005.

3. Mary Pipher, *Reviving Ophelia: Saving the Selves of Adolescent Girls* (New York, 1994), especially pp. 22–26. For historical perspective and neurotic responses to repression of girls, see Joan Jacobs Brumberg, *The Body Project: An Intimate History of American Girls* (New York, 1998). In a nutshell, I interpret Brumberg's thesis as this: A century ago,

American girls were bound by strictures demanding they "be good." Now, "be good" is sublimated to "look good." A sociological study of the predicament of adolescent girls comes from Patricia Hersch, *A Tribe Apart: A Journey into the Heart of American Adolescence* (New York, 1998).

4. Population figure and information about houses appear in Edwin Wolf, II, *Philadelphia: Portrait of an American City* (Philadelphia, 1975), 15, 26. On trade networks see Jack P. Greene, *Pursuits of Happiness: The Social Development of Early-Modern British Colonies and the Formation of American Culture* (Chapel Hill, 1988), 124–31. Also on trade see Mary Maples Dunn and Richard S. Dunn, "The Founding, 1681–1701," in *Philadelphia: A 300-Year History* (New York, 1982), 18–21; on West Indian emigration by prominent Quakers, see p. 19.

5. John Locke, *Second Treatise of Government*, ed. C. B. Macpherson (Indianapolis, 1980), 17; on Fox, see Mechal Sobel, *Teach Me Dreams: The Search for Self in the Revolutionary Era* (Princeton, 2000), 63; on Keith and on Penn's slave ownership, see Dunn and Dunn, "The Founding," 31, 30.

6. Quoted in Sobel, *Teach Me Dreams*, 55.

7. On Lay and Sandiford, see ibid., 63–64.

8. Ibid., 64.

9. Norbert Elias, *The Civilizing Process: Sociogenetic and Psychogenetic Investigations* (1939), rev. ed., trans. Edmund Jephcott (Malden, Mass., 2000); the quotation appears on p. 399 but see especially pp. 442–43.

MICHAEL DUNN

Skateboarding the Third Rail

The Risk of the Middle

Kathleen and I used to love camping. Hiking through pine-cooled air, romantic trysts by rushing streams, leaves lightly raining on our nylon ceiling. Now, with four young kids, not so much. Camping, like much of parenthood, is a struggle to keep the kids alive. Here's my "Ways the Kids Could Die" list from a recent adventure:

- tumble into fire pit,
- tumble down boulder-strewn, tick-infested, fifty-foot drop at edge of campsite,
- drown in bacteria-infested lake if somehow survive fifty-foot drop,
- trip over bungee cord stretched as barrier between campsite and fifty-foot drop,
- wander off while I chase other kids from bungee barrier,
- figure out butane lighter, bottle opener, Ginsu knives,
- *e coli,* West Nile mosquitoes, rattlesnakes, black bears, etc.

Not to mention the other humans, like the creepy drunk eyeing the bath-house door when I brought the kids to brush their teeth. Wrapped in my daughter's pink towel and armed with a nail clipper, I cut as menacing a figure as I could, glowering, "Don't think I'm afraid to use this."

As a people farmer, job one is to perpetuate the species, and my "Risk-Taker" hat is buried pretty deep in my Many Hats drawer. But even amid the dangers that make "safety first" our primal impulse comes the recognition of life's more vital impulse, that growing people really means letting them risk climbing over the bungee barrier to rappel the first few boulders down the fifty-foot drop, our hands outstretched like Holden in *The Catcher in the Rye.* While we need to protect our kids, our real job is to begin the heart-ripping process of gradually nudging them out of the nest. It doesn't make any sense, really: you fall in love in a tent near a rushing stream under pine-cooled air, decide to get married and have kids, then fall in love all over again with these tiny helpless beings only to have to push them slowly away from you each day.

But this seems to be the whole point—of parenting, teaching, life itself—to come eventually to the only big universal truth, that they have to figure it out by doing it themselves. Called "gradual release" in education-speak, it's Holden Caulfield's mini-enlightenment when he finally realizes it's okay to let his kid sister Phoebe reach too far off her carousel horse: "The thing with kids is, if they fall off, they fall off, but it's bad if you say anything to them." The warp and woof of parenting, it's Mary teetering up the stairs, Sean's big blue eyes as I wave through the pre-school window on my way to the car, Michael saying, "Let go, Daddy," and taking off on his bike while I stand on the driveway holding his training wheels, Fiona diving under the big waves for the first time while I stand on the sand holding my breath, all creating new possibilities by continually reinforcing the neurological pathways of the "I can" moment that only comes through risk, like a baby robin discovering her few ounces of feather and bone are enough to keep her from crashing to the cement.

Life is an eternal tango between these two survival impulses—one stretching bungee barriers, the other climbing over them—that constitute the Yin and Yang of the human condition. The only way to fulfill our first impulse, to survive, is to tap the second and evolve, but unfortunately the former often wins the day. Whereas the constant pull between protection and growth, fear and desire, creates the basic tension of life (even at the cellular level these impulses blend: cell walls that protect the life juice are also semi-permeable), the walls we build at the interpersonal level, of bungee cords or stone, ignorance or hatred, often thwart the growth impulse, and the imbalance can paradoxically threaten our survival. Perhaps our protecting impulse is more evolved than our risking one because our global campsite, teeming with extremist plots and terrorist bombs, is no less scary. But "something there is," Frost reminds us, "that doesn't love a wall, that wants it down," and since their mortar is fear, which it is the nature of the growth impulse to transcend, our walls symbolize not only how human conflicts concretize the abstractions of fear, but also the hunch that the impulse to protect, unbalanced by the equally vital impulse to risk, is what could blow us all up in the end.

We often think of risk occurring "out at the edges," as writer Russell Banks described Mark Twain. Pushing against what passes for the safe or acceptable in art, politics or lifestyle, risk-takers widen the bubble of the possible by stretching the ends of the bell curve of popular opinion further along the axes; and because stretching creates tension, they don't win popularity contests. But for an English teacher, metaphors matter, and perhaps the bell curve obscures risk's true playground: the middle. In contemporary parlance "the middle" is often characterized as "wishy-washy," "lukewarm," or "fence-sitting," and if we picture it only as the central button on the pillow of the bell curve, or the best place to hide from the edges, it connotes anything but risk. The risk of the middle becomes more apparent if we return to an older and wiser metaphor.

Contrary to bumper sticker wisdom, the Yin Yang isn't a homily of Hippie harmony, and in fact its magic is what makes it the world's first motion picture. Like other religious symbols, the Yin Yang emerged from pre-history as a natural expression of lived human experience. The ancient Chinese used its profound simplicity to convey the central truth that everything we perceive with the senses or conceive with the mind exists through the energy created by the interplay of opposites, like our two opposed survival impulses. The apparent harmony only exists because these opposites are balanced, not because they are at rest. In fact both sides are eternally and mightily pushing against each other with the entire force of the cosmos, and the resulting tension, according to both ancient Taoism and modern science, is the source of all energy and power, explaining everything from the unspeakable destructive force released by the splitting of the atom to the unfathomable creative power engendered in the coupling of lovers. The middle curve of the Yin Yang is the center of unimaginable power, the mother of all third rails (which lie, after all, smack between the uptown and downtown trains).

The risk of the middle is in skateboarding this third rail, venturing beyond protective barriers into the open field between the encamped armies, and the human story is full of evidence of how risky this is. Blessed though they be, a litany of peacemakers from Gandhi to Romero to Rabin, all of whom were martyred by extremists of their own camps, reveals how ultimate are their risks. Anything but wishy-washy, middle-riskers push against partisan walls to widen the common ground of understanding toward the tenuous equilibrium of consensus and compromise. From restorative justice mediation, where opposing sides sit down with a mediating attorney and thereby circumvent costly and time-intensive legal proceedings, to the student who leaves the invisible comfort of his cafeteria clique to say, "Hi" to the new kid, middle-riskers stretch outward to recognize complexity and acknowledge validity on both sides of issues, transcend fear by facing conflicts head on, and harness the energy of tension by finding the positive in the negative, like Rabbi Judea Pearl, the father of murdered journalist Daniel Pearl, who creates light from grief as he and his friend, Muslim scholar Akbar Ahmed, tour the country to engage in honest dialogue about what their faiths have in common.

Like the middle, tension also gets a bad rap, but without it, the interplay of opposites, there'd be no suspension bridges, no sex, actually there'd be . . . nothing, which is why the ancients liked the Yin Yang so much. As inevitable as night chasing day, the energy tension produces can fuel an intense game of basketball as much as it can a bomb. Instead of avoiding the discomfort it causes, middle-riskers pay attention to it to discover why the Yin or Yang is pulling so hard and what's out of kilter. They work in any conflict, external or internal, toward that moving center that strikes a balance between safety and growth, and then harness the tension in creative, instead of destructive, ways, even if it means stretching themselves thin in the process.

Our job, as parents, teachers, writers, artists, citizens, is to tap that "something there is" and take down walls, with pens or dynamite, flowers or votes, and stretch cords of connections, which spiders do to ensure their survival, but which we must do to ensure ours. We are truly at risk unless we raise our kids not only to stretch the bell curve of ideas and possibility but also to face the waves of tension head on. This is hardest when it means risking disagreement with our own side, letting go of what we've been taught to think or believe by our teachers, bosses, pastors or politicians. It means risking being the good referee, the one both teams accuse of not being fair, seeking out and welcoming dissenting points of view and "speaking truth to power," whether to the "it" kid on the playground, or to avoid the pernicious dangers of "group think" in an administration bent on war.

Skateboarding the third rail means taking the energy of opposing forces and creating new possibilities, and nothing could be more essential to teach our kids. The other day in class Tessa presented her research on Peace Players, who form basketball teams in areas of conflict made up of kids from opposing sides. Tessa focused on two boys, a Palestinian from East Jerusalem, who avoided pressure from recruiters to become a suicide bomber, and an Israeli living in West Jerusalem whose father turned a bedroom into a bomb shelter. Playing for the same team, they began to realize how much they have in common, which is the other lesson of the Yin Yang, that both sides are also doing the best they can to accommodate the other, as in the constant push and pull of marriage, recognizing that bit of the other at the core of ourselves.

Middle-risking challenges us to synthesize the best of conflicting paradigms, which in our schools, for example, means recognizing the need for "measurable performance data" but only in the service of stoking the fires of our children's innate curiosity and pushing them to fly on their own. It means encouraging them to read and think and write in ever more complex ways until they shout with Jefferson the rousing penultimate sentence of the Declaration of Independence, that they, and all of us, "are, and of right ought to be, free and independent." It means celebrating, like the sign over a colleague's classroom door, that "Mistakes are made here!" It's teaching them the art of concession and civil debate rather than fueling the polarized partisanship that constitutes much of what passes for public discourse these days. Mostly it means challenging them to explore various, often conflicting, points of view so as to ever expand their minds and stretch their hearts.

Through risk we transcend our limited notions of the possible, and the payoff is that the world opens up to us. On my classroom wall is a Polaroid I took in

Jerusalem of a fragment of wall by a roadside field drunk on the blood of centuries of human beings killing one another. Through a crack between the stones grows an intensely beautiful wild orchid, blood red, its fragile thirsty roots steadily dislodging grain after grain of loosened mortar until the wall, like all the walls, will one day come crashing down. "Something there is," after all, and the soft, according to the Tao Te Ching, will eventually overcome the hard. Life will have its way through our fears one way or another, whether as a tiny burst of color and fragrance or an explosion of deferred dreams. The high calling of artists and writers and teachers is to tap the tensions beyond our comfort zones in order to awaken us to the bit of the other at the center of our existence, and lead us to awareness expressed in action. Finding the middle requires collecting our balance closer to our core; and the greatest risk for us, both as individuals and as a species, is losing who we are by opting so much on the side of safety that the flower of our deepest selves can't find its way through the cracks.

The risk of the middle is the unsung risk, more kitchen table than bungee jump, and parenthood requires stretching bungee cords between trees instead of off of bridges. Sometimes between darkness and dawn, awakened by the thud of a kid falling out of bed, Kathleen and I have whispered about selling the house, shedding the suburban clutter clogging our closets, buying an RV and living in Thoreauvian deliberateness as the tires hum over the pavement, stopping from city to city to stay with friends and learn about who is skating third rails, and then turning it all into a family-friendly PBS series, complete with a book deal. Like George Bailey from *It's a Wonderful Life,* whose passion for building things found its way into building people's lives instead of "skyscrapers a hundred stories high," even if we don't get our PBS series, maybe we'll teach our kids to skateboard third rails and speak truth to power, transcend their fears and risk where they are planted, and evolve the species one dislodged grain of conflict, one leafy tendril of empathy at a time. Unlike the campground, the stakes couldn't be higher, but what a return we could get on the investment!

ROBERT JENSEN

∞∞

Choices on a Runaway Train

Imagine you are on a train that for many years has been barreling ahead at full speed, always with ample fuel to power the engines. You are seated at the front of the train, in the club car, where there is plenty of food, lots of beverages, and adequate entertainment on board. The pollution generated by the engine passes by your window pretty quickly. The waste generated in the club car either gets tossed out or shoved into cars in the back—in either case, it's out of sight and out of mind.

Over the years and along the way there have been occasional slow-downs and a rare derailment, but from your seat in the club car these have been only minor annoyances. The train has always gotten back on track, staying on schedule, full steam ahead. It has always seemed that the tracks would go on endlessly and that there were enough of all the necessary supplies to keep going, while the waste remained out of sight. From your view in that first-class car, things seemed fine.

Then one day, you look out the window and see that, in fact, the tracks end a ways up ahead—at the edge of a cliff.

Well, imagine that.

Now, imagine living in the developed world in the 21st century. Imagine that we are on that train, that the consequences of human hubris and First-World excess are coming due. Think about rapid climate change, peak oil, and a toxic environment, in the context of growing global inequality. Ponder the cliff.

What are the options of that club-car rider? What risks does each option entail?

OPTION #1: Shut the window, ignore the cliff, stay quiet, and order another round of drinks.

156

If it's difficult to imagine how the train can be slowed down in time to avoid going over the cliff, it could be argued the rational thing to do is to enjoy what's left of the ride. But two realities should trouble those who might lean this way. First, how can we know for sure the train can't be slowed, maybe even stopped? Should we really be so sure there's nothing to be done? Second, even if there is little or no chance of slowing the train, do we want to be the kind of people who ride in relative luxury while others in the cars behind suffer?

OPTION #2: Throw open all the windows, acknowledge the cliff, start shouting, and do things.

We live in a time that demands action without guarantees, in both intellectual and moral/political terms. That is, we can't be sure that we are capable of knowing enough to solve the problems that humans have created in this world. We also can't be sure that if we did know enough that we have the moral strength to shift politically, to change the distribution of power, in time. That leaves us facing the questions from Option #1.

First, precisely because we can't know for sure, our only choice is to act with an understanding that some suffering of the most vulnerable in the short term can be alleviated and that long-term change is potentially within our grasp. Second, by acting, we define ourselves as human beings in the deepest and most fulfilling sense.

I offer options starkly in black-and-white terms that, of course, over-simplify the situation. But such over-simplification is useful to remind us of the risks of the two stances.

There are two main risks in Option #2, one external and one internal. If one speaks openly and honestly about Option #2, one is likely to be labeled apocalyptic, unrealistic, sensationalistic. When one talks like that at a party, people tend quickly to find reasons to move across the room. Talk about it too often with friends, and one might find one has fewer friends. Even more difficult is the internal struggle of coming to terms with such a stark view of the world; it's not easy, and it takes one into intellectual, emotional, and theological space that can be difficult to traverse. In short, the risk of Option #2 is that people will treat you like you are crazy and that you will feel like you are going crazy.

But those risks seem minimal in the face of Option #1, which is the risk of losing one's soul, that one will no longer be fully human in any meaningful sense.

We might remember the line from the play *A Man for All Seasons*, about Thomas More, who resisted Henry VIII's claim to be supreme head of the Church of England and was executed for his principled stance. In the play, he confronts one of the witnesses against him, Richard Rich, who has testified falsely against More in exchange for appointment to the post of attorney general of Wales. More reproaches Rich, saying, "Why, Richard, it profits a man nothing to give his soul for the whole world. But for Wales!"

Are we giving our souls for Wales? For a comfortable seat in the club car? For a good meal and a soothing drink? For the ability to numb ourselves to the reality around us?

There is nothing in the world of enough value to risk losing those things that make us human—facing honestly the state of the world and struggling for justice in that world. Our options are clear, as are the risks.

HOWARD ZINN

A Kinder, Gentler Patriotism

At some point soon the United States will declare a military victory in Iraq. As a patriot, I will not celebrate. I will mourn the dead—the American GIs, and also the Iraqi dead, of which there will be many, many more. I will mourn the Iraqi children who may not die, but who will be blinded, crippled, disfigured, or traumatized, like the bombed children of Afghanistan who, as reported by American visitors, lost their power of speech.

We will get precise figures for the American dead, but not for the Iraqis. Recall Colin Powell after the first Gulf War, when he reported the "small" number of U.S. dead, and when asked about the Iraqi dead, Powell replied: "That is really not a matter I am terribly interested in."

As a patriot, contemplating the dead GI's, should I comfort myself (as, understandably, their families do) with the thought: "They died for their country"? But I would be lying to myself. Those who die in this war will not die for their country. They will die for their government.

The distinction between dying for our country and dying for your government is crucial in understanding what I believe to be the definition of patriotism in a democracy. According to the Declaration of Independence—the fundamental document of democracy—governments are artificial creations, established by the people, "deriving their just powers from the consent of the governed," and charged by the people to ensure the equal right of all to "life, liberty, and the pursuit of happiness." Furthermore, as the Declaration says, "Whenever any form of government becomes destructive of these ends, it is the right of the people to alter or abolish it."

"A Kinder, Gentler Patriotism," by Howard Zinn from *Newsday*, 2003. Reprinted by permission of the author.

When a government recklessly expends the lives of its young for crass motives of profit and power (always claiming that its motives are pure and moral ["Operation Just Cause" was the invasion of Panama and "Operation Iraqi Freedom" in the present instance]), it is violating its promise to the country. It is the country that is primary—the people, the ideals of the sanctity of human life and the promotion of liberty. War is almost always (one might find rare instances of true self defense) a breaking of those promises. It does not enable the pursuit of happiness but brings despair and grief.

Mark Twain, having been called a "traitor" for criticizing the U.S. invasion of the Philippines, derided what he called "monarchical patriotism." He said: "The gospel of the monarchical patriotism is: 'The King can do no wrong.' We have adopted it with all its servility, with an unimportant change in the wording: 'Our country, right or wrong!' We have thrown away the most valuable asset we had: the individual's right to oppose both flag and country when he believed them to be in the wrong. We have thrown it away; and with it all that was really respectable about that grotesque and laughable word, Patriotism."

If patriotism in the best sense (not in the monarchical sense) is loyalty to the principles of democracy, then who was the true patriot, Theodore Roosevelt, who applauded a massacre by American soldiers of 600 Filipino men, women and children on a remote Philippine island, or Mark Twain, who denounced it?

With the war in Iraq won, shall we revel in American military power and—against the history of modern empires—insist that the American empire will be beneficent?

Our own history shows something different. It begins with what was called, in our high school history classes, "westward expansion"—a euphemism for the annihilation or expulsion of the Indian tribes inhabiting the continent—all in the name of "progress" and "civilization." It continues with the expansion of American power into the Caribbean at the turn of the century, then into the Philippines, and then repeated marine invasions of Central America and long military occupations of Haiti and the Dominican Republic.

After World War II, Henry Luce, owner of *Time, Life* and *Fortune,* spoke of "the American Century," in which this country would organize the world "as we see fit." Indeed, the expansion of American power continued, too often supporting military dictatorships in Asia, Africa, Latin America, the Middle East, because they were friendly to American corporations and the American government.

The American record does not justify confidence in its boast that it will bring democracy to Iraq. It will be painful to acknowledge that our GI's in Iraq were fighting not for democracy but for the expansion of the American empire, for the greed of the oil cartels, for the political ambitions of the president. And when they come home, they will find that their veterans' benefits have been cut to pay for the machines of war. They will find the military budget growing at the expense of health, education and the needs of children. The Bush budget even proposes cutting the number of free school lunches.

I suggest that patriotic Americans who care for their country might act on behalf of a different vision. Do we want to be feared for our military might or respected for our dedication to human rights? With the war in Iraq over, if indeed it is really over, we need to ask what kind of a country will we be. Is it important that we be a military superpower? Is it not exactly that that makes us a target for terrorism? Perhaps we could become instead a humanitarian superpower.

Should we not begin to redefine patriotism? We need to expand it beyond that narrow nationalism which has caused so much death and suffering. If national boundaries should not be obstacles to trade—we call it globalization—should they also not be obstacles to compassion and generosity?

Should we not begin to consider all children, everywhere, as our own? In that case, war, which in our time is always an assault on children, would be unacceptable as a solution to the problems of the world. Human ingenuity would have to search for other ways. Tom Paine used the word "patriot" to describe the rebels resisting imperial rule. He also enlarged the idea of patriotism when he said: "My country is the world. My countrymen are mankind."

PART FIVE

Leaving Safety

ROBERT PINSKY

XYZ

The cross the fork the zigzag—a few straight lines
For pain, quandary and evasion, the last of signs.

ooo

Sunday Morning in Oakland

This morning while reading the Sunday paper, we hear shouting in the street, look out the window, and see the naked guy from the house two doors down. The naked guy is cut. Not bleeding. Chiseled. Ranting man, tight butt, muscled thighs, sculpted pecs: our neighbor has a body that screams institutionalization. In the past, his inner fires have driven him to the asylum weight room. It is a sign of our time that we're more likely to get the insane on an exercise routine than chain them to posts.

My husband Steve and I watch him from behind our blinds. The Floreses across the street watch him behind their screen door. The naked man struts in the middle of the street in front of his house, back and forth, back and forth, aiming a rifle wildly. We can see cars detouring at the end of the street. The man marches with a kind of exuberance. He is confident, perhaps, in his wild dance, and he is counting on us, perhaps, to do the neighborly thing: To save him from himself and us from him.

Snow Day

This has happened before. Early in the morning on a workday last November, our neighbor, armed and naked, stepped out. Somebody called, and Special Forces came. Though our neighbor and the Oakland P. D. have a relationship— we'll see squad cars outside his house once or twice a month—Special Forces come when the madness drives him out and onto public property. Last time, they came with pomp and circumstance.

First they seized the block, putting up barricades. Our neighbor immediately retreated to his house, but the game was in play by then and would play to the end. Mr. Flores, a plumber, tried to leave for work, but they shouted him back in through loudspeakers on their cars: "Go back in your house; go back in your house." Then, they began marching. Black-suited, helmeted, fully armed, they started at the top of the sidewalk. They marched in tiers, shield-bearers in front, sharp-shooters behind. They moved stealthily but in sync down the sidewalk. Then, walking backward, they retraced their steps, keeping their eyes triggered on the target. A woman pleaded through a loudspeaker: "Mr. Smith" (for that's his name), "please pick up the phone in your house; we just want to make sure you're all right."

For seven hours, the block was under siege. It reminded me of snow days during my childhood in Colorado when weather seized the streets. This was different, of course, but the effect was the same. By ten o'clock, it was clear kids couldn't go to school; workers couldn't go to work. Steve and I began doing indoor things but keeping an eye on the window. We were, of course, more distracted than we would have been by nasty weather. There was the allure of spectacle. There was the promise of a dramatic dénouement. Something would happen, but what? Would they shoot him? Would he shoot them? Or us? Or himself? Would it be on the evening news?

But today is Sunday, and the weather is fine. Who wants to be robbed of a Sunday, and the novelty? Arguably less the second time around. We can expect a long standoff. Then, around hour five, they'll deploy teargas. For this, they'll climb up on the roof next door and blow out his windows. Eventually, our neighbor will come out crying. Once his hands are cuffed, the cops will wipe the teargas from his eyes before helping him into the paddy wagon.

When he's on his meds, Mr. Smith is a perfectly regular guy. Funny, too, in a self-mocking kind of way. Sometimes, fully clothed, he dances. Up and down the sidewalk and into the street, he'll perform assault with an air rifle, swinging his trigger finger this way and that, ending each performance with careful aim, eye contact, and a smile.

The Block

We bought our house, a 950-square-foot bungalow in Oakland's Fruitvale district, just south of Interstate 580, in 2000. For years, the conventional wisdom was "You're not safe anywhere south of 580," but during the dot-com craze, when Silicon Valley's young professionals moved inland by the droves, property values skyrocketed and the conventional wisdom changed overnight. Steve, a musician, and I, a writer, were quickly being priced out of the rental market in Oakland's mid-town. We considered ourselves lucky when we found this place— the last affordable house west of the flatland "Avenues," where gangs and drug dealers have reigned for decades.

Our block has an appealing international flavor. Many of our neighbors are second-generation immigrants who've worked hard to buy bungalows like ours. Mr. Flores, the plumber, came from Mexico. There's a Tongan bricklayer a few doors down, and across the street, a Chinese family in construction. We used to have an old Laotian couple in the huge decrepit rental next door. They classed up the street, he always dressing in a suit, she in outdated but elegant dresses. They spoke no English. Each morning he would help her into the back seat of a Cadillac (vintage 1980), and they would drive somewhere, returning each evening at 6:00. Sadly, the place went on the market last year, they got evicted, and young entrepreneurs divided the house into three apartments that are now designated "Section 8" housing. A noisy crew has moved in, and many after-noons around 3:00 a woman can be heard yelling, "I got to have my candy!" We're not crazy about the new neighbors.

We like the view on this block. The houses were built on a hill, and we're near the top. Though we can't see the bay, we've got an eye-view of treetops, lovely sunsets, and fireworks on the 4th of July. We're also very fond of our drive-way, one of the few in the neighborhood, which means we don't have to park in the street. Our street is curvy and wide, a favorite of midnight riders. About twice a year, we have impromptu block parties. We'll wake to a sickening thud, thud, crunch of collapsing metal, and the neighbors all turn out to see whose cars have been taken out this time. Normally, a racer who doesn't make the curve will take out three parked cars at a clip, though the record since we've lived here is five, plus two porches. Astonishingly, there've been no human casualties.

Sundays are usually bustling, noisy days. There are signs of faith all over the neighborhood, but no more on Sunday than any other time. Daily, Muslim women in veils walk past our house with their children on their way to the Mexican grocery; *Watchtower* pamphlets constantly litter the gutters; Samoan men in lavalavas and women in muumuus gather throughout the week at the Samoan church around the corner. On this block, faith doesn't unite us.

It's hard to say what does unite us. We are distinctive for our differences. When the Raiders play, for example, somebody up the block usually has a TV party, inviting friends from outside the neighborhood to watch the game. Down the block, soccer fans gather, tuning in to sports on the Mexican language sta-tion. On a normal Sunday, you can't find curbside parking after noon. We track the dueling games by intermittent whoops and ahhs echoing from the party houses. The parties don't end when the games end. By then, barbeques are hot, stereos on. Button accordions jam with steel guitars into the night, getting louder as partiers get drunker. Frequently, the din continues into Monday morning. When we moved into this house, we installed double-paned, extra-thick windows to dull the roar from the street, but the noise still leaks in. We've learned to use earplugs.

We're a tolerant crew. We tolerate noise pollution, air pollution, litter. . . . We tolerate, for example, the Vietnamese scavenger who steals plastic bottles from recycle bins, leaving a mess of discards on the sidewalk. We keep mum about those hooded guys who like to park their cars in the middle of the street and have impromptu powwows. They'll get out to chat, air their dogs (Tupac blaring, pit bulls straining at the tethers), and stare the locals down. Nobody complains about the sidewalk mechanics with their famous wrecked cars that appear mysteriously overnight, flat tires turned curbside. We accept the ever-present broken glass in the street, and the loud people next door who may be turning the rental into a crack house. Nobody has ever said a word about the plumes of smoke issuing from our driveway. Next to playing the piano, Steve likes nothing better than roasting coffee. He sets up a 10-pound coffee roaster, and, on Sundays, will sit out roasting, smoking a cigar, and reading. Elsewhere, especially in neighborhoods north of 580, people might whine, but not here. We don't complain about our neighbors, and they don't complain about us.

911

If anything unites us on this block, it's probably our aversion to snitches. Yet we're not insensitive to a neighbor in need. Last time, after all, somebody did call on Mr. Smith's behalf. If we're hesitant this time, blame prudence. Experience has taught us that if we call, it will be an expensive day. These outings by the Oakland P. D. are costly. The gear alone is marvelous. How much do ballistic helmets cost? And face shields, and padded upper body armor? Forearm protectors, groin protectors, shin guards; stun guns; tasers; the precision Barrett M107; teargas dispensers? How much per unit, and how many units? The last time, no fewer than seven cars came, and those were only the cars we could see. There may have been more around the corner. With 2 officers per vehicle, plus the special units van, for a total of 20 some peacekeepers × 7 hours of work, not counting travel time, that's a big chunk of taxpayer change. As today is Sunday, will they get overtime?

And what's new this year in peacekeeping technology? Will they come with helicopter-mounted monitoring equipment? If the siege continues into the night, will they use surveillance and night vision cameras? As this is a repeat offense, will they initiate telephone-tapping systems in Mr. Smith's house? When they take him away, will they implant human identity recognition computer chips? Have they already?

We must take into account, too, the institutional expense. How much does it cost to admit and diagnose, to treat and feed? How much per day for a bed in the psychiatric wing at Kaiser, and if he's not a member of Kaiser—who am I kidding? On this block, we are a tribe of self-employed, under-employed, and now, Section 8 welfare families. I doubt anybody here has the means to join or the stomach for premier institutional healthcare in California, the Richard Nixon–endorsed, long-lived, but perpetually broken for-profit HMO, Kaiser Permanente. Okay, so how much per day will Medicare pay for the occasionally disturbed and off-his-meds Mr. Smith, and for how many days? Last time, he was back within the month.

Anyway, we needn't call when things go amiss. Somehow, word gets out. Once last year in the dead of night, somebody began raising havoc on our front porch. Steve was dialing 911, at the same time yelling, "Who the fuck's out there?" It turned out to be the Oakland P. D. investigating a shooting. They had been walking up and down the block, looking for broken glass, and found it in front of our house. There was a bullet lodged between panes in our front bedroom's double-paned window. There had been a gunfight on the street. One of the gun-slingers took a bullet and checked himself in at a local Emergency Room, whose employees, by law, must do their best to discover the location of the shooting. And so, through a circuitous and completely unsolicited though not unappreci-ated route, our city's peacekeepers heard about and responded to the gunfight on our street, which we slept through.

In our little country, this block south of 580, we are a citizenry bound by American rights: the right to privacy, which we honor by holding our tongues and averting our eyes. Like our forefathers, the rugged pioneers, we respect the individual's freedom of expression (how elegant, our naked dancer). We stand by the 2nd Amendment. Even Steve and I, pacifists by nature, schooled from the cradle in the art of conflict avoidance, would worry if the only Americans with the right to bear arms were the police.

Are we afraid of the gunman in the street? Of course. We keep our doors locked. We feel, to be honest, as if we're living in the American west during its heyday, when the rule of law was the rule of the gun. But we have no illusion about the police with their fabulous protection and repression technology, who will turn out in force for one disturbed citizen, Mr. Smith, initiating a peacekeep-ing extravaganza that could result in multiple disasters: lost time; lost money; potentially, lost lives. We'd rather put our trust in accidents—how wonderful, the double-paned window that does not stop noise but does stop bullets—than in the Cavalry.

Mr. Smith, drenched in sweat, has come to a standstill. He trembles, his finger on the trigger, eyes skipping from the sidewalk to a window, a door. His head moves in little jerks, and the rifle moves with it. He is listening to something.

Today is Sunday. Oh, let the voices be gentle. God, don't let him look this way.

∞∞

Island Journal

November with Hog's Blood

The stone steps leading to the village of Falatados are pooled with blood. Though the walk has been hosed down, leaving anemic puddles, their scarlet is unmistakable. Andonis's dog, Kika, grows vampirically excited. Andonis, our friend and guide, grabs her collar, shouts gruffly, and runs her to the top of the path, past the vanished source of the blood and into the village. We follow, my twelve-year-old son and my husband and I, along with Andonis's friend Nestor, trying not to imagine the scene in which two or three men must have held the animal while another slit its throat. Going farther from the village would have meant their having to haul it a long way uphill.

Why does this seem like the place to begin? We have come upon it at the end of a long walk on the island's traditional footpaths. There is something primal in the sight of blood from a slaughter—something connecting war, religion, and supper. But the reason it has meaning for me now, I think, is that tourists don't see the blood. We're not tourists anymore. It's November, and we'll stay on this Greek island through the winter, the winter during which the slaughtered pig, which we later see being butchered and tossed into metal tubs according to cut, will feed a family.

I am what Lawrence Durrell called an islomane. I love islands. They are somehow finite and knowable. You can drive Tinos end to end in an afternoon and along the way see it collapsing into the sea on both sides at the same time. You can count the villages—forty—and if you stay long enough, come to know the disposition of each, or at least the way it is situated in its landscape and what its people are known for locally: Volax for the basketmaking, Isternia for seafaring, Pyrgos for the sculpting of marble.

But islands are also infinitely nuanced. The sea alone, or the sea in combination with the sky and the wind, has an incredible repertoire of irrepeatable expressions and improvisations. Some days the sea is a body fathomlessly deep, turning over whitecaps like snow on anthracite and ready to take lives with ambivalence. Other days, when there is no wind, the sea and the sky are in such harmony that the horizon seems completely absent. The sea is ethereal and without depth. It might be a piece of satin—or lighter still—a revelation. An idea about air. When you add the ways the land can appear from various points as it enters sea, in terraced green pyramids or in smooth basins of marble, along with the sun or shadow on both, you have a genius of a composition perfected and yet always in progress.

Apart from these nuances, it is tempting to think of the island as a changeless, timeless place, an eternal present equal to the moment of one's arrival. I remember my first arrival on Tinos. I had come alone, leaving Jim and Conrad at home. It was May, slightly off season ten years ago, and the harbor road was quiet. There was only Pavlos in his shop among the marble reproductions of Cycladic statues, offering raki in the late afternoons, not drunk so constantly as he is now; and Dimitri, renting motorbikes then, though reluctant to rent me one since there had been a fatal accident the day before on a bike rented by Vidalis next door. The pension I had planned to stay in—O Iannis—was closed for renovations but it had not yet changed its name to Ianni's Rooms. I didn't know then that the O was the masculine article, used even with names. But I loved the wistful, annunciatory sound it gave everything it preceded. I took a room in the finest old hotel in town, the Tinion, for about seven dollars a night. The backside of the harbor hadn't been developed at all, and there were no vans meeting the boats to carry tourists to the "suburbs." I was the only tourist eating at the taverna O Kipos; the other patrons were old Greek men. I swam each day at Pakhi Ammos, the cove that was the ancient harbor and out of which three columns still rise, broken off toward the base. I ordered fried calamari from the little *cafeineo* below the chapel; it appeared through a small open window, held out by a muscular arm the owner of which seemed as absent as the gods to whom the harbor was once dedicated. The calamari was fresher and more tender than any I've had since. Beneath the little pink motorbike I rode over the interior of the island, a rugged landscape of gorse and poppies scrolled out and I felt immeasurably free until, rounding a bend in the road, I hit a loose patch of gravel and after a distended airborne moment during which I contemplated the likelihood of my own death, I landed with my face in the road. Then, as now, it was blood that awakened me from the island dream.

History, too, is willing to share with us the truth about the places we perceive as timeless: they are the products of violent fluctuation and vertiginous change. The landscape heaves and sighs in earthquake and fire. The Venetians and the Turks, the Germans and the allies, the dictators and the kings, the refugees and the tourists come and go. The developers come and keep coming. And though I am loathe to admit it, I myself have changed, am an agent of change. The island is sensitive to individual presences in a way that a city like Paris or Istanbul is not. When our little group sits down in the café in Falatados, where we end our day's walk, sweaty and hungry, it becomes a different café than the one it was before we arrived. People stare at us—even those whose hair and eye-color tell me they must, at one time, have been foreigners here themselves.

There is risk in making oneself foreign, and not a little of it for us has to do with the sore thumb our American-ness has become. The top story in headlines around the world is Bush's continuing threat to invade Iraq. When we arrived on the island, the beat-up sailing rig docked in the harbor, along with the nineteen refugees leaning from the windows of the pink municipal building where they had been held since their rescue, served as a daily reminder of how close Iraq was, and how imminent and likely America's decision to invade. Historically speaking, the United States has not kept its hands to itself where Greece was concerned either. The CIA's complicity in the overthrow of an elected government by a military junta in 1967 was one particularly bold instance of meddling.

So it is understandable that, at present, the Greeks are not kindly disposed to the United States or its political ambitions. Experience has taught them, however, that a government does not always represent the will of its people, and they don't blame us personally for what it seems is about to happen. Perhaps the only way I can justify my presence on the island is to demonstrate a love for the place without intention or demand. A love that lingers after the gyro stands have been boarded up for the winter and the tan lines have faded. A love that doesn't flinch at the sight of hog's blood.

A few days before Thanksgiving, it's difficult for me not to eye too lasciviously the fifteen or more pumpkins garnishing our neighbor's long driveway. Our friend Annette has told us that, as an American badly in need of pumpkin around the holidays, she has been burnt on pumpkin prices at the *laiki*, or local farmers' market. My neighbor's display confirms what I have heard—that the Greeks themselves don't use the pumpkins in their kitchens. "Are the pumpkins from your garden?" I ask.

They don't look at all like American pumpkins, but rather like winter squash pumping iron. Still, when I see them, I know what they must be, just as my instinct honed in yesterday on the little clutch of turkeys I hadn't noticed before, being raised in a small lot just off the road down to the sea. When Annette told us she was having a hard time ordering a turkey from her grocer (largely because the EEC won't import from the US products affected by genetic engineering), a murderous impulse rose up in me. I imagined climbing the fence in the dark, selecting the plumpest of the brotherhood. I find this surprising and somewhat funny, since Conrad and I recently dismissed the idea of an insect collection for home school because we couldn't justify killing the insects for our acquisitions. I feel suddenly and conspicuously American—allied not only with those who wish to feast but also with the whole acquisitive impulse of my country, which I have denounced daily since our arrival on the island.

"Take one, Paula," cries Dimitri. "They are from Frankiskos's garden." Frankiskos is our common landlord; he has just introduced us to one another. I hesitate long enough for Dimitri to think it's quantity I'm worried about. "Yes, as many as you like," he says. Frankiskos, who doesn't speak English, stands by with a tickled expression that charms me. He grins, lowering his chin and looking shyly down and away for a moment, as if beside himself with the pleasure of pleasing me. I explain that I want to make pie, and as I leave, a fat, gourd-shaped squash in my arms, I promise them both a piece.

On Thanksgiving morning, I awake with a small, persistent ache for home. We haven't done much in our miserable little kitchen yet. Frankiskos has replaced the compact two-burner stove (one tiny burner for Greek coffee) with a three-burner stove (one tiny burner for Greek coffee), which still looks suspiciously like a top-of-the-line toaster oven. I have demonstrated for Jim a system of doing dishes seated with your knees inside the cabinet under the sink. It has the beauty of bringing you closer to the cleaning site and saving your neck and head from the interference of the cabinets, which are hung directly above. The fluorescent halo suspended over the table completes the atmosphere of an Odd Fellows hall.

Even so, I call Annette for instructions on cooking fresh pumpkin.

Annette is our go-between with the Greek world. An American herself, and an artist, she has lived on Tinos for eighteen years, since she met the Greek sculptor Petros Dellatolas and married him without being able to talk to him. (Instead, she tells us, they drew to one another.) Annette has since learned Greek, raised two children on the island, and established, with Petros, a marble sculpting studio that is open to aspiring marble artists from abroad in the spring, summer, and early fall.

Since she tells me she has found her own pumpkin and made her pies already for Sunday, when we will celebrate Thanksgiving together, I'll make this pie now for the sake of the process—just to be working in the kitchen at the same time that my mother and my sisters at home are waking up to chop celery and onions and squeeze handfuls of stale bread soaked in water. Annette says I have a choice between baking the pumpkin and steaming it. Then she says I'll need to strain it through cheesecloth. She reads my silence accurately. "Look, Paula," she says, in her endearing take-charge way. "You take a pair of Jim's old underwear and you tie up the legs." This is a woman who faked her way into a successful career as a textile designer in New York City. "Fresh or seasoned?" I ask.

Jim resists this idea, since I paid five euros apiece, after much searching, for two pairs of "classic" jockey shorts when we found that by some error in packing he'd ended up crossing the Atlantic with only three pairs. Greeks, it seems, wear a flyless bikini type undergarment by which Jim would, I suspect, feel emasculated. To the great amusement of passersby, I spent a long time with the clerk, holding various pairs up out of the package, eyeballing them for size. So we steam the pumpkin and lay the pieces face-down in a colander, hoping gravity will spare the contents of Jim's top drawer.

It shouldn't come as a surprise that you can't buy a pie plate here. In America, our entire sense of proportion—even as evidenced in our understanding of national defense spending—derives from the shape of the pie. In Greece, *pita* may mean "pie," but it involves phyllo dough—a crisp, buttery, multi-layered pastry that settles like a feathery shale above and below a stratum of filling that is more often savory than sweet, like the cheese in tyropita, or the spinach in spanikopita. In the event that it is baked in a circular shape, a pan with straight vertical sides is used. But all in all, the shape is not important. It might be a rectangle, or it might be the shape of a dumpling, its size bearing little or no relation to defense spending.

When we get to Annette's house, she tells us she cried for a day when she broke one of her pie plates. The other two are in the freezer with pies in them. I'll have to snip the edges of an aluminum cake pan and encourage an outward flare. Annette shows us how to eyeball butter measurements, imagining the European tub divided into American-style sticks and then into tablespoons. As a final gesture of friendship, she offers a beaten length of cheesecloth she takes gingerly from her clothesline. I am beginning to get some idea how much this means to her. "This cheesecloth is really old," she says. "A family heirloom?" I ask. "Your grandmother was married in that cheesecloth," Jim says and, willing expatriates all, we marvel at the irony of our sentimentality for things American.

It's Friday, the day after Thanksgiving. We've had the little cat for just three days and she has not been well from the beginning. I have been tempted to sacrifice a pair of Jim's underwear for her cause, since she has had diarrheic episodes all over the house, on the tile, the multicolored rag rugs, and, occasionally, in the litter box we've provided. Yesterday, we got her a pill from the pet store since we'd seen evidence of worms. In spite of all of this, she's been supremely affectionate, sitting on Jim's shoulder as he reads, nuzzling Conrad's chin. Though we found her, she's not at all like the dirty, feral creatures Annette has warned against taking in. But now she's begun to cry a lot and her bowel problems have not subsided. She seems tired and has stopped eating altogether. Last night she hid somewhere in the garden, among the hibiscus and the bougainvillea, refusing to come in, and we found her this morning looking languid and fragile.

When Jim and I return from town, where we have gone to buy her some canned food, thinking the smell of it might raise her from her lethargy, we climb the steps to find Conrad sitting in a plastic chair on the terrace, his hands stained with blood—whose, we don't know—his face stained with tears, the cat stretched out unnaturally with her mouth open, in his lap. He is calm in a way that terrifies me. Beyond him, and us, the sea and the sky are indistinguishable from one another, both the color of waxed paper with just a hint of blue.

"What took you so long?" he asks, stricken. It's difficult for us to get the story from him—how she lay so still he thought he should hold her, how he held her in his lap on the couch, how she began to thrash and bite his hands. She leapt down and tried to run off; he caught her and held her again.

"She's dying, Connie," I say. "You need to put her down." We lay her on a bit of fleece lining from an old coat and wait. Her eyes wide open, her body is slack and heavy. Suddenly, she convulses, flipping like a fish on the bottom of a boat, and then she attempts to drag herself toward the stairway. Conrad lunges for her and saves her from falling.

The necessity of leaving our own cats at home was the greatest obstacle to Conrad's willingness to come to Greece for the year. Having to push his chair away from the computer and leaving neighborhood friends were a close second and third. It is only at this moment, seeing the anguish on his face—an emotion I have never before seen there—that I understand how many assurances he has been forced to give up. And how few Jim and I are able to offer in this place that surprises us daily. We wipe the blood from his hands and put the cat in a box.

By the end of the day, the cat has taken the needle of mercy from the live-stock vet and lies in the ground behind Petros's marble workshop, her grave marked with a carved marble stone—a scrap that, having been discarded in the field, fell in definition somewhere between beauty and litter. Conrad stands unhappily in the back room of the pharmacy while I hold his pants down to reveal one muscular buttock and the pharmacist administers a tetanus shot. Having watched the very young doctor at the clinic who wrote the prescription for the injection check the book several times and, not once but twice, cross out and change numbers, I pray to whatever gods preside over this place that we will witness no more bloodshed or death for a while.

The pies are pretty much a success, though one burns on the bottom. The other is beautiful, a little orange-peel and cinnamon helping the crust transcend its structural role. We carry a piece up to Dimitri's and, finding the shutters sealed tight and the jeep gone, we hurry home to finish it off, stealing another pumpkin along the way for soup. In December, the rain arrives, driven by a heavy south wind that sends salt spray fanning up over the breakwater in the harbor. New traffic patterns form as cars and trucks pull a wide curve inland, all driving on one side of the road to avoid the briny surf that crashes in, spouting ten feet over the harbor wall. An old man in a caution-orange rain suit rides a donkey patiently along the coast road. A colonnade of salt pines wags theatri-cally on both sides of the road as he passes. The sky turns a darkened eye on the sea, which answers with bituminous resolution and a widespread spackling of whitecaps.

The town of Tinos, too, is a theme in grays and whites. Against the animated backdrop of sky and sea, the starched masonry of the buildings holds still. A flock of white doves lifts suddenly from the monument at the center of the traffic circle and careers up toward the sheltering eaves of a neoclassical façade. The pelican that lives in the harbor sits atop an old Toyota, watching the sea with disinterest. He is fed by the owner of a fish market. The souvenir shops closest to the water are boarded up. Since the tavernas are closed for the season, the stone patios beneath their wooden trellises are being used as parking spaces.

It would be difficult to describe what happens here on the island as a storm. Storm implies a kind of integrity or isolation of the phenomenon. What you experience here is more a condition—pervasive and chronic—of wind and rain, thunder and lightning, hail and spray and insurrection of the sea that makes you want to lay in supplies and hunker down for days or weeks at a time. Surrounded by the sea as you are, you feel it could go on forever, though in truth the serious lashing of the wind and rain—the tree-breaking sort—is only spasmodic.

At home we are generally well insulated from the weather. But on this island, weather is a constant factor in our experience, a presiding presence like that of a cook in a big open-air kitchen. It stirs and stews, bakes and chills, soaks and dries, each day blowing over great atmospheric spoonfuls before serving up the local specialty. Today, we open the shutters, curious to see what's brewing: a formidable cold custard, served with whipped topping. Bring your own rum.

It's of no small consequence what the weather is like out there. For instance, since the wind has worked itself up to a Beaufort nine, it's too cold in the bathroom for showering. The laundry we've been wanting for several days now to wash will wait, and that means dirty clothes longer than is pleasant, since no one on the island has a dryer. Jim's heavy cotton sweater has been wet for five days and is becoming a promising site for a mold colony. There are no ferries "goingcoming" on account of the wind, at least for the next two days. That means the Greek verb lexicon we ordered two weeks ago certainly won't arrive, and our proud nouns will languish a while longer in a state of being. The book we sent Jim's stepfather via registered mail this morning with the guarantee it would arrive in five or six days won't even leave the post office for two more. The newspaper won't make it here, so if Bush invades Iraq, there will be a period of grace before we know about it. It means, too, that rather than going to Athens today or tomorrow as we had planned, we'll stay home. I'll huddle over the computer keyboard in the back room, wrapped head to foot in a blanket and wearing my cycling gloves to type, choosing the cold over the subtly noxious odor emitted by the propane heater Annette has loaned us. In all of this there's an enforced sort of humility that makes me aware of the insignificance of my plans.

Conrad, on the other hand, doesn't subscribe to the enforced humility thing. He feels a sudden and compulsive need to cook sausage—on a Saturday afternoon, when all of the butcher shops are closed. Jim has driven the Fiat Panda into town for dinner items at the supermarket (which, contrary to Conrad's belief, doesn't sell sausage). Having nearly come to blows over the alleged impossibility of Conrad's plan, and perhaps, beneath it all, over the shortcomings of my plan to winter on this island—a plan that has brought us into close proximity to the proverbial hog's blood but failed to acquaint us with a single sausage maker—Conrad and I agree at last, in desperation, to put on our jackets and walk to the sea. Perhaps we'll meet Jim on his way back.

Along the road that parallels the beach, it starts to rain again, lightly, almost as soon as we set out. At high tide, the sea roils frothily against the retaining wall. Together we pause and look down into its vertigo-inducing surge and retreat. Wind pummels the salt pines. The sky grown almost black overhead, lightning flashes in the direction of Syros. We continue toward town, not meeting the headlights of the Panda as we had hoped but sharing, instead, the perverse excitement of walking into the island's wet maw.

KRISTEN KECKLER

Devil's Work

Sometimes a new job promises the same thrill of possibility as falling in love again, with someone even better, sweeter, and more suitable than your ex. Pammy Gomez's rented kitchen was on the ground floor of an old mansion. A massage school occupied the top floors. A half-wall split the kitchen into two rooms—one for cooking, the other for assembly and packaging. As I manned the industrial deli slicer, I thought about how much I liked my new white apron. The twelve-burner stove. The two shiny silver fridges. Long aluminum prep tables. Shelves of exotic spices. A sink the size of a bathtub!

I liked Pammy, too. She was built like a boxer, compact and muscular. I liked the way she seemed to bounce, to roll between heel and toe. She wore her short black hair under a ball cap—white with a black Nike swoosh—and a white t-shirt with the sleeves rolled up. Her skin was naturally brown, like mine after tanning all summer. She dreamed of a world taken over by vegans, envisioned herself ruler of an extensive seitan empire. Her favorite mantra was: "Lift with your legs, not your back."

On my first day managing Pammy's seitan business, I found myself riding shotgun in her van, my astrological chart in the console between us. We were on our way to a food fair to hand out samples of her vegetarian deli slices to college kids. Seitan (pronounced "say-tan") is wheat meat. We passed half-frozen, glassy lakes and fields of brown tassels—remnants of corn—poking through snow. A rainbow gay pride sticker stretched the length of the van's bumper, the only hint of color in the landscape.

"I would have guessed Cancer moon 'cause you have that little worry crescent between your eyes. All Cancer moons have it," she had said, looking at the road. My finger instinctively felt for my crease, marveling at Pammy's almost eerie psychic ability. I wondered if she had found something in my chart that had made her hire me.

I had just quit the psychiatric home where I had worked for three years, giving up health insurance and all my benefits. I realized that despite my best efforts, my clients, many of them diagnosed as schizophrenic, would never get better. In care-giving professions, when the stress starts to eat the caretaker alive, we called it "burnout." But burnout is just a nicer way to say you no longer give a shit. It's not like I wasn't interested in psychology, or the mind's bent corners. I just took more pride in being known for my eggplant parmagiana than for my counseling. Eager for the more predictable world of food, I found Pammy through a mutual friend. I wanted to work with my hands instead of my heart. I wanted to create, to eventually attend the Natural Cookery School in New York City. Maybe someday even open a restaurant. Host my own cooking show on the Food Network (which I had watched obsessively at the group home.)

My first morning in the kitchen, I followed Pammy around as she explained each process thoroughly. I asked a lot of questions. What's "liquid smoke" made of? How do they separate gluten from the wheat? Bosses, like teachers, liked questions.

Soon after, we started each day by filling a dozen plastic tubs with the wheat gluten, spices, and wet ingredients, each for a different flavor (Szechwan, Original, Mexican, BBQ, Cuban, Bac-Un, Pepperoni). Wearing plastic gloves, we mixed with our hands, kneading the mélange like bread dough, the spices stinging our eyes and nostrils. She told me stories about growing up in Miami, of running with the fast crowd, of drinking and drugging her life away. I imagined a lesbian West Side story, the butches defending their lipsticked femmes, wielding knives, dancing in lines. She played astrology tapes, complex readings by her friend Shara in Florida. *A sextile between Mercury and Venus is a rare astrological pearl. When the planets are this close to the sun, they move closer together as well. So look forward to a new harmony between your mind and body, your ideas and actions*, she told us. We listened reverently, kneading the ingredients, then weighed gobs of the sticky mixture. We cupped our hands around it, forming long mounds, and wrapped these mounds in tin foil, tightly, making logs approximately two feet long and four inches in diameter.

There was a precise trick of the wrist, of folding the foil just right, of pressing in as you spun. If the logs were not wrapped precisely, I knew they would come undone while steaming. Be ruined. But I couldn't quite get it. After my third try, Pammy sighed loudly and flipped off her gloves, wiping her hands dramatically on her apron as she stalked to her office. My hands trembled. I tried again, squeezing the soft gluten into the foil. *Pluto is moving retrograde through Capricorn*, Shara warned, soothingly, like my first-grade teacher. I struggled along, wrapping some halfway decent logs.

Ten minutes later Pammy appeared. "Where were we?" she asked cheerfully. I showed her my logs and she examined them carefully, like a surgeon.

"Better," she said. "I really need for you to get this, to be present," she added.

"I'm trying," I insisted, my voice squeaky and childlike.

She softened, punched me lightly on the shoulder. "It'll take practice."

Even when wrapped, each raw log had a gelatinous spine, and had to be delicately cradled. We steamed them in deep roasters, piling layers of three or four. Halfway through the cooking process, we had to rotate them. Holding a partially solidified five-pound log in tongs was like picking up a piece of cake with tweezers. I breathed deeply, prayed. The windows had fogged with their mist.

Each task was a Russian doll, holding a mini-task inside it. A lapse in concentration could quickly undo jobs I had spent half the morning on: like the time I pasted "Pepperoni" labels on fifty packages of "Original Flavor" and had to re-vacuum pack them all. I stuffed the discarded packaging to the bottom of the trash, tied it up, and took it to the curb, thinking about precision. Kitchen work took mental toughness. What if one day when I'm an important chef, I spill a five-pound bag of rice? What if it is the only rice I have on hand?

Pammy did her best to instill in me her Zen of slicing: *Feel the motor vibrate in your hand, your wrist. Never look away, get out of your rhythm. Always be aware of the blade, humming and spinning. If it gets stuck, turn it off before fixing it.* She showed me how to disassemble it, clean it, and put it back together. I was amazed at my uniform discs of wheat meat. My eyes followed a chunk of Portobello mushroom baked in like a fossil in marble, a perfect cutout, getting smaller and smaller with each slice. I heard a table saw in a country barn, alongside fields of alfalfa and dandelions, and a horse named Seven. My log, the color of redwoods, flavored with anise.

On Tuesdays and Thursdays, I catered lunch for the massage students upstairs. I lived for these days. Pammy saw this as a way of making extra money as well as developing name recognition for her business. I scoured my cookbooks for innovative and inexpensive vegan recipes. As Pammy only gave me an hour to cook, I often went in early to prep. All morning, recipes ran through my mind like ticker tape. I made curried butternut squash soup with herbed crostini; BBQ-tofu over brown rice pilaf; lentil chili with cornbread; broccoli-cashew-seitan stir-fry over basmati rice. The kitchen smelled of ginger and garlic and the starchy comfort of rice. I brought the lunch upstairs in a cart, and the students lined up to buy it. As I packed up, I secretly watched them eat, tried to gauge their reactions.

Then, Pammy and I would sit and eat the portions I had set aside for us on the picnic table outside the kitchen, overlooking Cayuga Lake.

One afternoon she told me, "You're an amazing cook."

I blushed. Nothing I made ever tasted as good to me. I perpetually feared something would backfire and was ecstatic when it didn't. Pammy had taken off her apron, folded it into a neat square on the table. It was early spring, one of those warm days when the sun hints at the warmth yet to come. Pammy dreamed openly about someday owning the first ever vegan Cuban restaurant, where I could be her chef.

"I love hot, I love spicy," she said, shimmying her shoulders. "The idea of centering meals around rice, beans, and peppers."

I nodded. "And for dessert—pan-fried plantains over coconut soy ice cream, all drizzled in pure chocolate," I said.

"Yum!" Pammy had a sweet tooth. "See, you're a thinker." She tapped her head. "It's your Capricorn," she said, as we imagined a day we could be free of the seitan, when the kitchen would magically run itself, or perhaps, just finance bigger and better ventures.

By the time I got off work in the late afternoon, I felt I deserved a beer or two. My body was exhausted but laced with endorphins. I felt effervescent, cocky, strong. I was sweaty with wheat meat lodged under my fingernails. I showered, then headed to the bar to hang out with my restaurant friends, who had just finished their shifts around town.

Stan bought a round of shots he called "woo woos," or chilled citrus vodka with a hint of cranberry. I downed two, as Jake, a pizza cook, chanted "Satan! Satan!" while making devil horns with his fingers. Chris said, "Now, let's be serious." He swung his arm around me, pulling my head close, and asked conspiratorially, "So, what's it like to work with Lucifer?" These were people who couldn't understand the concept of wheat meat—people who had carefully reduced veal stock and stuffed pig intestines all morning. So I rolled my eyes and wrote 666 in place of my name on the dart scoreboard.

On my walk home, however, I wondered: what *was* I doing with my life? My parents thought I was crazy, in the way that I always had been—stubbornly idealistic and independent. That this was another phase. "Satan?" my father had asked. He didn't get it, and wasn't really that interested in my explanation. "Much snow?" he'd inquire instead. "How's the car running?"

I'd been a proud and vigilant vegetarian for six years, had taught myself to cook to accommodate for the lack of options in restaurants and dining halls. I subscribed to *Vegetarian Times*. I did not want to eat what I was unwilling to kill. I believed (and still do) that animals had souls, perhaps different types of souls than humans, but ones that come with having consciousness, central nervous systems, and the ability to feel pain. The other issue was environmental, of course, the amount of land and water and oil we use to produce one pound of beef, that overgrazing leads to desertification. All of that. But seitan, and the natural food industry, went beyond these beliefs. Producing seitan, I realized, was a life's work. There was a step between believing in something and devoting your life to it. I was missing this step, and trying my best to swing myself to the next rung. Often, I felt I dangled in midair, reaching.

Then, I dreamt I was on fire. I was in my childhood bed and flames had ignited my bed ruffle in a glowing rectangle. They crept up my comforter, licking my hands, which flailed desperately like fly swatters. I woke robed in sweat, my hands numb with pain and whaling on my mattress. I shook myself awake. Then it hit me: carpal tunnel. I had experienced mild carpal tunnel syndrome while cooking at a restaurant several years earlier, but only after my prep shifts, and only in my right hand. I had rearranged my schedule so that I didn't work two consecutive prep shifts, and loaded up on B vitamins, and the pain had abated. Somehow, when taking this job with Pammy, I had conveniently forgotten about my predisposition.

I popped three Advil, though I knew they wouldn't help. Pain relievers, even anti-inflammatories, had never helped me before. I paced my apartment, shaking out my hands, their frozen veins of pain. The nerves inside them were like wires ripped apart in a storm, live and sparking in the winter air. My cat Cleo followed me from room to room, meowing, as if to say, "What? What is it?"

I hid the carpal tunnel from Pammy, hoping I could find some way to cure it. If I wanted to inhabit the world of food, I knew I had to pay my dues, which included long hours and a little physical discomfort. Somewhere, though, deep in my psyche, I thought I was being punished for some kind of karmic debt I owed, and that, certainly, I deserved it. I visited an herbalist, who suggested Devil's Claw and yoga. I tried to alter my routine, slicing for an hour, then vacuum packing, and then slicing for another hour. But soon, I began to hate the seitan. I even began to detest the taste of it. It had a certain . . . aftertaste. It seemed too . . . sweet, too acidic, like raw tomato paste. The slicer became my nemesis, and as I fed in the two-pound logs, I imagined it was eating my very own limbs. Consequently, I cut myself for the first time, while cleaning the blade, a painful gash in the odd crease where the thumb meets hand.

I thought about my Sicilian immigrant grandparents, long dead. My grandfather had been a bricklayer and my grandmother, a seamstress. They had worked with their hands their whole lives, day after day, so that I wouldn't have to. What would they think of me, armed with my college diploma, descending into a life of manual labor? I considered it a mark of my generation to choose performative, physical work over a more intellectual career. But I realized that somewhere along the lines, my genes had been weakened, the hardy peasant stock of my ancestors given way to a slight American body not made for real work.

Vacuum packing was one of the few tasks that were easy on my wrists. All I had to do was close the lid of the large machine, push the button, and listen for the long hiss. I was working on putting together a twenty-case order for our distributor. Pammy was in the main kitchen, finishing the morning's batch. Suddenly, I heard the crash of metal, like a cymbal in a drum kit. A normal kitchen sound. Followed by Pammy's guttural growl: "You fucking son-of-a-bitch." Then the timber of tongs, followed by a solid *whump*, like a deflated basketball hitting the floor. I stifled an involuntary stress-giggle.

Pammy muttered, "Can't get ahead, can't get any help around here," and I saw her shadow stalk out the door, pointy red tail trailing behind her. The water, I realized. She had forgotten to check the water levels on the pans so the bottom logs had burned. And she was mad at me for not checking them either, even though I was just as busy as she was. The kitchen was silent, except for Shara, advising: *After slogging through Capricorn, when Pluto squares with Venus, she will be in crisis! We know our own weaknesses—sugar, coffee, bad relationships. Beware of codependency.* I sighed, picked up the lone log splayed on the floor, its edges charred, its flesh cracked like a wound.

Each passing day was like a photo slide, flashing color on a white wall, then gone. I began to stay later at the bar, having discovered that a few shots of Irish whisky helped me to sleep longer before I would inevitably wake up to the highway of pain stretching from my fingertips to elbows. Carpal tunnel, like a functional drunk, only reared its ugly head at night, when my body was relaxed, lying flat. I would pace my apartment, shake them out, in order to dull the pain enough to sleep. But, I woke to hands as stiff as my half-frozen steering wheel. I drove to work with my pinkies (the only fingers not controlled by the median nerve). I was hung over, and the smells of the spices I mixed into the gluten made my stomach lurch. While scrubbing the caked pans, I watched the massage students out the window, sitting at the picnic table, joking and rubbing each other's shoulders. They looked happy. Sleep deprived, I nodded off at the sink, lulled by the rushing water, the steam.

I finally broke down and paid $75 to see a doctor. He performed a Tinel test on me by tapping on the median nerve in my wrist. My fingers tingled, grew numb. He told me I would need to have to have surgery if I kept it up. That I risked wasting away the muscles at the base of my thumb. Risked not being able to feel hot and cold. Risked being unable to hold a spoon, make a fist. "You'll have to find another job," he told me. "And of course, another line of work." In the meantime, he patted my back and gave me two wrist splints.

I didn't want to quit. But I didn't want to stay, either. I was relieved that someone else had made the decision for me.

One April morning, my hands were too stiff to open a can of cat food. Cleo circled me, crying hungrily as I tried to pull the flimsy tab with my teeth. I threw down the can, filled up her dry food instead, spilling kibbles over the linoleum. I thought about Pammy, how she acted like she was paying me *so much* money ($7.50 an hour). How the seitan had bought her a modest house, at least. How the seitan was paying for her girlfriend to go to law school. How the seitan provided their occasional weekend trips to Provincetown, Mass., and how I walked and fed their dogs while they were gone. What would make sense, I thought, would be to invest in an automatic slicer and an industrial sized mixer. Why did I have to *be* her damn equipment?

Armed with my fury and the wrist braces, I told Pammy everything: the pain, the herbalist, the doctor, my hungry cat.

She looked at me skeptically. "Did you take some Advil?" she asked. Then she buried herself in the silver fridge, marking inventory on her clipboard.

Now I can see that Pammy, too, felt trapped by the seitan, and had seen me as a way out of a life married to physical labor. She wanted to concentrate on marketing, introducing her product to new customers, and inventing other vegan recipes to complement the seitan. She had put nearly three months into training me essentially, for nothing. She had to start over with someone else.

After letting the information sink in, and after a pow-wow with her girlfriend, she came around. She told me she understood and was sorry to lose me. We made an uneasy peace. I continued to cook lunches for the massage students until their six-month term was over and Pammy found a stout Chinese woman to take over the rest. She and her girlfriend invited me to their commitment ceremony later that spring. I bought them a pretty teapot.

The psychiatric home had not hired anyone to replace me, so I was able to slip into my old job, gratefully. Though I quickly got my clients on a regime of fresh vegetables, my life with food slowly faded to the background, like music does when you're thinking about something else. It was a relief to hear the chatter of real voices again (even my client's bizarre ponderings about the devil speaking through Beatles lyrics). I guessed it was just in my stars to work with people instead of wheat.

ANDREW GREIG

Camping out of the Comfort Zone

One evening twenty years ago I sat on a Karrimat below the Baltoro glacier in Upper Baltistan, waiting for the dusk-blue light to die. I was with my friend and Himalayan mentor Mal Duff; we were on our way home to Scotland after an expedition to climb the Mustagh Tower in the Karakoram Himalayas. It had been a time of risk and high endeavour, and of the sustained unpleasantness and deprivation, anxiety, irritation and hilarity that goes with six weeks on a big mountain.

Four of us had summited, the second ascent ever, and got back down safely. (In pure mountaineering terms, if you don't get back down, the ascent doesn't count—a marker of the outlook of those apparent risk-obsessives). It was over. Now we wanted to get home.

What did we talk about, Mal and I, in the long days of our walk-out? The expedition, naturally. Possible future trips. But mostly we talked of the pleasures and comforts of Home. Of bacon and beer and wine; of the luxury at sitting on a chair pulled up to a table to eat; of lying on a soft and level bed with our partners; of the familiar, gentle weather of our country. We missed golf and fishing, old friends and watching television.

In short, what drove our blistered feet and battered knees on across the hours and days of glacier moraine towards the first villages was a vision of our Comfort Zone. But on the sixth day a stream flooded by glacier melt cut us off from all our gear and porters. We looked at crossing it, but it was too wide, too fast, too full of loose churning boulders. We hadn't come this far to get injured crossing a river.

Nothing for it but to spend the night this side of the river. In the morning, with the high ice fields freezing up, it would be manageable. The trouble was we had absolutely nothing but our Karrimats, a bar of chocolate and half a pack of cigarettes. No food, no stove, no tent, no sleeping bag, no torch. We would just have to sleep as we lay.

I remember still the mix of emotions as night came on. Irritation and frustration—we were so near to comfort, food and warmth, but we couldn't get to it. Mild apprehension—I'd never slept out completely unprotected and unsheltered before, and had no idea how cold it would get at six thousand feet. Most of all, I was intrigued.

We unrolled our mats in the lee of some large rocks. We shared out the cigarettes and let the night come on. Sometimes we talked—of home and its comforts—sometimes we were silent, just lying, smoking, looking up at the astounding stars. At one point it rained lightly, tickling our faces, then fortunately stopped again.

When people ask about my first Himalayan expedition, it's not the moments of acute stress, risk, effort, anxiety or achievement that first come to me. It is not even the afternoon we came off the mountain alive and well, stumbled into Base Camp and were handed our brew and cigarette by Jhaved. It is that night we lay unprotected and chilly under the stars, feeling every puff of wind, hearing each night sound, exposed on the turning Earth as we waited for morning. That was the best. That was It.

As we go through our lives we try to create our Comfort Zone. A new place, a new job, a new relationship—we arrive stressed or astonished, then work to make it manageable, familiar, workable. Comfortable. It's like pitching a tent in the wilderness, zipping it against the weather then crawling into the sleeping bag with torch, food, stove, maybe a Walkman, all in easy reach.

It's hard-wired, this urge. Without it, we wouldn't survive long or function well. Nietzsche observed wryly that boredom is modern Man's supreme achievement—to have reduced the unpredictable chaos, impersonal shambles and ruthless impermanence of existence to something so safe and tame we can actually feel bored, that is astounding.

And bored we get. Riding alongside our desire to make comfort zones around us is a need—just as fundamental, just as hard-wired into being human—to do the opposite. To push outside and beyond, to leave the known and predictable, to explore what we do not yet know, with control and outcomes uncertain. To risk.

Without that drive, we would never have extended ourselves as a species or as individuals. For myself, I am not a brave or risk-intoxicated person. I love and value my Comfort Zones of country, friends, lover, familiar books and pursuits. Despite the decade or so I spent climbing somewhere near the sharp end, I remain scared of heights and exposure. Like most of us, I fear rejection, yet living as a writer and performer, I constantly court it. I fear failure, yet every day I must try to write something I haven't written before, do something I can't already do.

It's possible for the non-brave to do this because even stronger than caution and comfort is boredom. Repetition and stagnation eventually become insupportable. Our restlessness is even stronger than our fear.

The irony is that when we do break out, move to a new town, new job, open our hearts to a new relationship, or even just try eating something we haven't eaten before, reading something we haven't read before, we will then work very hard to make those in turn comfortable, familiar, known. It's what we do.

Whoever said that the source of most of our suffering is the inability to sit quietly in a room (or Comfort Zone) was partially correct. That inability is also the source of most of what is interesting about us. The tension between these opposing drives for Risk and Comfort is the tension of being human. It creates the arc of our journey.

We have these drives to different degrees. There are a few for whom the urge for Comfort and the aversion to Risk (i.e. *change*) is so pronounced that their whole lives move very little—though even then, parents have to die, and we ourselves age, work, retire and die, so change can never be entirely banished. Complete aversion to risk and the unfamiliar may look unspectacular and normal, but is a near-psychotic condition.

I've known one or two—a mountaineer, a rock and roller, a poet—whose boredom threshold is so low that their lives must be constant risk, crisis, flirtation with catastrophe. Naturally, they tend to be short-lived. They also, if they are honest and live long enough, have to confront another trap: *risk has become their Comfort Zone*. At that point life-affirming risk-taking often hardens into the destructive and suicidal.

The rest of us go through our life with this balancing act. The balancing act *is* our life.

Risk comes in many shapes and sizes, hues and guises: physical, emotional, artistic, intellectual, experiential, political, financial. Risk is about encountering and exploring where the outcome is uncertain, where control is at best partial. The Comfort Zone is an area of control, and Risk is its antithesis.

Mountaineers present an interesting, though probably not unique, case. They try to exert control in ever more uncontrollable circumstances. That is the game they play. The object is to go closer and closer to the edge, and still survive. The climbers I have known share a very strong life wish. That is what drives them to these situations, because sustained comfort is not life enough.

Perhaps once in a while we get both at the same time, Adventure and Security, the novel and the familiar. I think of being driven through the night as a child, warm in the security of car and family, excited with the uncertainty of where we were going and what would await there.

And I think of that evening and night below the Baltoro glacier, where Mal and I lay out on our mats, smoking, talking, silent under the stars and the blue-black night.

JIM SHEPARD

Males and Risk

How stupid *were* my friends and I, growing up in Lordship? It goes without saying that we were unsupervised (in the early sixties, most parents—at least mine—expected their kids, once past the age of say, seven, to disappear, on nice Connecticut Saturdays, and not return until dinner time) and, in that unsupervised state, it fell to us to keep ourselves entertained. We always came up with something. And all of it fell into two categories: things that were stupid, and things that would have been fine, had they not been done stupidly. We gloried in the brainlessness of both. We had such an appetite for the kinds of activity that would cause a parent to despair that my father ran out of ways of insulting us, and he was easily one of the most verbally inventive people I knew. He got tired of announcing that I had the brains of a squirrel, for example, and started substituting around in the animal kingdom, and beyond: an ant, a flatworm, a walking doorknob.

Why can't you entertain yourselves the way the normal kids do? he would plead, searching for just a glimmer of reason. And we were always contrite to have upset him so much. So for a few days we would. We'd play basketball, and everyone who wore glasses would come out of the games with pince-nez, or monocles. We'd play tackle football and tear shirts into court jester–like strips and rip the knees and seats out of pants, and when none of that or none of the bloody noses and sprained ankles generated any stir, we took to playing on the empty fields above our beach, Russian Beach, with one sideline the edge of the bluffs. That lasted until two of us, Milton Harrigan and myself, caught a runner on a sweep and slung him out of bounds high out over the brambles. I remember an involuntary sound of awe on all of our parts, including the

---

runner's, as we realized just how much air he'd achieved before he experienced his Wile E. Coyote moment.

Who's "we"? Well, in my particular little pod there was probably a rotating group of six or seven kids, but three of the mainstays were my best friend and the bane of my father's existence, Jimmy Swift; my brother, John; and *his* best friend and the *other* bane of my father's existence, Kenny Swift. The Swifts and the Shepards were good friends and Joanie, their mom, was hilarious and sharp-eyed and more or less at her wit's end when it came to her boys. Bill, their dad, I remember as hard-working enough that most of his disciplining occurred long after my brother and I had had to go home for the evening.

My father was a worrier, and perhaps because of that he had an invincible need to believe that his sons weren't psychotics; that the Swifts were the problematic influences. It wasn't a bad theory—they almost always had better ideas than we did, in terms of the sheer inventiveness of the havoc—but adults always tended to overestimate the importance of the guy who came up with the idea. Sometimes you'd put forward a notion and everybody else would be more excited about it than you'd be, and *they'd* be the ones who made sure it happened.

However you dished out the responsibility, though, we were a precocious foursome when it came to mayhem. When we were eight or so without any discussion we all piled into our crabby neighbor's prized rhododendron bush, stomping it flat. He was nearly ungovernable with rage for more than a week, and we were grounded, but each of us in our private cell rode out the storm unconcerned. Less than a year later we spent an afternoon slinging marble-sized rocks long distance at cars until one guy jerked his Rambler up onto the lawn and threw open his door and chased us for a good three minutes. He stalked back to his car and sat there. We hid behind some bushes, then decided we had to disguise ourselves in order to slip past him, since we'd chosen as the place to pelt cars *our own front yard*. Kenny put his shirt on his head like a turban. I took mine off and held it behind me. You get the idea. We were grounded that time for more than twice as long as the rhododendron episode.

Where was my mother during all of this? She came from a big Italian family in Bridgeport, so she'd pretty much seen it all. Her role devolved into spending all of her time trying to suggest to him why what we'd done—whatever latest news had followed us home—was not the end of the world. And then later privately making clear to us that what we'd done *was* pretty stupid.

Joanie Swift was also her best friend. So she operated as the Swift family's defender throughout my father's rants.

"The night riders," he called Kenny and Jimmy, partly because they seemed to always want to hatch something at the borders of our bedtime: *could Jimmy and Johnny stay out just a few more minutes, Mrs. Shepard? There's something very cool down at the vacant lot that we need to show them.*

A year or two after the car stoning—my brother would have been about thirteen, and I would have been about eight—we were sitting in Kenny's upstairs bedroom when we heard Joanie's car pull in. Kenny and Jimmy looked stricken. It turned out that because of some other offense, they'd both been strictly forbidden from having anyone, especially us, in the house. "We have to jump out the window," Kenny told us. We all nodded and crowded up to his window. There was no "What are you, crazy?" or "Why do we have to jump out your window?" Joanie called up the stairs something like, "You better not have anybody *up* there." Of course she'd already heard us. "Jump," Kenny urged. He jumped, hit the grass, and rolled. There were big stones bordering the little flower garden along the house and we were glad he missed them. He yelled anyway, having, it turned out, broken his arm. Already caught and already having seen him get hurt, we all followed him out the window. Let me repeat that: already caught and already having seen him get hurt, we all followed him out the window. The good news was that he was the only one who broke anything.

I'd have to suppose it was inevitable, then, that some of us would have developed our game of lying on the runways at Bridgeport Airport while the aircraft were coming in. The airport wasn't very big, and it still isn't, but it also had a fiercely committed if understaffed security force, and that's where we got the idea. We'd been playing down the airport—that's what we called it when we roamed around in the brushy acres surrounding the thing—jumping a natural canal to see who'd be the first to land in the muck (which you also wanted to avoid because of the occasional rats) when a yellow army surplus jeep rolled up to us, we were all piled into it, and driven home. We hadn't been particularly close to the runway—maybe seventy yards?—but we were told we were being picked up because we *might've* gotten close to the runway. We got into a lot of trouble for that: Sikorsky Aircraft, where my father worked, had many ties to the airport, and he took seriously the notion that what his kids did in one place might impact him in the other. And so a nemesis was born: the yellow jeeps. I'm not sure the four of us even had to talk about it. It would now all be about the yellow jeeps.

We started going down there at night, and flirting with the runway's margins until we could see the headlights of the yellow jeeps fire up and head our way. Then we'd sprint for the chain-link fencing surrounding the airport—it was a few hundred yards uphill—scrabble underneath, and disappear. We waited to see who'd be the last to run, to generate closer and closer calls. The jeeps started hiding in the brush to ambush us. They finally did, successfully, and our parents' resultant punishment was so draconian in length that my brother and Kenny lost interest in the whole thing and declared themselves out of yellow jeep baiting business.

That left Jimmy and me, when we were finally allowed back outside. We weren't out of anything. There was a scene in a goofy Western that was sometimes on The Million Dollar Movie—John Sturges' *The Magnificent Seven*—in which Steve McQueen, handed his gun and one last chance to come to his senses by the beneficent-feeling leader of the army of Mexican banditos, says by way of explaining why he's heading back into town to fight those same eight million banditos with his six friends, "No one hands me my gun and tells me to ride. No one." It was like that with Jimmy and me.

We decided to lie *on* the runway, just short of the huge numbers of the runway designation. It was at night. We lay on our backs with our feet toward the incoming planes and our head toward the touchdown points. Whose idea was it? I think it was mine. I'm pretty sure it was mine. We didn't tell our older brothers. I think we knew that we'd strayed into a territory even they would no longer support.

We lay there in the darkness and waited and eventually we heard a plane and when the engine noise got loud enough and we looked, our chins on our chests, we caught the landing lights full in the face and then came the red and white running lights and the underside of the wings and fuselage and the wheels swaying below them and the whole thing thundered to the tarmac a hundred or so yards up the runway. Not that close, really. But it *felt* like the trailing wheels had parted our hair.

Of course the pilots would have reported us; of course the jeeps were immediately on their way. We ran all the way home. We were too happy even to shriek. We were grinning with terror, beside ourselves with gleefulness, shaking with joy. Now *that*, we thought: *that* was stupidity.

I wrote a short story about it. Years later, in graduate school, my teacher, John Hawkes, was nudging me away from the niche in which I seemed to be most comfortable—wry suburban comedy, and sensitive suburban children—and toward the weird. It was by far the most valuable instinct he helped instill in me: that instinct to ferret out and further distress the unexpected strangeness wherever it surfaced in my work. You want weirdness? I remember thinking. And I wrote an account of what we did on the runways. I made the narrator adult, and solitary, and happy with his life, because I remembered that what was most striking about what we did was the way it seemed to coexist with our everyday and mostly happy existence. In order to put pressure on the situation for the purposes of the story's dramatic development, though, my guy had resolved to move farther and farther toward the touchdown point of most aircraft: in other words, his actions were designed to become progressively more and more stupid, by which I suppose I mean more and more inevitably catastrophic.

This is all by way of saying that for all our gender stereotyping about the way men fetishize the rational, here's one of the more notable things about us as a group: we often seem to make bad choices. Shoot-ourselves-in-the-foot kind of choices. The kind of choices that make our loved ones cluster in little informal discussion groups afterwards, trying to figure out what on earth their boy was thinking.

It's not an unimportant point. Whether we're falling off the wagon or gambling away our families' savings or having to resign the Governorship, the impact we generate through those choices never goes away. My father to this day has never recovered from my night rider days. He's still waiting for the news that I've done one more calamitously stupid thing to undo all the good fortune that he feels I've enjoyed up to this point. How many other parents or wives or siblings or children are living, one way or the other, under the shadow of the very same thing?

Adult, and solitary, and happy with his life: that character of mine was a guy who at the same time cherished his intimate connections and sought to undermine them. That paradox turns out to explain a lot of seemingly inexplicable behavior. Of course we wanted to believe that the sorts of things we did as boys had nothing to do with aggression toward our parents; we loved our parents. And of course those things had everything to do with aggression toward our parents. It was as if at the same moment we were grateful to have been granted the space and the trust to maneuver and to screw up, if we had to, and simultaneously enraged at having been left to do so: was there really *no one* minding the store? Was someone really going to suggest to us that *we* should have agency? It made for a state of mind, familiar to so many of us, in which you take a risk and deny the risk at the same moment, out of rage. It's a way of protesting and subverting a feeling of individual impotence, perhaps: *I'm not helpless. Look: I can shoot myself in the foot.* Even at eleven or twelve or whenever I did it, when I spread myself out on that runway, a familiar part of me found it inconceivable that one of those aircraft would touch down early and turn me into a gruesome local mystery. But the other part knew the risk and could begin to imagine the damage to those who loved me and went ahead with its activities nonetheless.

One thing that is certain is that we'll never get men to fully explain themselves on that score. That's one of the reasons the laconic is and always has been so deeply attractive to men in all genres of popular entertainment. In that same Western I mentioned earlier, *The Magnificent Seven,* the Mexican bandit chief asks Steve McQueen why he came back to face impossible odds: why he'd commit, cheerfully, something like near-virtual suicide. McQueen tells him, "Well, it's like a fellow I once knew in Waco. One day he took off all his clothes and jumped into a cactus. I asked him why he did it." And the Mexican bandit chief says impatiently, "Well? What did he say?" And McQueen smiles bemusedly and tells him, "He said it seemed like a good idea at the time."

The Politics of Hope

Somewhere toward the end of a fall semester class in public speaking at a junior college in New Hampshire, I learned that an attractive female student of mine was homeless. Her mother, a schizophrenic, tossed her out of their home shortly after a traumatic event in her daughter's life. As a result this young woman, whom I will call Jill, had been living for the past few weeks in her car, an old Chevy Impala. While attending classes full-time, she also held at job at a local factory. Jill worked weekdays, 3 PM to midnight, and after she became homeless, steadily increased her working hours in an attempt to postpone as long as she could, the inevitable return to her car.

Her car was not just a lonely and cramped space containing her few worldly belongings. Nor was it even a fragile refuge from her recent past. It was worse than imaginable: it was once, just before her mother evicted her, a crime scene.

About a month prior to the disclosure of her living conditions in class, Jill had gone out with some girlfriends after work on a Friday night to a popular bar in downtown Manchester, New Hampshire where they were regular customers. Since they were "regulars" and attractive young women, they never stood in line and often got discounted drinks. On the night that was to change her life, a bar fight erupted between some male patrons just a few feet away from the table where Jill and her girlfriends smoked and drank. During the melee, a drink was hurled at one of the battlers, and its contents found its way onto Jill's clothes. The fight soon ended, but disgusted, Jill decided to quit the bar and go home wearing her wet clothes. As she started to leave she was dissuaded by the bartender, who offered her a drink on the house. He also offered her another drink, paid by the man who had spilled his drink on her. Wisely, she refused the drink offered by the stranger, but chose to stay, returning to her table of friends with a drink the bartender offered to her as reparation.

Getting the free drink from the bartender was the last thing she remembered before she regained consciousness the following day. She was last seen by her friends talking to "some big scary guy" on her way to the ladies' room.

The next day she awoke lying half-naked on the cold pavement beside the open passenger's car door. As her head slowly cleared, she discovered her car was parked alongside the Merrimac River, its engine still eerily and gruesomely running with the gas gauge pointed at empty. She was covered in blood, and blood smeared the car seats. It was her blood. Her purse was gone. She had been beaten and cut and raped and robbed.

She later discovered at the hospital that a combination of two "rape date" drugs had been secretly slipped into her drink: GHB and Ketamine. She felt the effects of these drugs for a full week after the incident; during that time she suffered nausea, amnesia, convulsions, dizziness, and blurred vision. Because of her rape and its aftermath, she was unable to attend my class and others during the early weeks of the fall semester.

I know this story because this was the final speech she delivered in my public speaking class. Earlier I had been informed by one of her classmates she was homeless. Classmates learned this when Jill informed her and two others in her small discussion group. One of the members of that group immediately offered her a place to stay. The college gave her professional counseling, and her professors allowed her to rejoin and to make up all the assignments she had missed. She took a risk by informing everyone of her situation, and because she had done so, she was offered another opportunity to resume her studies, and a chance to find a path, however tenuous, to survival and peace.

About fifteen years earlier during another fall term, I was approached at the end of a high school American Literature class I taught by a 17-year-old student, whom I'll name Nora. Nora told me she had been raped a few weeks earlier at a summer party. Nora was a cheerleader. She was pretty and smart, and at the time I knew her, besieged. She explained she had been raped at an outdoor party where "funneling" alcohol had taken place, and she had participated. Addled and dislocated Nora was escorted by a boy with whom she had attended school since kindergarten into some nearby woods just out of sight of the party-goers, and was raped. When she managed to free herself from him, she returned to the party, running toward her classmates with clothes torn, screaming for help. Though she was quickly comforted by her girlfriends at the time of the assault, and a hospital report supported the contention that a rape had occurred, she was shocked by the reception she received upon returning to school a few weeks following the incident. Her female classmates instantly abandoned her, even the ones who had earlier comforted her at the party. The male students unanimously sided with her attacker. Nora suddenly found herself alone and reviled. For some reason she took a risk and chose me, a male teacher, for comfort and support. Unlike my role in the story of the first young woman, I had somewhat more to do with assisting this victim of a violent crime by providing a friendly ear and a bolstering voice to alleviate her distress. I told her I believed her story was true, and attempted to get her counseling with professionals specializing in helping women who had been sexually assaulted. But she was not interested in any of it. Gender did not matter; she eschewed all assistance from professionals who had experience with these matters, men and women. Nora only wanted my support and counsel, and I tried to give her that during those dark days. Later, during the spring semester, her attacker was arrested after attempting to rob, with a knife, a local convenience store. News spread across the school of his arrest, and soon those who had forsaken her, became her advocates, and she began the long process of healing.

Just a few years later I received a series of letters from another student in my American Literature class, another 17-year-old female. Call her Megan. During the spring semester of Megan's senior year, her mother had her involuntarily committed to an adolescent psyche ward at a hospital in Boston. Over the next weeks, she struggled to survive. She fell in love with a male inmate, and was involved in several riots on her ward, and was repeatedly subdued and shackled to her hospital bed. During this intense time, she refused to communicate with anyone in the "outside" world except me, her English teacher. Though saddened by her plight, I felt surprised and moved that she had chosen me as her correspondent while she was incarcerated. And though her supervisors kept her under heavy medication, she managed to keep a journal and read a couple of novels during her stay. Her letters expressed her desperation to leave the hospital, her nostalgia for the loss of her school days, and her rage at the injustice of her imprisonment. Years later she told me she had received no psychological benefit from her time away from school, only great anxiety. Megan mercifully remembered little; drugs erased much of her memory. She confessed that her discharge from the hospital only came when she learned how to play "their" game. She gave the institution's supervisors the answers they sought, was pronounced healthy enough to return to normal life, and sent home. I was just about to visit her at the hospital, when I entered the high school corridor outside my classroom and found her walking toward me.

It was a day after her release.

These three stories of Jill, Nora, and Megan are stories about young women who took risks at a horrific moment in their lives. Part of that risk involved turning to a teacher who could provide a security of a classroom for a student to share a brutal experience from a recent past; in the case of the first student, Jill, the small college—and some of her classmates—supplied the rest. It was not enough by itself, but it was a start, and if she had not been attending school at the time, I'm not sure where she could have sought and received help.

What was it—I have often asked myself—that allowed these three young women to feel comfortable enough to articulate their pain to me—a middle-aged man—or, as in the case of Jill, to other students in my classroom?

Of course, a significant portion of this has to do with personality: the persona the teacher is projecting in class, and the consequences of that projection. Their comfort in seeking my help certainly made me feel good about myself and my profession. But if that is all there was to it, I would have nothing to convey.

I believe the risks these young women took had as much to do with the method and substance of the literature and writing (and speaking) I taught, as to who I am, and although these things are inextricably linked, I don't believe my personality alone—without the purpose of content—would have delivered the sense of security they felt when they came forth to tell their stories to lighten their burden.

Teachers of writing and literature are especially privileged. By taking young minds on a journey into the difficult country of discipline and concentration and understanding, we are able—on our best days—to inspire and liberate.

Through literature we teach the power of the story, and the beauty of language by perception, analysis, and rigor. We imply a philosophy built on the pinnacle of the very best of civilized creation, and with it, we convey a spirit of liberation, achieved through the disciplining of mind and the understanding of human aspiration and motivation. Since all of human behavior is contained in great literature, there is a full portrayal of the human condition in its sentences, and there is an implicit forgiveness (if only, at the very least, an understanding) of the worst of that behavior, and a celebration of the best. We read about the great risks characters in novels have taken, and the great tragedies they have experienced and survived. We examine these fictional characters as real people at the most vulnerable and important moments in their lives. We rejoice in their triumphs, and empathize with their faults. We imagine ourselves beyond our own existence. We imagine ourselves as them.

As teachers of literature, we ask our students to become wise beyond their years, to probe with investigative zeal into the motivations and actions of human beings in times of great crisis. We ask them to consider and to articulate—orally and in writing—what they have carefully read. Before long, they understand and embrace, if they have not before, that great quote from Terrence, "Nothing human is ever alien to me."

If, as instructors, we can create a love of language—the arrangement of words and their meanings—then we can transform that love into a liberation from insecurity and despair and ignorance to those at the bottom of their lives. To appreciate and rejoice in a vivid, wonderfully created sentence is to sensitize and elevate our notion of beauty; all that follows becomes the possibility of sustained excellence and tastefulness, or to quote another poet, Carolyn Forché,

"Taste is involved in the politics of hope." The task of creating "taste" in quality literature in our students—more than any of the other arts—is an ancient and sacred one, for inherent in the act of teaching the value and purpose of literature, is the inherent belief of ennobling man's mind, and with it, the enrichment of human experience.

Through writing we beckon our students to engage in a rigor that cannot be replicated in any other form. By attempting to create articulate beauty on a page—and later, after the task has been completed, by witnessing the triumph that comes from sustained labor after producing a compelling sentence, paragraph, page, essay, story—our students are able to know the power they possess, a power born of discipline and resolve. It is a discipline that can find lodgment and use in their lives. If a student can find confidence through rigor in writing, he may also find the faith to believe he can summon that same confidence and aesthetic love in times of great distress and tumult. The foundation of taking risk is built upon the edifice of nerve derived from a passion for words, ideas, and a search for meaning.

The classes the three female students attended focused on the power and humanity of the written word, and a comprehension of the universal truths great writing conveys. That comprehension allowed these three young women the audacity to take risks at the bleakest moment in their lives, and to find—along with some peace—a rejuvenating spirit they had read about, and then communicated with sustained courage and grace.

LYNN PHILLIPS

Everyday Courage and the "How" of Our Work

As we live our lives with dignity and integrity, we affect the people around us whether or not we are aware of our influence. We are each teachers of bravery.

–Sarah Pirtle

Never one to shy away from the big, existential questions, I spend a lot of time thinking about the contributions I am compelled to make with this one, unique life. I find myself alternately invigorated and daunted by the enormity of responsibility for the footprints—from carbon to moral—I will leave in my time on the planet. I like to think I have contributed to social change efforts through activist research; through advocacy for victim/survivors and clinical work with perpetrators; and through teaching, writing, and speaking about media, violence, culture, and a wide range of injustices. Increasingly, though, I find myself pondering not just the "what" of my work, but the "how" of it—my way of being and what I am modeling as I go about working for social change. In what ways am I a "teacher of bravery"?

When it comes to fighting injustice, I tend to associate words like "bravery," "risk," and "courage" with dramatic acts of self-sacrifice. For me, these words conjure up immediate images of Tiananmen Square, Greensboro lunch counters and the Freedom Riders, Stonewall, or young carpet weavers daring to speak out about child labor. I think of radical acts motivated by outrage, of knowingly throwing oneself in harm's way for the greater good, of speaking truth in the face of oppressive forces, or of selflessly daring to expose corruption, abuse, inequity, and greed.

But when I move beneath the surface of these more obvious forms of risk and daring, my mind settles on a different, more subtle kind of courage—the kind of courage that the musician and peace educator, Sarah Pirtle, writes about in the introduction to her album, *Everyday Bravery*. Although these acts of bravery may never make the evening news, I have come to believe that they are, in their own quiet way, nonetheless radical. This is the type of everyday courage we are called upon to muster if we are not only to speak out about injustices perpetrated

199

by others, but also to make the changes we know in our hearts are necessary in our *own* lives if we are to live and work with integrity. Indeed, even more courageous than angrily fighting injustice is daring to do so in ways that keep compassion in our hearts and that embrace the complexities of human experience.

Though I'm not likely to stand in front of a tank or move to a war zone, I am faced daily with the opportunity to take "little risks"—to decide whether I'll exercise the courage to act in ways that promote the peace and justice I'm working for, or whether fear, self-righteousness, or moral indignation will seduce me into the very closed-mindedness I am combating in others. More and more I am distressed by the intolerance I witness not just among those who perpetrate injustice, but also among those who fight it, as though moral conviction entitles us to dehumanize those we deem to be "the problem." And so I ask myself, how can I use my anger to energize me without defining my way of doing my work? For me, this question plays out around four recurring themes:

- Will I allow the conventions of my discipline and the fear of looking "unscholarly" to silence the part of me that needs to speak beyond the intellectual, to acknowledge and embrace the emotional connection I feel with those with and for whom I am advocating?
- Will I on settle on simplistic explanations that support the views I wish to promote rather than daring to explore complexities that may lead me to conclusions I'd rather not consider?
- Will I have the courage to see those whose actions I abhor with the same three-dimensional lenses I would expect for myself?
- Will I indulge in the opportunity to throw barbs at those working against causes I believe in—especially when I know, sadly, that those barbs will earn "points" among some in making me seem more radical or my critique more scathing?

My point here is not to compare the risks involved in dismantling systems of oppression with those involved in leading with our hearts and our ethics in our everyday lives. Rather, it is to suggest that each can inform the other—that compassion and embracing complexity do not undermine political work and scholarship, but can join with our outrage to fuel and ground our efforts toward change.

What follows, then, are some musings on the ways these questions play out in my own life as I strive, in small ways, to bring everyday courage to the "how" of my work.

The Courage to Bring My Heart to Work

When my daughter was four, she asked me what my book, *Flirting with Danger,* was about. Not yet ready to tell her that I study rape and battering, I explained, "I write about why people are mean to each other, and I work on ways to help them be kind." While I'd like to think that readers would find my analysis a bit more sophisticated than that, I've come to realize that, in a very real sense, that is a fair description of the concerns that propel my work. As someone who has spent over twenty years studying and fighting injustice, I can offer up quite a nuanced analysis of power, moral exclusion, and victimization. I theorize hegemony and oppression, and I use the tools of social science to study injustice in a rational and systematic way. But the truth is that on some deep-in-my soul level—a level that at first glance seems childlike, yet actually transcends the intellectual—it *is* about "meanness" and "kindness," and I find myself in a perpetual struggle to fathom the heartlessness I witness both globally and interpersonally. Even as I teach and write and conduct research by day, I go home and weep for everyone from victims of hate crimes to dogs in puppy mills to children toiling in sweatshops, and I grieve for a planet ravaged by rampant consumerism and a cultural disconnect between consumption and environmental and human consequence. Beneath the analyses of ideology and power structures that make oppression intellectually comprehensible, cruelty and intolerance still rattle me to the core. All of this quite literally keeps me up at night.

I have mourned for victims of oppression and neglect for as long as I can remember. Some of my earliest childhood memories include deep distress upon hearing of children living in poverty, worry for elders forgotten in nursing homes, and sorrow at the realization that inmates in the local prison would not be home to celebrate Christmas. Even now, despite my training as social scientist to be an "objective observer," and despite the activist reminder, "don't mourn—organize," I cannot separate my intellectual and political work from the deep sense of grief and soul-level connection with those who are hurting.

I worried early on in my academic career that this made me "soft" or meant I did not have a rigorous mind, and even now, I am powerfully aware that to share the fact of my emotional vulnerability and spiritual dismay is, in many circles, to risk compromising my credibility as a social researcher. It seems that anger is an acceptable emotional accompaniment to political and intellectual work, but sorrow is seen as an indication of Pollyannaish hand wringing or naïveté.[1] I have spent most of my life in academe, a realm where the clear-cut, dispassionate argument prevails—we don't often hear social scientists lamenting over the water cooler, "Why can't we all just get along?" After all, we researchers are supposed to investigate social problems, not grieve over them.

After years of striving to compartmentalize the emotional and the intellectual, though, I am summoning the courage to stop pretending. The more I study and teach and work for justice, the more I have come to see deep emotional connection to the issues I study as a vital force in my effort to advocate. Indeed, I think oftentimes the problem is not that intellectuals shed too many tears, but too few. Or at least we don't risk admitting to the tears we may shed in private.

Much like the bumper sticker that says, "if you're not outraged, you're not paying attention," it seems to me that if we've so intellectualized our concerns that we've forgotten to cry, we're not fully alive to the injustices we fight.

And so, I still collect and analyze data systematically. I turn to social theory and statistics and analyses of power. But at the risk of appearing "soft" or "irrational," I no longer apologize when my eyes well up as a student or interviewee shares her experience of abuse and degradation. I no longer pretend that my work is merely an intellectual pursuit. And I no longer censor myself from writing essays, like this one, that dare to speak of and from both the mind and the heart. It's not exactly staring down a tank, but it's my little act of everyday courage, and though it may come with professional costs, it has enhanced my sense of integrity in my work.

The Courage to Honor Complexities

I love complexity and paradox. When a research participant tells me how she feels about an issue, my next question is, inevitably, "Now tell me about a time when you didn't feel that way." And, inevitably, she can quickly come up with a counter example. I am trained in a discipline—psychology—that prides itself on reducing complex phenomena to measurable variables, stripped of context and ambiguity. But that has just never worked for me. I don't know anyone who lives his or her life in a social vacuum or who, when really pressed, has completely consistent, clear-cut attitudes and experiences that are not marked by complexity and nuance. And so in my work I explore those seeming contradictions in order to better understand and give voice to the twists and contours of people's complicated lives.

While intellectually rich and fascinating, this is not always a comfortable perspective from which to work. In fact, this orientation has sometimes taken me places I'd rather not go. Deeply committed to anti-violence struggles, I have situated my work within social movements in which it is often important to make definitive statements about right and wrong in order to press for change, advocate for victims, and hold perpetrators accountable for their actions. In a still-victim-blaming society, advocacy for survivors of rape, battering, harassment, and other such crimes often rests on legalistic dualisms like victim/perpetrator, guilty/innocent, and consent/coercion. Fueled by a sense of social and political urgency, acknowledging nuance and contradiction can seem to me to be decadent, if not downright dangerous. Activists have worked for decades to impress upon us that "no means no and yes means yes," that violence against women is solely men's responsibility, and that if women don't "just leave" abusive situations, it is because they lack the social and material support to get out. This work has been vital in bringing much-needed attention to the plight of victims/survivors and highlighting the ways in which our society condones and promotes male violence. I am deeply committed to these goals and certainly don't want to risk undermining that vital work by introducing findings suggesting that it's not so straightforward after all.

But my desire for effective here-and-now advocacy continually bumps up against my desire for long-term change and my commitment to honoring the textures and wrinkles of people's own stories—stories that are always far more complicated than our political slogans would seem to suggest. On the one hand, to go public with the complexities and contradictions in women's and girls' experiences is to risk having their own stories used against them. If we acknowledge that sometimes women say "yes" when they want to say "no" (or vice versa), or that many refuse to consider themselves victims even in cases that fit legal definitions of rape, battering, or harassment, we risk adding fuel to the argument that women really want to be raped, that they lead men on, that they're fickle and confused, or that they must not mind being abused or else they would just leave. This is a defense attorney's dream come true. On the other hand, though, if we continue to iron out all of the wrinkles and contradictions from survivors' stories in order to make them more legally or politically palatable, we perpetuate the myth that "real" victimization is always clear-cut, physically violent, and "comes out of nowhere." And as long as our dominant cultural scripts insist that abusive experiences fit these very narrowly proscribed criteria, we preclude women with complicated stories (which is just about everybody) from acknowledging their experiences as victimization and, thus, from seeking advocacy and redress.

As I have written elsewhere, I land, albeit with great trepidation, on the side of complexity, for it seems to me that without an acknowledgment of women's lived realities, however "messy," we cannot work meaningfully toward prevention, education, and true social change.[2] The responsibility, though, is enormous—if we are to go forward with this work, it is our absolute obligation to situate discussion of the nuances and seeming contradictions in women's experiences within a thorough analysis of the cultural forces and gendered power asymmetries that give rise to their sometimes counterintuitive perspectives. Otherwise, we risk pathologizing victims rather than problematizing the contexts in which they form their decisions and attributions.

The Courage to See the "Other"

Going public with the complex stories of those we wish to defend can feel risky enough. Acknowledging the complexities of those who perpetrate injustice and victimize others can be downright scary. The challenge for me is: can we both hold people accountable *and* see them three-dimensionally? Can we hate and refuse to tolerate what people do and yet acknowledge that, like the rest of us, there may be complicated reasons why they do it?

Early in my career I worked with incarcerated sex offenders—convicted rapists, child molesters, and incest offenders. It was challenging work on many levels, and I'm not sure I would have it in me to do it again, particularly now that I'm a mother. At the time, though, it felt like a logical (though certainly emotionally and politically charged) extension of my commitment to feminist anti-violence work. Having worked with rape survivors, I realized that if I could work with men who, without benefit of therapy, were highly likely to reoffend against multiple victims, I could potentially help prevent the victimization of hundreds of women and children I would never even meet.

Over many months, as I listened to these men talk about their crimes as well as their early developmental experiences, I was confronted with two competing sets of feelings. On the one hand, I was angry and disgusted by what they had done as adults—I ache to this day for their victims. On the other hand, I felt deep sorrow about the abuse every one of them had suffered as children. I imagined the frightened and victimized young boys they had been, molested by strangers or, more often, trusted adults. Many had been subjected to horrific acts of physical and sexual violence, and although they were reluctant to talk about these experiences, the emotional scars were often glaring. I also witnessed the abuse and humiliation they endured from the general prison population. Although I was clear that I would not advocate for their release from jail and I would never minimize the horror of their crimes or the damage to their victims, I nonetheless felt defensive for them as they absorbed taunts and threats from other inmates.

These men were despised, both in and out of prison. Yet knowing their stories, I could not help seeing them as three-dimensional human beings with developmental contexts that in no way excused their horrible deeds, but did help to explain them. And seeing them as such, I could not write them off as monsters, even though what they had done was surely monstrous. As I struggled to make sense of my feelings of genuine sympathy for people who had done the very things I was so passionately committing my life's work to fighting, the image of "musical chairs" kept running through my head. Had the music stopped one generation ago—had we stepped into these men's lives when they were children—we would have sympathized with them and despised their abusers. But when the system finally intervened, it was they who were "standing" and now the objects of our scorn. And, in light of the prevalence of abusive histories among those who abuse, it's likely that if we had gone back generations further, the same pattern would have played out, again and again.

I am not seeking to absolve perpetrators of violence or other injustices from responsibility for their actions. People need to be held accountable for their crimes. But hate does not strengthen our work. It does not further our understandings or our ability to prevent others' cruelty. When we deny another person the basic compassion we would ask for ourselves, it is we who lose our way. And who, then, will model the integrity we claim is lacking in others?

The Courage to Fight without Trying to Wound

When I first came to an awareness of the notion that some people's oppression was linked to other people's privilege (including my own), I was, like many newly political students, outraged and disillusioned. I was disgusted by "the system," and eager to expose conspiracies and find "bad guys" to blame. I joined others around me in knee-jerk claims and an ironic willingness to stereotype those who stereotype—to other people for othering people. Even as we conducted diversity and cultural awareness workshops on campus, we somehow never problematized the fact that our case studies and examples posed whole groups of people as the inherent carriers of prejudice and indifference ("How do you handle the football player who doesn't care about this stuff . . . ?"). Certain "types" were taken, unthinkingly, to be fair game, symbols of ignorance, malice, bigotry, and greed. At the time they were football players, fundamentalists, "pro-lifers," and Republicans. And heaven help you if you were a straight, white, middle-class man.

Not long into this period of self-righteousness and accusation, though, I received a humbling lesson in the limits of othering as I volunteered as an escort for women seeking abortion and other services at a local clinic. It was a tense and angry scene every Saturday morning, as barricades were erected to separate patients and their advocates from the scores of protesters doing their best to dissuade women from entering the building. I listened as insults and accusations were hurled from each side of the sawhorses: "Baby killers!" shouted one group. "People who don't support women's choices are just angry white men who want to control women's lives!" shouted the other. The people on each side seemed so sure of themselves and so ready to collapse their opponents into a monolithic and malicious entity. Yet despite firmly supporting women's right to reproductive freedom, and despite my anger at the protesters who were screaming obscenities at often-terrified women at such a vulnerable moment in their lives, I found myself on those mornings thinking, "If I actually thought people were inside killing children, I would be trying to stop it too. How could I not?"

One morning, as I stood on that street corner, I heard a young woman across the barricade talking with a fellow protester, explaining the animal rights button she had on her collar. "I'm pro-all-life" she declared, and went on to describe an animal rights march she had attended the previous weekend—a march in which I had also participated. Her fellow protester registered a look of disgust and retorted that she didn't believe in animal rights. I suddenly realized that this young woman and I were on the same side of one barricade the previous weekend and now were standing on opposite sides of another, with groups that were dehumanizing one another as unequivocally ignorant, self-serving, and brutal. And her ally on this Saturday morning might well have been one of the people shouting insults at us as we marched down the street the weekend before. While it might have been more psychologically and politically convenient to write this young woman off as "one of the bad guys," how could I do that when I now knew that she took the same position as me on a difficult issue that is dear to my heart? And if I could not write her off, how could I demonize anyone else in her group? While I might always disagree with them about the issue and about their tactics, I could no longer stand smugly by and judge them as less ethical, compassionate, or enlightened than me.

It is a difficult task to disagree to our very core and yet still acknowledge the other's vantage point. In a world where most of us find comfort, however misguided, in claiming moral superiority to our opponents, this is not a popular position to take, and it's certainly not as comfortable as dismissing or demonizing those who disagree with our views. To consider that our political opponents might be well intentioned and reasonable, even if we are sure they are wrong, is to forfeit that delicious claim to the moral high ground as well as to risk being seen as an apologist for oppressors. Certainly there are far too many who do act with malice, selfishness, and hate. But to presume that everyone on the "other side" *must* be motivated by ignorance or malevolence seems to me too convenient and morally or intellectually self-serving. If we are truly sure of our positions, then we shouldn't be threatened by the possibility that those working against our causes might be just as intelligent and ethically motivated as we are.

It takes strength and courage to be angry without hatred, to challenge without demonizing, to fight without secretly hoping to wound. But I find the more I resist the temptation to other the other, the more I rise to the occasion of doing the hard work of defending my positions only on their own merits without presuming I'm right and the other is ignorant, mal-intended, or simply wrong. This ought to be self-evident and automatic practice. But it's amazing how often I watch us slip.

Conclusion

How do we acknowledge the level of turmoil in the world and in our lives and at the same time chart a course toward a life of integrity . . .? In these times of the world out of balance, what I experience is that the light inside us calls us to be part of restoring the balance through the deeds in our lives.[3]

The very act of publishing this essay is, for me, a small act of courage. If I were a poet or a novelist, a religious scholar or a philosopher, the appeal to bring our hearts to work might not feel like such a stretch. I am choosing to write past my worry that this will be seen as a trite plea to "play nice" or an appeal to some superficial read of the Golden Rule—on par with all those truisms that, if taken seriously, might make us think, but by now have become so clichéd as to make us wince at the naïveté.

The commitments I am calling for are by no means earth-shattering. They will not change dominant power arrangements, feed those who are hungry, interrupt violence, or protect the environment. That is for the "what" of our work. It's a bit like recycling, carrying my mesh bag and travel mug, and eating low on the food chain. I have no illusion that these small acts will solve our environmental ills. For that we need systemic change—we need to compel multinational corporations to stop spewing pollution into the environment, we need to address peak oil and the global water crisis, we need government to actually regulate industry rather than massage it. Whether we are biologists, community activists, teachers, or poets, we can use the "what" of our work to press for these and other systemic changes that may begin to turn things around. But if our focus outward on the "real" source of the problem keeps us from challenging our own behavior—whether it's what we do with our trash or how we treat our opponents—then we become part of the problem we are trying to solve. Imagine the arrogance of demanding a level of integrity from others that we are unwilling to match ourselves.

Challenging the "how" of our work is daily practice. It's not glamorous, and many times it's tempting to skip it. We can certainly do a lifetime of important work without reflecting on the spirit we bring to it. We can push for change without challenging ourselves to live our values in those everyday moments of fighting for what we believe in. But how much more energized, authentic, and ultimately effective might we be with that everyday courage enriching our work?

NOTES

1. However, marginalized groups still risk being seen as "uppity," irrational, or having a chip on their shoulders if they show anger when advocating for their own needs.
2. Lynn M. Phillips, *Flirting with Danger: Young Women's Reflections on Sexuality and Domination* (New York: New York University Press, 2000); Lynn M. Phillips, "Recasting Consent: Agency and Victimization in Adult-Teen Relationships," in *New Versions of Victims: Feminists Struggle with the Concept*, ed. Sharon Lamb (New York: New York University Press, 1999), 82–107.
3. Sarah Pirtle, "Introduction: Thoughts on *Everyday Bravery* and Songs of Personal Courage," *http://www.sarahpirtle.com/lyrics/lyricsEB/htm*.

Mutually Assured Destruction and Jumping Horses

I might be the only woman I know my age who is still jumping horses. I didn't realize this until recently, when I looked up and noticed that in the riding arena I was surrounded by teen-aged girls and that my trainers—those who are still jumping—are all ten to twenty years younger than I am. What ambitious old lady riders do is dressage. When I tell them I am taking my jumper to a show, they are amazed. I trace my willingness—no, eagerness—to keep jumping to a life of fear.

I was born in 1949. On the back of the newspaper clipping announcing my parents' 1948 wedding is another headline, announcing the theme of my childhood—"Russians Explode Hydrogen Bomb." The two things I remember most in my experience of childhood—that tent of immediacy that is the small, intense perspective of every child—are wanting a horse and feeling that within any given half hour, the world might come to an end (a half an hour would be the interval between the launch of the Russian missiles and their arrival in my neighborhood).

Fear and desire. Simple, isn't it? The fears proliferated—tornadoes, especially, but midnight intruders, men who might pull up to the curb and open their passenger doors, house fires, trains derailing, rolling down the embankment and on up the street, knocking houses over. Gas leaks. Carbon monoxide (invisible! undetectable!). Lightning. Rarely, flood (though if we were walking in the nearby creek, flash floods always crossed my mind). Remember Jeanne Dixon? Nostradamus? I was sure they were on to something. The desires, though, did not proliferate. There were things I missed—that twin I should have had, or, failing that, a mere sister or brother—but there was only one active wish, the horse the horse the horse. Fury, My Friend Flicka, The Black Stallion or Flame, Silver Birch, Hi Ho Silver.

1962 was a turning point. On the one hand, on the evening of the Cuban Missile Crisis, my stepfather told me that if the bombs came we wouldn't even try to survive, which was liberating in its way, because he was so matter of fact about it—that would be that, and possibly a relief, in the end. On the other hand, I started jumping horses. I had a friend who was fearless. We did it together, first on the school pony, down behind the barn, and then out riding at the club my parents joined. The idea that I would jump horses made my mother nervous, but I defied her, and even after I broke my arm (high jumping, not riding), I kept at it.

But her nervousness infected me. I knew my job—look up, go forward, stay with the horse's motion—but I was always tempted to look down in horror at the jump. Still am. By this time, I have probably resisted that temptation thousands of times. But I still have to resist it.

I have given up jumping horses several times. I didn't ride at all between the ages of twenty-four and forty-two. I couldn't afford it, and I thought I'd lost interest, but when I got back on in my forties, I realized that horsefever was still there, like trichinosis or TB, encapsulated for a while, but ever-ready to spring back to life. When I came back to riding, with three kids, a career, and all the obligations those entail, I assumed that I wouldn't jump again. How little self-knowledge I had. The jumps were in the ring. The horse was willing. Over we went. It was thrilling, and yet it was terrifying. And so I did it again.

The Vietnam War, which I opposed, was reassuring to me. I saw it as a valve on the pressure cooker. I never thought it would escalate, I always thought it would distract. But that didn't mean that the world wouldn't end. Even during the period of my greatest fearlessness (in my twenties), my boyfriend came home from his job at a bartender late one night to find the basement light on. It was a moonlit, breezy, balmy evening. When he went to turn out the basement light, I was sitting in the southwest corner with all of my dearest possessions, waiting for the tornado to hit.

Instead, the panic hit—when I had children. Once, when my older daughter was a baby, I sat up in bed and woke my husband with the news that there was a tornado coming, and we had to get to the basement. We hurried to her room, and then crawled to the basement, through the dining room. The dining room had giant windows. As we crawled past them we noticed that the weather was perfectly clear. As for misadventures, accidents, SIDS, I knew every horror story, from the child who was born without a face to the one who grew only on the right side to the one who stepped through the door of the subway train as it was closing, dropping his mother's hand. It was all I could do not to follow my children to school every morning.

I've fallen off my horses many times, but not while jumping. Nevertheless, I'm not afraid to ride, but I am afraid to jump. I don't know what it is. There have been periods when my fear actually put me to sleep—that is, upon entering a show ring, I began yawning and longing for the surcease that would only come if I were rendered unconscious. It seemed possible and appealing to simply fall off my horse and sleep, right there in front of the jump.

When I did subsequently break my leg (he bucked and turned left, I drifted off to the right and came down easy, except that the footing was hard and my heel hit like a whiplash), it was no big deal—at least in comparison to the dread I had been feeling. It was a practical task, or a series of practical tasks—crutches, physical therapy—nowhere near as paralyzing as the fear. After four months, I was back on the horse. After six, I was jumping again.

My friends who no longer jump, who say it is too scary for them, are the ones for whom fear, dread, and caution came as a surprise. They started out like those teen-aged girls I see in the ring with me, dedicated, single-minded, maybe unimaginative. At some point, and only sometimes because of an accident, they realized what might happen.

After that, they did the smart thing, I suppose.

Sometimes I watch my trainer jump my horse, Essie. We set the fences at 3'6" or 3'9", and I lounge as Samantha canters Essie around the ring and over the fences. It's amazing to me how undramatic the horse makes it look. She gallops, she gathers herself, she jumps, and gallops on. She is never daunted, in the way that a person is never daunted by an activity that person is perfectly familiar with—let's say in the way that I am never daunted by baking a cake. The cake will be baked. The jump will be jumped. Then Sam gets off and I get on. She lowers the jumps, and it's my turn. Once again they loom. Once again, each is a climax. Once again I distract myself from my fear by keeping time, one two one two one two. Once again, we are up and over, up and over, and I feel my anxiety rise and pop, rise and pop. When I've done my course properly, I am relieved and ready to quit. As I'm walking Essie out, I feel the usual mix of exhilaration and gratitude that nothing bad happened. Essie, I know, never thought that anything bad would happen (I have another horse who is always sure something bad is going to happen, so I know her attitude isn't universal).

I used to think that I could become a not-fearful person. Now I don't. SARS, bird flu, bombing Iran (a moral danger, if not a physical one for me), a semi veering across the yellow line, fire in the valley, financial ruin, an intruder, the events of 2012, you name it, I've pondered it in the night and made my plan. The gift that the horses have given me is not that they have erased my fears, but that they have helped me not flee them; they have helped me see them from the outside as well as the inside, as an aspect of my temperament rather than a feature of the world—danger is a feature of the world, and best not dealt with through fear.

Jump

The first time I was ever in an airplane, I jumped out. I was nineteen, skydiving with friends on a lark, on a dare, with a sense of immortality that must be the province of youth. The moment I remember most is standing in the open doorway of the plane at 2,500 feet. My friend had jumped seconds before, becoming a speck in the distance with remarkable speed, and I had watched his parachute blossom in the air. There was another jumper behind me, and the jumpmaster signaling me to go. So I did. I stepped out into the sky. And fell. Or briefly flew—in those few seconds before the static line pulled my parachute safely open, there was an exhilarating sense of freedom, and strangely, no fear.

I write about this with a certain incredulity, looking back. I never jumped out of a plane again, and my sense of immortality has long since disappeared. I'm a mother now, and there's no way I want my lovely children, each unique in the world and full of promise, jumping out of airplanes. It's hard enough to let them cross the street. So where did it come from, this desire of mine as a young woman, to take such a risk? And what has it meant?

In the days when I talked of sky-diving with my friends, I also lived at home, and I worked 20 hours a week in a grocery store to put myself through community college, where I was majoring in business. I dreamed of becoming a writer, but I had no idea how a person did that. It was such an unlikely dream, and I was probably the only person to take it seriously. Yet I never questioned this, myself. However unlikely or impractical, I understood writing to be my vocation, a calling in the true sense, something that was choosing me as much as I was choosing it. Perhaps my impulse to jump out of that plane was really a willingness to break free of the expected, a chance to announce different, and less predictable, possibilities for my life.

The first real story I ever wrote, for a college class I took with Fred Busch at Colgate University, (once I'd followed my heart to major in English, and transferred) was a 32-page opus about sky-diving. It was short on character and long, very long indeed, on technical details and parachutes. Still, the story caught Fred's eye, and when I went to his office to confess my unlikely dream, I suddenly had another person who took me seriously. Over the next several years, as I took more risks of various kinds, going to Iowa, moving to Malaysia and Japan, flying into Cambodia to spend a year when the Mekong was flooding and the country was still closed to Americans because, as one official put it, "of the weight of history," I revised that story again and again. Eventually, it was published in *The Threepenny Review* and won a Pushcart Prize. It appears in my collection *The Secrets of a Fire King* as "The Way It Felt to be Falling." I still think of this as the story on which I learned to write.

I'm thinking now, as I write this, how the various risks I've taken in my life could be seen collectively as a metaphor for the creative life. Each story, each book, is its own new landscape, a place full of unknown delights and dangers, a journey one begins without any idea of how the narrative will unfold—except that it will be impossible, on this path, to hide from the truest voices of the self.

CRAIG WALZER

◇◇

The Only Word I Heard Was "Abeeda." That Means Slave

Abuk told her story of abduction, enslavement, liberation, and resettlement while drinking tea in her den in suburban Boston. It was clear that she is well-practiced at this: she often speaks at churches and community centers on behalf of anti-slavery campaigns. During the interview and throughout the editing process, she remained insistent that her involvement not be limited to her storytelling alone. She needed to know that we would use her narrative as a platform to launch concrete action for rebuilding South Sudan.

I am from Sudan. I was born in 1975 in South Sudan, in a small town called Achor, in the region of Bahr al-Ghazal. My family was wealthy, but not wealthy with money. In our lives, we didn't have money. Our cows and goats were our wealth. My grandfather and my father all lived in the same area in Achor. I had two brothers and three sisters. We were close. We laughed and played, you know? We were still young. I was the oldest. I lived with my cousins around, and my grandfather and grandmother, aunts and uncles. We didn't have a lot, but we had a normal life. We were happy.

My father was a farmer. The children did not work, but we helped around the house. We just stayed home, took care of the animals and checked on the cows, brought the water from the river, washed the dishes, and cleaned the floor. We didn't have flour so we needed to mill it so we could cook. Most women and girls did that. I would do that. I would take care of the baby cows, and I helped take care of the children too.

This oral history, conducted and edited by Craig Walzer, appears in *Out of Exile*, an anthology edited by Walzer and published by McSweeney's as part of its Voice of Witness series. The book also features an introduction and additional interviews by Dave Eggers and Valentino Achak Deng. Reprinted by permission of the publisher.

In the village, we had a garden to grow something to eat, and there were mango trees. We had a small lake nearby, and the kids would go swimming and fishing. We went into the jungle and looked at animals like monkeys, giraffes, and elephants. When you were sleeping, you heard the sound of a lion. Most boys went to the jungle with the animals, and the girls were usually at home.

At night we danced, sang, and played games. I had a favorite game where you put small beans on the floor to play and took, like, five in your hand, and you had to jump them.

We didn't have school over there, and we didn't know how to read. It was hard because when you're a kid and you need to go to school, you need to go to the city, like up in Khartoum in the North. It's hard to go and live up there. Most people in the North were Arabs. You couldn't go to the city because you didn't know if something would happen there, and when you go there you need to know Arabic; we just spoke Dinka. We had heard some Arabic words, but nobody usually speaks Arabic when you go to the South, just Dinka.

I Heard the Fire

The Second Sudanese Civil War began in 1983. The Sudan People's Liberation Army SPLA was formed when John Garang encouraged a series of mutinies in South Sudan. Approximately two million people were killed and four million southerners were displaced from their homes during the twenty-three-year war. Abuk's village was among those affected.

I was twelve. We were playing in my yard outside the house. It was in the morning, around noontime. We were playing and we heard gunfire. Suddenly we heard people running and guns being shot. They set fire to the houses and we all ran in different directions. We didn't know where to go. The children were screaming, and the people were being shot and killed. Mostly they killed the men; when they saw men, they shot them right away. My father was running; he hid and I didn't see him, but I thought at that time that he had been killed. I didn't have any idea because they shot a lot of people, all men. The militiamen wore a *jallabiya*, a long robe, and something on their head. They spoke Arabic. Some had light skin, but some had dark. Some of them looked like us. They came with horses, all running with horses. They came by groups, like, a hundred or two hundred, village to village.

People said the Arabs were taking control in the South. We had heard that they had come to other towns to take cows and other valuable things. The people were fighting; we were all Christian, and they are Muslim. When the British came to Sudan, they brought Christianity everywhere, but the Arabs didn't want us to be Christian. We heard there was fighting, and we didn't know if they would come to the village. We heard about the SPLA and John Garang, but we thought it was just for politics, for the capital city, you know? In my village, we didn't have a lot of people go off to the SPLA, and I never met any of them. We didn't know they could come in the village and kill people. The Arabs that came to the village to do business didn't look like soldiers.

Sometimes my grandfather would say, "Maybe the Arabs are here. We should go into hiding." My grandfather would take us to the jungle to hide, and we would be scared. We hid in the jungle, so many people. Sometimes we hid for a month, because we didn't know if the militia would come to the town. We didn't know. We hid by the trees and the children could not cry there. We had to be quiet, because maybe an animal could come and eat you, you know?

We thought that people from the North came to the South for business. In my village, we didn't have sugar, or tea. People used to come for business, to bring sugar, tea, and such things to South Sudan. We didn't have money but we paid them by trade, with things we grew. We knew the people that came for business. Even my grandfather said those people just came to do business, you know? I thought they were there to trade and that's it. Then they came back to kill us, to set fire to the houses and kill the men and take the cows.

The day the Arabs came to the village, my grandfather came to where we were playing and he ran with us. We were crying, me and my cousin and my brother, and we didn't know what we were doing. We were just running. Then they shot my grandfather. I was running and I heard the fire. When they shot him, he never got up. They shot him, even though they knew him, because he was the chief. They killed him right away. I ran back to him and I was screaming. I tried to take him but he never got up. That's how I knew he had been killed. At that time I saw my aunt, the sister of my father, and we started running. I didn't find my mom at that time, or my brother or anybody.

They took us. The Arab militia took the women and children. They killed many people and the city was quiet. They grabbed us and tied us all together by the neck, with a rope. We walked. We didn't know where they were taking us. We walked all day. It was so far. They gave us no food or water, nothing. It was very hot. My aunt talked to me as we walked, trying to calm me down, telling me things would be okay. I thought we would die.

We walked north. I didn't know where we were going, but when we arrived there we heard that they called it Ad-Da'ein. When we got there, they put us in a big place that looked like a market. They sold horses there, food and spices, anything a market sells. It was a small town, and we weren't in the jungle anymore. We were in the desert. It looked different than in the South. All the people there were Arab, and all wearing *jallabiyas*.

Young Baby, Get Up!

We were so scared. We didn't know where they would take us. They could kill us. The men that captured us went to talk to the people who were in the market.

They came and called us one by one: "You need to go with this person. You need to go with this one." At that time I knew they were selling us. You sat down and they came up and said, "Oh, I need this one," and they called you, "Young lady, come up."

When someone came and called you, you couldn't say no, because they could kill you. We were afraid, and we didn't know Arabic. I don't speak Arabic; how could I even say something I needed to tell them? The men said to me, "Young baby, get up!" I was crying so much because I saw my aunt nearby with the baby; some women and some children from my village were all tied together with me. I was screaming for my aunt because that's the person I knew. They told me, "You need to go with this man. You need to go with us." As they grabbed me, my aunt told me to be calm.

A man named Mohammed Adam put me on a camel and tied up my hands. I didn't see him pay for me, but he was talking with the people who brought us. I don't know what happened to the other people. Maybe the same thing that happened to me.

Mohammed Adam took me to his house. When I got to that place they made me a slave. Mohammed Adam had a wife, Fatima, and two children, and his house was different than the houses in my village; it was like a big tent, something they could move, but they never moved when I was there. In the day, Mohammed Adam went into town. I didn't know what he was doing. Maybe he had work to do. Maybe they had to do business, to go and kill people; I don't know. I didn't see any job or office, nothing. Fatima didn't work or go anywhere. Usually she was just at home and doing things in the house. She was always quiet, but she was happy. The children were quiet, normal children. They just went walking around and came back. They were just a normal family. I didn't see anyone really angry or fighting.

I worked from morning until night. I didn't speak Arabic, only Dinka, so Mohammed Adam pointed and showed me how to do things. I cleaned the floors and took care of the cows all day. I carried water on my head from the well. It took twenty minutes to get to the well, and they would tell me to come right back. I couldn't run away. I couldn't. I didn't know how. They were all Arab in the city, and maybe if I ran, they could kill me. I didn't have a choice. I was twelve years old. When he called me, the only word I heard was "abeeda, abeeda." That means slave. They would call "abeeda," and I would go over. I have a name, you know? Sometimes they would call my name, but usually they just pointed to me.

When I wasn't working I would just sit. I would sit in one spot and the family would sit in another. When the father talked to me, he looked angry, and the other people in the family didn't talk to me at all. They gave me leftovers when they finished eating. They just threw some flatbread down or left a bowl of soup. Sometimes I ate. Sometimes I was sad and angry, so I didn't really feel hunger.

Some days I didn't eat anything. Sometimes when I was very hungry, I would steal some food when nobody was looking. They never caught me, but I had such fear. If I had been caught, I know they would have beaten me.

I slept in the kitchen, in a small place on the floor. They just put some dirty clothes down and I slept on them. I didn't have any clothes of my own, really. Sometimes I just wore something small. I didn't really care. I didn't think about clothes; I thought about my family. I was thinking about how I could get to my mom and my father. I didn't know anything about them. I wished I had friends to sit with, and to play with, and to talk with. Sometimes I cried all day and all night, until the next morning. Maybe I wouldn't find my family again.

I was with Mohammed Adam for ten years, and I didn't meet anyone else from South Sudan during that time. I didn't speak at all. I didn't learn Arabic, because I didn't play with the children. Nobody played with me. The children were a few years younger than me, but they never tried to talk to me. I was some-one to come work with them, to do some housework and everything; they didn't think I could be a friend. Maybe the father told the children, "Don't be close to her, she's *abeeda*." They could beat me and they would; maybe their father told them to. If I ever said, "I'm tired; I can't do it," they would beat me. They'd bring a stick like the one you hit a horse with, and they'd beat me and beat me, calling me *"abeeda, abeeda."*

They were religious people. They taught the children the Koran, and I saw them call the children to sit down together and pray. They tried to teach me the Koran too, but I didn't speak Arabic. They taught me to wash my hands and feet in the Islamic way. They have some special water when they pray. They would open the Koran and say, "Wash your hands," because you don't touch the book when your hands are dirty. But I didn't know the words. They said, "Sit down," and tried one time to make me pray with them. I was so confused. I had never seen it before and I didn't know what it meant. I learned *"Allah hu Akbar,"* because they said that all the time. They prayed and they screamed loud, made a loud sound. I wanted to know what that meant but I didn't understand. They tried to get me to pray and bow like them but I couldn't. Sometimes they were angry because I didn't know what I was doing.

Maybe God Is with Me and I Can Run

When I was twenty and I was grown up, Mohammed Adam tried to rape me. One night he came and grabbed me. When I said no and pushed him off, he stabbed me with a knife in my right leg. I started crying, and he left. He was worried about his wife. He was a religious man, and she would have been angry about it if she had found out.

I thought maybe the next time he would kill me. I said to myself, No more. I started running. I said, Maybe God is with me and I can run. It was the middle of the night, and they were all sleeping. My leg was bleeding, but I ran, and ran, and ran.

In the morning I came to a town, and I saw a big truck taking animals to market. I snuck in and hid on the back of the truck. The drivers were Arab, and if they found me, they would have brought me back to Mohammed Adam. The driver didn't see me, though, and they drove the car to another town.

When the truck got to town, I saw a lot of people walking and selling everything. Most were Muslim, but some people looked like Dinka. They called the city Babanoussa. It looked like a marketplace town. I saw one Dinka man from South Sudan. He was sitting down and he looked so honest, I trusted him before I even spoke to him.

I went over there and I said, "I speak Dinka," and he said, "Oh! Why did you come here? Who has brought you here?"

I said, "I walked by myself. I was with the militia." The people in that town knew what was happening in South Sudan.

The man said, "Oh, you come from a master." He asked, "What's your father's name?" And I told him my father's name and my grandfather's name. He said, "Oh! I know this man! I know your grandfather's name. It's good now that you found me."

This man's name was Majak, and he was older than me, maybe thirty-something or forty. He bought me a train ticket to join his family on the way to Khartoum. The trip took two days. There were other Dinka on the train, and when we would stop at a station, the guys would say, "Okay, I'm going to bring water," and they would get off to run and buy something to eat and drink. I didn't go down because I was worried someone would take me away again, so the guys would get things for me. Majak's wife helped me clean my wounded leg, using salt water and wrapping it in clean clothes. We had no medicine, and it took such a long time to heal.

I spoke with the people on the train about my mom, my family, everything. They said they had heard a lot of children were taken. They said a lot of South Sudanese people lived over there in Jabrona, where Majak lived. It was a place for the people who were running from the fighting back in South Sudan; when they set fire to the villages, nobody needed to see that, so they all came from the South to the North, to Khartoum, and they lived in this special place. There were a lot of tribes there and a lot of Dinka people. They said, maybe you can find your mother or your brother, you know, because a lot of people ran from the South to the North.

So we came to Khartoum, and Majak put me in his house in Jabrona camp. He opened his house to me and said, "You can do anything you want." He had a wife and five children, and they took care of me. They were good people and I was happy there. Happy because I found some people that looked like me and spoke my language.

I said to myself, Oh, this will be okay now; I found some people who know my family and my language. Majak can help me a lot and he can find my dad. I thought I could find my mom and everything.

In the morning I would get up and go to the market where Majak worked. At the market, people searched for their families. People were missing their children. I kept looking and I didn't find my mom or my father. Nobody. I kept asking and telling people my mom's name. I was there for three months, just talking to people and asking and asking and asking.

Sometimes the police came into the market when people were fighting. I would get so scared that they would take me again.

I didn't talk to the police; I was worried. I had been enslaved, and maybe the police could take me back. I didn't trust the police.

Majak was worried too. Maybe the people would hear, "Oh, Majak, he helped this lady that the Arab militia took a long time ago." Maybe the people would talk. Maybe the Arabs could hear it. They didn't need to know. People couldn't know about that, that there was a slave in the city.

Maybe His Brother Would Be a Good Guy, Too

After I was there for about three months, Majak said, "You've been here awhile now. I will keep looking to find your father and your mom, but you need a place to go in case there is trouble. I'd like you to marry my younger brother, Atak." His brother was in Egypt, in Cairo. And the good thing was, he was originally from Marial Bai, close to my home of Achor. His family had known my grandfather a long time ago. And I trusted Majak; I saw that he was a nice guy. Maybe his brother would be a good guy, too.

Majak said we could go to the big Catholic church in Amarat to help me get passport documentation.[1] When the people got in trouble they wrote a note to the church. You wrote them your note, saying you've been running from the war back home, and they would help you set up your case and bring you a passport so you could leave the country. The church had taken some young kids, some eighteen-year-olds and sent them to Rome, to Italy, or Syria. They didn't want to be conscripted into the Sudanese government's army, made to go back and fight in South Sudan, because that was their people they would have to fight against. So the church helped them to run away. They helped a lot of people. My husband-to-be had run away. He went to Egypt because the Khartoum government had wanted to take him in the military, and he didn't want that. The church helped him, too.

It took a long time to get my documentation. Sometimes they could do your papers quickly, but for me it took, like, a month. Because the government doesn't usually allow ladies to travel by themselves, Majak also wrote me a note explaining that I was going to marry his younger brother in Egypt. I took the train from Khartoum to Halfa. I took the train, and I came to Halfa by bus, by minibus, and after that, another bus to Port Sudan. From Port Sudan, we took the boat to Cairo. The boat ride took about a week through the sea. You could see Saudi Arabia on the other side.

I took the bus to Cairo, where Atak was waiting for me at the station. He knew I was coming, but he didn't know me, and I didn't know him. When he came he just saw we were sitting down and he said, "Abuk Bak?" And I said, "That's me." He just said, "Okay" and I said, "Hi, hi," because I didn't know him. He wasn't really nervous, but I was nervous. I thought, Oh, who is this I am going to be with? I don't know him and he doesn't know me. It was strange thinking that this man would be my husband. It was really hard, but I tried. Maybe it would be different later. Maybe we could know each other.

When I had been there for a week, we went to the church and had a wedding. A lot of Sudanese were there—my husband's friends. They rented a special place to have the party. I had a white dress and we danced. It was happy but I was thinking of my family. When I left Jabrona, I still knew nothing about my family in Sudan. I was still thinking of my mom and how I could find them.

In Egypt, life was hard for a lot of people. You had to wait for a month to find work and you didn't have money to pay for an apartment. You couldn't rent an apartment because it was too expensive. For some people who came, like single mothers whose husbands had died, it was very different. They didn't find a place to live, or they lived in a house with five or seven people, and the landlord didn't want that. They would get thrown out. So some people just went out into the desert and made a tent. Some children got sick.

I stayed in the apartment Atak rented, near Abbassia. It was two bedrooms, and we shared with a woman, her daughter, and her husband. There were five of us. The apartment wasn't very big: just a dining room and two bedrooms, a bathroom and a kitchen. The kitchen wasn't very big, just a small one. Their family had one room, and I had one room with my husband.

Cairo was very confusing. It was a nice city, but when you don't know a place you worry. I didn't speak English or Arabic, so Egypt was really hard for me. I got lost all the time. I didn't know the bus schedule. Some Egyptians were friendly and nice, but some of them are crazy. When you go walking outside they call you *hunga,* referring to your color. That means like chocolate. And sometimes they would just come up and smack you. Some people were nice, but some people were bad.

Sometimes, when you walked at night they could come and beat you. That never happened to me, but some people said that. They hit them, they broke their arm, they broke their head because they didn't want them to walk in a certain neighborhood. I have a friend who was pushed down and punched in her teeth. Some police were no good; they would see you and laugh at you. You didn't walk at night because you didn't know what could happen. At night I stayed in the apartment.

My husband worked in a store that made belts. He worked morning to night, working, working all the time. At that time, I said to my husband, "We need money. I should go work." Some women did work, like doing housekeeping. But working in a house, you didn't know what would happen. Sometimes you would work and they wouldn't pay you, and if you talked back they could even kill you. I heard that one lady was working in a house and they didn't pay her. They killed her and threw her off the second or third floor and she died from the fall. So when I said to my husband that I should work, he said no. He was scared. He said I could work in a market or a store, but working in a house was too dangerous.

When I came to Cairo, I was pregnant very quickly with my son, Majak. We named him after Atak's brother, who had helped me. He was born in the refugee hospital. The refugee hospital gave me food and checked me every week while I was pregnant. The Egyptian hospital didn't care; they didn't do anything for us, and it was too expensive. When women went to the Egyptian hospital they would give them a C-section and they would take a kidney out; they would steal something. The doctors don't do the C-section like here in America. They start up higher and they take something from inside you; they steal it. A lot of Sudanese who went to the Egyptian hospitals will have another baby here in America, and the doctor says, "Where's your kidney?" So I went to the refugee hospital. Majak was born on June 27, 1999.

At that time, I talked to my husband and said, "Maybe you can keep calling your brother to ask if he can find my mom and brother." After some time, Majak found my mom. When we were separated she had gone to northern Chad. She stayed over there to raise the younger children because she was running with them. My brother was there and my sister.

Now my mom was running back to Khartoum, because when you come to Khartoum they have people that can help you. They have some organizations that give you food and clothes in Jabrona. People over there were always talking, talking; we are Sudanese and we know each other. My mother kept asking people about her daughter, saying that she was missing for a long time from the fight, from the war when the people came to the village to kill. She would say, "My son, my baby is missing, my daughter."

Majak met my mom, and when she asked him, he said, "Oh, I found your daughter. She was here with me and she didn't find you, and she married my younger brother." At that time my mom was so excited, and Majak called us right away in Egypt.

I thought, Oh my God! I found my mom! My husband was really happy, too. We sent money for my mom to come to Egypt with my brother and sister.

This was in 1999, around Christmastime. When my mom came, it was a small apartment and we all lived together in that small place.

We Had Two Choices

When I had been in Egypt for a year, I got my visa to go the United States. During that year, I went a lot to the United Nations, to the UNHCR, because I wasn't allowed to stay in Egypt. They just gave us visas, like a yellow or pink one, and it expires when it expires.[2] If the Egyptian authorities found you without papers, they could send you back to Sudan, so you had to apply to the United Nations for documentation.

At the United Nations, you had to wait in line to go inside. You went in the morning around three or four A.M. to get in the line. You waited until you got to the door, and at the door they didn't need you to go inside; they just took your passport and your papers. After that they might call you to make an appointment. They said, "On this day you need to come here to see someone." They wanted to know if you deserved to be a refugee.

So I came in the morning and I waited. When I went in for my appointment, the electricity was out, and the man said, "Now we cannot do anything because the computer is not working. You need to go back and come again." They made me another appointment, but I was so angry. I was telling my husband, "It's been really long now. How long do I have to wait to go back there?" It was far from home, and you had to take three buses. The buses were crowded, and some days you missed it. You went over there, and maybe you didn't find the number and you missed the bus. Then, when you get there they say, "Now you're late." Some people, they just didn't want to talk to you. It was hard to go over there. They were mean.

I got my interview appointment. The people at the office were Egyptian, but they looked like Christians, you know? The woman who interviewed me told me she was Christian. She was nice. They had a translator, and I told her my story. She said, "Abuk, your case is sad. I'm sorry for you." She said it really touched her heart. At that time I was pregnant and she wished me good luck. She said to come back in three months for my result, to see if they accepted my case. If they accept you, they give you documentation to stay legally in Egypt, and after that they can send you anywhere.

So after three or five months they called me and said, "Okay, you need to choose where you want to go." They said, "We have openings for people in Canada, Australia, and America, and you can go anywhere." To get to Australia you had to pay for your ticket, and we didn't have any money. America paid for your ticket. My husband and I decided to go to America. They said, "Oh, America is good; when you go there, you can work hard and your life will be changed." They gave me papers and made everything ready for me.

My husband had a cousin living in Iowa. I had a cousin in Buffalo. It's easier to go to a place where you have someone when you don't know English. If you have a Sudanese friend, they can help show you how to do the shopping. We had two choices, and we went to Buffalo.

It was my first plane and, God, I was so scared. We left at four A.M., and I was so confused. We stopped in Holland first. We sat for five hours in the Amsterdam airport. My baby was six months old at the time, and he was tired, and so was I. I had never sat in one place for so long. When I tried to walk, I fell down. I fell! Around eight o'clock that night, we went to another airplane and came to America. We flew to New York, to J. F. Kennedy.

When we got there, it was snowing. Oh my God! It was the first time I saw snow. We had a jacket but it was so cold, it wasn't enough. In the airport, they checked our passport and asked us where we were going. They said everything was okay, welcome to America. Then someone came and took us on a bus to another smaller airport. It was night, so we didn't see New York City or anything. Our flight to Buffalo took around one hour, I think.

So when we got there, we saw that people were waiting for us, people from the International Institute.[3] And my cousin was there, too. They had blankets to keep us warm. They had everything for us, and they put us in a nice, nice house. I thought the rooms would be really cold, but it was warm! It was good because it was warm in there, but it was so funny, too, to have heat. The house had one bedroom, and they gave us food and everything for the inside. It was nice. People from the International Institute helped us to learn English and find a job.

In Buffalo I started to work with the American Anti-Slavery Group.[4] I was so excited to share my story. That was the first thing I needed to do, because back then no one knew what was going on in Sudan, and people needed to know. That was my reaction.

I worked a lot with them, and after I was in Buffalo for a year they bought me a ticket to move here to Boston so I could be close to them for speaking engagements. They found a place for my family to stay until my husband found a job, and they helped us rent an apartment. They sent someone to my home to teach me to speak English, and my husband got a job doing banquets in a hotel.

We traveled, and I even went to the United Nations in New York to speak out when I heard that Omar al-Bashir was coming. We went in front of the United Nations building to protest and speak out about why Bashir was coming here to tell lies.

I spoke at churches, high schools, and colleges in many cities. I was happy because people sat down and listened to me tell my story. It was good to talk to young people too. I knew they were children and they didn't know anything about Sudan, but it's good to share your story with another person. I told them, "Children are dying. They took our children away. People can go into the village and kill your mother and your grandfather in front of you, in front of your eyes. How would you feel if they took you? How would you feel?"

People got excited because they had never heard what was going on in Sudan. Their hearts were really touched. I gave people our website and told them, "People should know. Your friend, your father, anyone." I told them they could write a letter to the government about civil rights, about how people are dying for nothing.

I think the United States didn't pay attention to us a long time ago, but now a lot of people have opened their minds. I'm not saying all people, but some. When you see what is going on in Sudan, you see it's just because of religion and racism. The Sudanese government wants everyone in the country to follow *sharia* law. For example, if women are raped and pregnant with the babies of the Arab militia, they can't say, "That's not my baby, it's the Arab militia's baby." That's your blood and you have to keep and take care of them, even though it's really painful. No one talks about that in Sudan.

That's Why We Came Here

In 2003, we saved enough money to bring my mother, my brother, and my sister here as refugees. I had never heard from my father, but my mom said he was back in Sudan after years in Kakuma refugee camp in Kenya. I said, "Thank God, he's not dead, he's okay!"

I spoke to him a few years ago, when he was in Kakuma, and it was so scary. He told me a lot of things about the war and people who died. After our village was destroyed, he married again, to another wife, and the militia came back and killed this wife. They killed my stepmom and her baby, who was three months old. My father thanked God we were okay. We didn't talk a lot because there was no phone over there in Kakuma. We could only talk when he went to the city, to Nairobi, which is a long bus drive away.

When the Comprehensive Peace Agreement was signed in 2005, my father decided he wanted to go back to Sudan. But it's still dangerous. You don't know. You can die. Now my father is back in South Sudan, in the city of Aweil.

People say it is good now in Sudan; that it's getting a little bit better. That's what they say. Even in Aweil they now have a phone. But it's hard to connect when you call.

I'm thinking that I need to visit Sudan now. I'm married, I have three children, and my father doesn't even know my kids. I really need to see my dad. I thank God we are all alive and just hope that we can meet someday.

Now I work in an assisted-living center taking care of old people. I like my job; you feel like it's your grandmother you're caring for. My husband works at the airport, driving the shuttle bus. We have a very nice house. When you work in America, it's very good. When you work hard, you can pay your rent and get anything you need. You work your job, and the kids can go to school to learn. We became citizens in 2005. We're really here in America, our home is here, and it feels right to be a citizen here.

My kids speak better English than me! Sometimes when I say something in English, they correct me. They say, "Oh, Mom, you don't say that!" You work for your children, you know?

I've started speaking with my son Majak about my story. He asks me questions all the time. "Why do they take people for slaves?" He knows the story and he knows why I left Sudan, but it's all so far away for him and hard to understand. We watch news all the time in the house, especially news about Sudan. My kids will ask, "Why is there so much fighting? Why are all the people dead?"

I say, "That's why we came here." I tell them that someday we'll go back and visit. They want to go, but not right now. Not until it's all quiet.

NOTES

1. Amarat is a district in Khartoum.
2. For more on refugee status determination, see Walzer's *Out of Exile.*
3. The International Institute of Buffalo assists immigrants and refugees resettling in the United States.
4. The American Anti-Slavery Group is a nonprofit group working with former victims of human trafficking.

ABOUT THE EDITORS
AND CONTRIBUTORS

Luke and Jennifer Reynolds are both passionate about human rights causes and literature. Currently they live in Massachusetts with their son, Tyler. Luke is a teacher and freelance writer. Jennifer is a freelance writer and a full-time mother.

Steve Almond is the author of five imperfect books and the father of one perfect daughter. He lives outside Boston with his small but hopeful family.

Beth Alvarado is the author of the short-story collection *Not a Matter of Love*, which won the 2005 Many Voices Award from New Rivers Press and was published in 2006. Her fiction and creative nonfiction have been published most recently in the journals *Ploughshares, Cue,* and *spork.* She teaches at the University of Arizona in Tucson and is currently working on a memoir called *Anthropologies.* Everything takes place in the desert.

Jane Armstrong's work has appeared in *Newsweek, North American Review, Beloit Fiction Journal, New Orleans Review, River Teeth,* and *Brevity* and on National Public Radio's *All Things Considered.* She teaches at Northern Arizona University.

Born in New Mexico of Indio-Mexican descent, Jimmy Santiago Baca was raised first by his grandmother and later sent to an orphanage. A runaway at age thirteen, Baca was eventually sentenced to five years in a maximum security prison. After that he began to turn his life around: he learned to read and write and unearthed a voracious passion for poetry. Instead of becoming a hardened criminal, he emerged from prison as a writer. Baca sent three of his poems to Denise Levertov, the poetry editor of *Mother Jones.* The poems were published and became part of Baca's *Immigrants in Our Own Land,* published in 1979, the year he was released from prison. He earned his GED later that same year. He is the winner of the Pushcart Prize, the American Book Award, the International Hispanic Heritage Award, and, for his memoir *A Place to Stand,* the prestigious International Award. In 2006 he won the Cornelius P. Turner Award. Baca has devoted his post-prison life to writing and teaching others who are overcoming hardship. His themes include American Southwest barrios, addiction, injustice, education, community, love and beyond. He has conducted hundreds of writing workshops in prisons, community centers, libraries, and universities through-out the country. In 2005 he created Cedar Tree, Inc., a nonprofit foundation that works to give people of all walks of life the opportunity to become educated and improve their lives.

Ishmael Beah came to the United States when he was seventeen and graduated from Oberlin College in 2004. He is a member of the Human Rights Watch Children's Division Advisory Committee and has spoken before the United Nations on several occasions. He lives in New York City. In 1993, at the age of twelve he fled attacking rebels who destroyed his village in Sierra Leone. By thir-teen he had been picked up by the government army and been made a child soldier. His memoir, *A Long Way Gone,* tells his story.

John Bensko has an MFA in creative writing from the University of Alabama and a Ph.D. in twentieth-century poetry and narrative technique from Florida State University. He is an associate professor at the University of Memphis. Previously, he taught at the University of Alabama, Old Dominion University, Rhodes College, and, as a Fulbright Professor in American Literature, at the Universidad de Alicante, Spain. Bensko won the McLeod-Grobe Poetry Prize for 2000. He was director of the River City Writers Series for the 2005–2006 season. His books of poetry include *Green Soldiers, The Waterman's Children,* and *The Iron City.* He has also written a book of stories, *Sea Dogs.* He teaches in the MFA pro-gram at the University of Memphis.

Sherwin Bitsui is originally from White Cone, Arizona, on the Navajo reserva-tion. Currently, he lives in Tucson. He is Dine of the Todich'ii'nii (Bitter Water Clan), born for the Tl'izilani (Many Goats Clan). He holds an AFA from the Institute of American Indian Arts Creative Writing Program and is currently completing his studies at the University of Arizona. He is the recipient of the 2000–2001 Individual Poet Grant from the Witter Bynner Foundation for Poetry, the 1999 Truman Capote Creative Writing Fellowship, a Lannan Foundation Literary Residency Fellowship, and, more recently, a 2006 Whiting Writer's Award. Sherwin has published his poems in *American Poet,* the *Iowa Review, Frank* (Paris), *Lit Magazine,* and elsewhere. His poems have also been anthologized in *Legitimate Dangers: American Poets of the New Century. Shapeshift* is his first book.

Robert Boswell is the author of novels (*Century's Son, American Owned Love,* Mystery *Ride, The Geography of Desire, Crooked Hearts*), story collections (*Living to Be 100, Dancing in the Movies*), a cyberpunk novel (*Virtual Death*), a prize-winning play (*Tongues*), a book of essays on writing (*The Half-Known World*), and a nonfiction account of a treasure hunt (*What Men Call Treasure*). He has received two fellowships from the National Endowment from the Arts, a Guggenheim, and numerous prizes for his fiction. His stories have appeared in *Esquire, New Yorker, Best American Short Stories, O'Henry Prize Stories, Pushcart Prize Stories,* and many literary magazines. He teaches at New Mexico State University and the University of Houston and in the Warren Wilson MFA program. He resides with his wife, Antonya Nelson, and their two children in Texas, New Mexico, and Colorado.

Paula Closson Buck is the author of two books of poems, *The Acquiescent Villa* (1998) and *Litanies Near Water* (2008). Her poems have appeared in journals such as *Antioch Review, Denver Quarterly, Gettysburg Review, Shenandoah,* and *Southern Review.* She is a three-time recipient of the individual artist fellowship from the Pennsylvania Council on the Arts and is currently at work on a novel set in Berlin and Greece as well as a book-length memoir of the year in which she and her family lived on the Greek island of Tinos. At Bucknell University, where she is on the creative writing faculty, she edits the literary magazine *West Branch.*

Lindsey Collen took risks riding a motorbike around Mauritius, as she took risks in the anti-apartheid struggle in South Africa. She still takes risks, standing up for women's liberation in a patriarchal society, working for children's use of their mother tongue in a country under the double assault of *la Francophonie* and English hegemony, and venturing with her husband, Ram, into the big Indian Ocean in a small pirogue. She has been arrested twice for her activist work—once in South Africa, once in Mauritius. Collen's novels include *There Is a Tide, The Rape of Sita, Getting Rid of It, Mutiny,* and *Boy.* She has twice won the Africa section of the Commonwealth Writers Prize—in 1994 for *The Rape of Sita* and in 2004 for *Boy*—and *Getting Rid of It* was long-listed for the Orange Prize.

Ann Cummins is the author of a short-story collection, *Red Ant House,* and a novel, *Yellowcake.* Her stories have appeared in the *New Yorker, McSweeney's,* and elsewhere and have been anthologized in *The Best American Short Stories, The Prentice Hall Anthology of Women's Literature,* and *The Anchor Book of New American Short Stories.* A 2002 recipient of a Lannan Literary Fellowship, she divides her time between Oakland, California, and Flagstaff, Arizona, where she teaches creative writing at Northern Arizona University.

Gail Dines is a professor of sociology and chair of the Women's Studies Department at Wheelock College in Boston. She is a nationally known researcher, an award-winning speaker, and a prolific writer. She is also a long-time feminist activist and co-founder of the organization Stop Porn Culture.

Dines is co-editor of the bestselling textbook *Gender, Race and Class in Media* and co-author of *Pornography: The Production and Consumption of Inequality*. She has written numerous articles on pornography, media images of women, and representations of race in pop culture. Her work has appeared in academic journals, edited books, newspapers, and magazines; and she is a recipient of the Myers Center Award for the Study of Human Rights in North America.

Judy Doenges is the author of a novel, *The Most Beautiful Girl in the World,* and a short-fiction collection, *What She Left Me,* which received the Bakeless Prize, a Ferro-Grumley Award for Best Lesbian Fiction, and a Washington State Governor's Writers Award and was named a *New York Times* Notable Book. Her fiction has appeared or is forthcoming in the *Georgia Review,* the *Kenyon Review, Nimrod,* and elsewhere; and her reviews have appeared in the *Washington Post* and the *Seattle Times.* She has received grants and fellowships from the National Endowment for the Arts, Artist Trust, the Ohio Arts Council, and Bread Loaf Writer's Conference. She is an associate professor at Colorado State University.

Christopher L. Doyle teaches history at Farmington High School in Connecticut. He worked as an academic historian for ten years and has previously held a tenure-track post at the University of Northern Colorado. Doyle has published articles on race, gender, and law during the early years of U.S. history, and his work has appeared in the *Journal of Southern History,* the *Magazine of History,* and the *Virginia Magazine of History and Biography.* Recently, his writing has shifted to address a more general audience and to critique public education and the norms of contemporary childhood. He is married and has two teenage children.

John Dufresne grew up in Worcester, Massachusetts, where he wasted his youth playing baseball and going to movies. He attended Worcester State College and the MFA program in creative writing at the University of Arkansas. Dufresne is the author of the story collection *The Way That Water Enters Stone.* His novel *Louisiana Power & Light* was a Barnes & Noble Discover Great New Writers selection. It was also a *New York Times* Notable Book, as was his second novel, *Love Warps the Mind a Little.* His most recent novel is *Deep in the Shade of Paradise.* He has also written *The Lie That Tells a Truth,* a book about writing fiction. He teaches in the creative writing program at Florida International University and lives in Dania Beach, Florida, with his wife and son.

Michael Dunn teaches English, religion, and creative writing at Farmington High School in Connecticut. He pioneered the Adventure Challenge program there, in which students break through fears and form bonds through wilderness experiences. He writes poetry, drinks Guinness, and loves his wife and four children immensely. He graduated from the University of Notre Dame.

Kim Edwards is the author of a short-story collection, *The Secrets of a Fire King*, which was an alternate for the 1998 PEN/Hemingway Award, and has won both a Whiting Writer's Award and the PEN/Nelson Algren Award. She is a graduate of the Iowa Writers' Workshop, and her most recent book is *The Memory Keeper's Daughter*.

Nadine Gordimer was born in Springs, Transvaal, South Africa, in 1923 and has lived in Johannesburg since 1948. She was an ardent opponent of apartheid and refused to accommodate herself to the system, despite growing up in a community that accepted that system as normal. As a result, several of her books were banned in South Africa. Gordimer has published thirteen novels and ten short-story collections in forty languages, beginning at the age of fifteen, when she published her first short-story in the liberal Johannesburg magazine *Forum*. Eventually, in 1951, the *New Yorker* took one of her stories. Her story collections include *A Soldier's Embrace* (1980), *Something Out There* (1984), and *Jump and Other Stories* (1991). Her first novel, *The Lying Days* (1953), was based largely on her own life and set in her home town; and her next three—*A World of Strangers* (1958), *Occasion for Loving* (1963), and *The Late Bourgeois World* (1966)—deal with master-servant relations in South African life. In 1974, *The Conservationist* was joint winner of the Booker Prize for Fiction. Her latest novel is *Beethoven Was One-Sixteenth Black* (2007). Gordimer has been awarded fifteen honorary degrees from universities around the world. In France, she was made a Commandeur de l'Ordre des Arts et des Lettres; and she is vice president of International PEN, a fellow of the Royal Society of Literature, and a founder of the Congress of South African Writers. In 1991 she was awarded the Nobel Prize for Literature, and in 2007 she received France's Chevalier de la Légion d'Honneur.

Andrew Greig was born in rural Bannockburn, Stirlingshire, Scotland, in 1951. He won the E. C. Gregory Award for Poetry in 1972 and published his first poetry collection, *White Boats* (with Catherine Czerkawska), in 1973. *Men on Ice* (1977), once called "the first (and only) Scottish post-Modern longpoem," became something of a cult in the climbing world. Years later, thanks to a misunderstanding about the metaphorical nature of poetry, it led to his being asked to join an expedition to climb the Mustagh Tower in the Karakoram Himalayas. The story of this improbable and oddly successful trip appears in *Summit Fever* (1985), which has never been out of print. That book was followed by *Kingdoms of Experience* (1986), chronicling expeditions to the Northeast Ridge on the Tibet side of Everest and to Lhotse Shar. Both climbing books were short-listed for the Boardman-Tasker Award for mountaineering literature. His books of poetry include *Surviving Passages* (1982), *A Flame in Your Heart* (with Kathleen Jamie) (1986), and *The Order of the Day* (1990), which was a Poetry Book Society choice. His novels include *Electric Brae* (1992), *The Return of John MacNab* (1996), *When*

They Lay Bare (1999), *That Summer* (2000), and *In Another Light* (2004)—the Saltire Scottish Book of the Year. His latest book, *Preferred Lies* (2006), is an unusual book about being alive, mediated through the practice of golf; and recent poems are included in *This Life, This Life: New and Selected Poems, 1969–2006* (2007). He is married to the novelist Lesley Glaister, and they live in Peebles and Orkney, Scotland.

Tom Grimes is the author of the novels *WILL@epicqwest.com, A Stone of the Heart, Season's End, Redemption Song,* and *City of God.* His fiction has twice been finalist for the PEN/Nelson Algren Award; and individual works have been chosen as *New York Times* Notable Book of the Year, Editor's Choice, and New and Noteworthy Paperback. He received a James Michener Fellowship from the Iowa Writers' Workshop and has edited the fiction anthology *The Workshop: Seven Decades of Fiction from the Iowa Writers' Workshop.* His play *SPEC* premiered at the MET Theatre in 1991, won three Los Angeles Dramalogue Awards, and was revived at the Alliance Repertory Theatre in October 2004. Another play, *New World,* premiered at the MET in 2001; and his latest play, *Rehearsal,* premiered there in 2004 along with one-act plays by Sam Shepard and Beth Henley. Recent essays have appeared in *Tin House,* and "Bring Out Your Dead" was honored as a Notable Essay of 2007. He directs the MFA program in creative writing at Texas State University.

J. C. Hallman is the author of *The Chess Artist* and *The Devil Is a Gentleman.* A book of short fiction, *The Hospital for Bad Poets,* is forthcoming in 2009. He is working on a book about modern expressions of utopian thought, and he lives and teaches in St. Paul, Minnesota.

Ron Hansen is the bestselling author of the novel *Atticus* (a finalist for the National Book Award), *Hitler's Niece, Mariette in Ecstasy, Desperadoes, Isn't It Romantic?,* and, most recently, *Exiles,* as well as a collection of short stories, a collection of essays, and a book for children. *The Assassination of Jesse James by the Coward Robert Ford* was a finalist for the PEN/Faulkner Award. Hansen lives in northern California, where he teaches at Santa Clara University.

Linda Hogan is an internationally recognized public speaker and the author of poetry, fiction, and essays. Recent books are *Rounding the Human Corners* (2008) and *People of the Whale* (2008). Her other books include the novels *Mean Spirit,* winner of the Oklahoma Book Award, the Mountains and Plains Book Award, and a finalist for the Pulitzer Prize; and *Solar Storms,* a finalist for the International Impact Award. Her poetry collection, *The Book of Medicines,* was a finalist for the National Book Critics Circle Award. Other poetry collections have received the Colorado Book Award, a Minnesota State Arts Grant, an American

Book Award, and a prestigious Lannan Literary Fellowship. In addition, she has received a National Endowment for the Arts Fellowship, a Guggenheim, and the Lifetime Achievement Award from both the Native Writers Circle of the Americas and Wordcraft Circle. Her nonfiction includes *Dwellings* and *The Woman Who Watches Over the World*. With Brenda Peterson, she has written *Sightings* for National Geographic Books; and she has edited several anthologies on nature and spirituality and has written the script *Everything Has a Spirit*, a PBS documentary on American Indian religious freedom. Inducted into the Chickasaw Hall of Fame, Hogan has also worked with Native youth in horse programs. A professor emerita at the University of Colorado, she is now the writer in residence for the Chickasaw Nation and lives in Oklahoma.

Ann Hood is the author of nine books, including the novel *The Knitting Circle*. Her work has appeared in the *Paris Review*, *Tin House*, and *O Magazine*. She lives in Providence, Rhode Island.

Uzodinma Iweala is the author of the novel *Beasts of No Nation*. A Nigerian American, he was born in Washington, D.C., in 1982. *Beasts of No Nation*, his first novel, was published soon after his graduation from Harvard University and won the John Llewellyn Rhys Prize, the American Academy of Arts and Letters First Fiction Award, the New York Public Library Young Lions Award, and the *Los Angeles Times* First Book Award. The novel was long-listed for the IMPAC Prize and short-listed for the Commonwealth Writers Prize. It was named a best book of the year by *Time*, *People*, and *Entertainment Weekly* and was selected as one of the *New York Times'* one hundred best books of the year. Iweala has written pieces for the *New York Times Magazine*, the *Independent*, the *Spectator*, and the *Financial Times Magazine*. He has also worked with internally displaced peoples in northern Nigeria and the Millennium Villages Project at the Earth Institute at Columbia University. He is currently working on a book about HIV/AIDS in sub-Saharan Africa and attends Columbia University's College of Physicians and Surgeons.

Robert Jensen is an associate professor in the School of Journalism at the University of Texas at Austin, where he teaches media law, ethics, and politics and directs the Senior Fellows Program at the College of Communication. He joined the faculty in 1992 after completing his Ph.D. in media ethics and law at the School of Journalism and Mass Communication of the University of Minnesota. Before becoming an academic, he worked as a professional journalist for a decade. Much of Jensen's work has focused on pornography and the radical feminist critique of sexuality and men's violence. Recently, he has addressed questions of race through a critique of white privilege and institutionalized racism. He also writes for popular alternative and mainstream media on subjects such as foreign policy, politics, and race; and he is involved in a number of activist groups working against U.S. military and economic domination around the world. Jensen's books include *Getting Off: Pornography and the End of Masculinity* (2007); *The Heart of Whiteness: Confronting Race, Racism and White Privilege* (2005); *Citizens of the Empire: The Struggle to Claim Our Humanity* (2004); and *Writing Dissent: Taking Radical Ideas from the Margins to the Mainstream* (2002). With Gail Dines and Ann Russo, he has published *Pornography: The Production and Consumption of Inequality* (1998); and with David S. Allen, he has co-edited *Freeing the First Amendment: Critical Perspectives on Freedom of Expression* (1995).

Nancy Johnson is a former broadcast journalist who left the world of steady salaries to write. Her poems have been widely published in magazines, and her book *Zoo & Cathedral* won the White Pine Press Poetry Prize. She is the author of the forthcoming memoir *The Accident Is My Mother*.

Kristen Keckler's work has appeared or is forthcoming in *Ecotone, Sonora Review, Iowa Review, Flashquake, Cold-Drill, Concho River Review, Palo Alto Review, Sport Literate,* and the *Dallas Morning News.* She is a regular contributor to the Art&Seek blog of NPR's Dallas affiliate, KERA. She received a Ph.D. in English from the University of North Texas, where she currently teaches. In her spare time, she coaches Dallas Mavericks basketball from her loveseat.

Lynne Kelly is professor and director of the School of Communication at the University of Hartford in Connecticut, where she teaches courses in interpersonal and small-group communication as well as communication technologies and relationships. Her research deals with communication reticence and electronically mediated communication, particularly its role in the development and maintenance of interpersonal relationships. She has published many articles in academic journals and has co-written *Teaching People to Speak Well: Training and Remediation of Communication Reticence* with Gerald M. Phillips and James A. Keaten.

Betsy Lerner is the author of *The Forest for the Trees: An Editor's Advice to Writers* and *Food and Loathing: A Lament.*

EJ Levy's essays have appeared in *The Best American Essays, 2005,* the *2007 Pushcart Prize XXXI: Best of the Small Presses,* and *The Touchstone Anthology of Contemporary Creative Nonfiction: Work from 1970 to the Present,* as well as in *Orion, Salmagundi, Utne Reader,* the *Nation,* and elsewhere. Her short stories have been published in the *Paris Review,* the *Gettysburg Review,* and the *Missouri Review;* and two have been recognized in *Best American Short Stories* as among the year's distinguished stories. Her anthology, *Tasting Life Twice: Literary Lesbian Fiction by New American Writers,* won the Lambda Literary Award. She divides her time between Washington, D.C., and Columbia, Missouri, where she is an assistant professor in the graduate program in creative writing at the University of Missouri—Columbia.

Phillip Lopate has written a dozen books—novels, poetry, film criticism, and personal essay collections—such as *Portrait of My Body, The Rug Merchant, Being With Children, Totally Tenderly Tragically,* and *Waterfront.* He is also the editor of *Art of the Personal Essay, Writing New York,* and *American Movie Criticism.* He teaches at Hofstra University and lives in Brooklyn with his wife and daughter.

Frank McCourt taught in the New York City public schools for twenty-seven years, the last seventeen of which were spent at Stuyvesant High School in Manhattan. After retiring, Frank and his brother Malachy performed their two-man show, *A Couple of Blaguards,* a musical review about their Irish youth. McCourt's memoir of his childhood, *Angela's Ashes* (1996), spent 117 weeks on the *New York Times* bestseller list. The book has since gone through more than sixty-five printings and is available in eighteen countries. McCourt was the winner of the 1997 Pulitzer Prize for Biography, the National Book Critics Circle Award in Biography/Autobiography, the *Boston Book Review*'s Nonfiction Prize, the ABBY Award, and the *Los Angeles Times* Book Award. The Alan Parker film of *Angela's Ashes,* starring Emily Watson, was released to wide acclaim in 1999, the same year in which the second volume of McCourt's memoirs, *'Tis,* was published. The third, and probably final, volume, *Teacher Man,* was published in 2005.

James McPherson's work has appeared in dozens of journals, magazines, and anthologies. His awards include a Guggenheim in 1973 and the Pulitzer Prize for Fiction in 1978 for his short-story collection *Elbow Room.* His other books include *Hue and Cry, Railroad, Crabcakes, Fathering Daughters: Reflections by Men* (co-edited with DeWitt Henry), and *A Region Not Home: Reflections from Exile.* In 1995 McPherson was inducted into the American Academy of Arts and Sciences and in 2002 was awarded a Lannan Literary Fellowship. He has taught English at the University of California—Santa Cruz, Harvard University, Morgan State University, and the University of Virginia and has also lectured in Japan at Meiji University and Chiba University. He is now a professor of English at the University of Iowa.

Lynn Phillips has taught in the Department of Communication at the University of Massachusetts since 2005. Previously, she taught at the University of Pennsylvania and the New School University, where she received the Distinguished University Teaching Award. A social and developmental psychologist by training, she teaches courses in media and critical cultural studies, with a focus on issues of gender, race, class, and sexuality; on how the media affect children's well-being; and on the health and environmental implications of consumer culture. Her publications include *Flirting with Danger: Young Women's Reflections on Sexuality and Domination*; *Unequal Partners: Power and Consent in Adult-Teen Relationships*; and *The Girls Report: What We Know and Need to Know about Adolescent Girls*. Committed to participatory activist research, she has collaborated with organizations such as Planned Parenthood, battered women's shelters, sexual health and education programs, and grassroots programs and foundations supporting girls and youth development. Her current research explores consent and coercion in adolescents' sexual experiences, the subjective and social implications of media images of hypermasculinity and the hypersexualization of young girls, and children and adult caregivers' experiences of the commercialization of children's culture. She is currently working on a documentary film with the Media Education Foundation based on her research. Phillips has appeared on NPR, CNN, ABC, Fox News, and other television and radio programs; and her research on adolescent girls has received front-page attention in the *Washington Post* and other national and international news publications. She has delivered keynote addresses in forums ranging from violence prevention conferences to the National Science Foundation.

Robert Pinsky recently published *The Life of David,* a prose account of the biblical figure, and a chapbook of poems, *First Things to Hand.* A new full-length collection, *Gulf Music*, appeared in fall 2007.

John Prendergast is co-chair of the ENOUGH Project, an initiative to end genocide and crimes against humanity. During the Clinton administration, John was involved in a number of peace processes in Africa while he was director of African Affairs at the National Security Council and special advisor at the Department of State. John also has worked for members of Congress, the United Nations, human rights organizations, and think tanks, as well as working as a youth counselor and a basketball coach in the United States. He has written eight books about Africa, including *Not on Our Watch*, a *New York Times* bestseller co-authored with Don Cheadle. Currently he is working on a new book that focuses on his twenty years in the Big Brother program. Prendergast has helped produce two documentaries on northern Uganda and been involved in three documentaries on Sudan. He has been part of three episodes of CBS's *60 Minutes,* a series that earned an Emmy Award for Best Continuing News Coverage, and is helping to develop two additional episodes. He is now helping to spearhead a campaign involving the NBA and Participant Productions to widen awareness about Darfur and another to end the violence against women and girls in the Congo. Prendergast travels regularly to Africa's war zones on fact-finding missions, peace-making initiatives, and awareness-raising trips.

He is a visiting professor at both the University of San Diego and the American University in Cairo.

John Robinson is the author of two novels: *January's Dream* and *Legends of the Lost*. His short stories have appeared in *Ploughshares,* the *Sewanee Review,* and other literary journals and have been nominated for a Pushcart Prize. As a dramatist, he has written (and performed in) two plays, *Through the Looking-Glass Diner* and *Kansas,* which was a finalist in the *Boston Globe* Drama Festival One-Act Competition and a finalist in the New England Drama Festival. A new play, *Cape Echo: The Final Battle,* premiered in Massachusetts in 2009.

Bill Roorbach's newest book is *Temple Stream,* which won the 2006 Maine Literary Award for Nonfiction. Others books of nature writing are *Summers with Juliet, Into Woods,* and *A Place on Water* (the last is essays with Robert Kimber and Wesley McNair). He's the author of the bestselling book of instruction, *Writing Life Stories,* and editor of the Oxford anthology *Contemporary Creative Nonfiction: The Art of Truth.* Roorbach also writes fiction and is the author of a novel, *The Smallest Color,* and a collection of short stories, *Big Bend,* which won the Flannery O'Connor Award in 2001. His short work has appeared in *Harper's,* the *Atlantic, Playboy,* the *New York Times Magazine,* and dozens of other magazines and journal, and has been featured on the NPR program *Selected Shorts.* He currently holds the Jenks Chair in Contemporary American Letters at the College of the Holy Cross in Worcester, Mass. He lives in an old farmhouse in rural western Maine and tries to keep it standing.

George Saunders, a 2006 MacArthur Fellow, is the author of six books, including the short-story collections *CivilWarLand in Bad Decline, Pastoralia,* and *In Persuasion Nation,* and an essay collection, *The Braindead Megaphone.* He teaches at Syracuse University.

Jim Shepard is the author of six novels, most recently *Project X* (2004), and three story collections, including *Like You'd Understand, Anyway* (2007), which was nominated for the National Book Award and won the Story Prize. His short fiction has appeared in *Harper's, McSweeney's,* the *Paris Review,* the *Atlantic, Esquire, Granta,* the *New Yorker, Playboy,* and elsewhere. He teaches at Williams College.

Jane Smiley is the Pulitzer Prize–winning author of *A Thousand Acres* and more than ten other works of fiction as well as three works of nonfiction, including a critically acclaimed biography of Charles Dickens. In 2001 she was inducted into the American Academy of Arts and Letters. She lives in northern California.

Debra Spark is author of the novels *Coconuts for the Saint* and *The Ghost of Bridgetown* and editor of the anthology *Twenty under Thirty: Best Stories by*

America's New Young Writers. Her most recent book is *Curious Attractions: Essays on Fiction Writing.*

Sarah Stone's novel, *The True Sources of the Nile,* was a BookSense 76 selection and has been translated into German and Dutch, adopted for classroom and book-club use, and discussed in Geoff Wisner's *A Basket of Leaves: 99 Books that Capture the Spirit of Africa.* She is also co-author, with Ron Nyren, of *Deepening Fiction: A Practical Guide for Intermediate and Advanced Writers* (2005), published in a trade version as *The Longman Guide to Intermediate and Advanced Fiction Writing* (2007). Recent publications include pieces in *The Future Dictionary of America* and *The Believer Book of Writers Talking to Writers* and in the journals *Ploughshares* and the *Writer's Chronicle.* Stone has written for and taught on Korean public television; reported on human rights and worked with orphan chimpanzees in Bujumbura, Burundi; and has taught writing at University of California, Berkeley, and San Francisco State University, among other places. She is now a faculty member in the MFA program in writing and consciousness at the California Institute of Integral Studies.

Peter Turchi is the author of a novel, a collection of stories, and two books of nonfiction, including *Maps of the Imagination: The Writer As Cartographer.* He co-edited, with Charles Baxter, *Bringing the Devil to His Knees: The Craft of Fiction and the Writing Life* and, with Andrea Barrett, *The Story Behind the Story: 26 Stories by Contemporary Writers and How They Work.* He also edited and co-wrote *Suburban Journals: The Sketchbooks, Drawings and Prints of Charles Ritchie.* The recipient of fellowships from the National Endowment for the Arts and the Guggenheim Foundation and of North Carolina's Sir Walter Raleigh Award, he directed the MFA program for writers at Warren Wilson College for fifteen years. He now teaches at Warren Wilson and Arizona State University.

Craig Walzer has traveled extensively in Sudan, Kenya, and Egypt. He is currently working toward graduate degrees from Harvard Law School and the Kennedy School of Government.

Howard Zinn is a historian, playwright, and social activist. He was a shipyard worker and air force bombardier before he went to college under the GI Bill and received his Ph.D. from Columbia University. He has taught at Spelman College and Boston University and has been a visiting professor at the University of Paris and the University of Bologna. He has received the Thomas Merton Award, the Eugene V. Debs Award, the Upton Sinclair Award, and the Lannan Literary Award. He lives in Auburndale, Massachusetts.

For more information on the Save Darfur Coalition, please visit the website *www.savedarfur.org.*